and... just like that

Essays on a life before,
during and after
the law

and...
just like
that

MARK SHAIKEN

*For Loren and Zac,
and also for all the friends, colleagues,
co-workers, clients, judges,
and opposing counsel,
whose paths crossed with mine
during my legal career*

CONTENTS

FOREWORD

I WAS AN ATTORNEY for a very long time. Now I am not. This is a collection of compositions about what my life was like before and during my law life, and after my law life ended (what I call my afterlife). That period after three years as a law student, two years as a bankruptcy law clerk, and thirty-six years as a practicing bankruptcy attorney at large law firms, including a fourteen-year stint when also I taught bankruptcy law to law students at the University of Kansas at the same time I practiced law. Forty-one years of a life in the law, and then, one day, no more law. Just like that.

The compositions are a selection from the many verses of my life's songs written and played in the live concert that has been my existence before, during, and after the law. I like to dream. To dream: the transitive verb, to think of the possibilities. For me, possibilities other than a life in the law. The law got in the way of dreaming. It resisted me and fought me. The compositions address my dreams... perhaps to dream my way out of the law life.

In my thirty-six years of working in law firms, as I reserved the right to seek greener pastures, I saw things, felt things, laughed at things, cried at things, loved things, despised things, and became resigned to things. I have selected some of those things, and present them in the coming essays. Nothing I have written here is about a particular law firm, attorney, or even person. Think of these essays as a mixed pot-luck stew of things that happen in any and every law firm, especially the large ones, where I resided for my career. My views truly are therefore firmless, regionless, attorneyless, associateless, partnerless, clientless, colleagueless, managementless, and sometimes even thoughtless. My views sometimes drove my family crazy, oftentimes drove my friends crazy, and almost always drove my colleagues crazy, and left me a bit crazed for extended periods.

Each essay explains my perspective and offers my observations. Sometimes, they are my thoughts on my life. Sometimes, they are my thoughts on my life as an attorney. Sometimes, the two are not easily distinguished.

Life as an attorney taught me to enjoy being busy, so in the afterlife, I am very busy, but I no longer give out legal advice, write briefs, go to court, make oral arguments, call witnesses to the stand, cross-examine witnesses, and deal with my law partners on a day-to-day basis. I do not like the word "retire," because there is no "retirement" for me – rather, I chose to do many other things, such as that I smile a great deal. I swear less. I spent a great deal of my law life not necessarily making the world a better place. Now I try to make the world a better place, little by little, day by day, person by person, project by project, cause by cause, and I hope I am making up for lost time. As Vincent Van Gogh said, "I would rather die of passion than of boredom." In my law life, while I wasn't bored, I lacked passion or at least if I had it, I eventually lost it. Now I have passion, and there is no boredom in my afterlife. The afterlife is a good deal for me... so far. More on that as you get to know me better.

Take note: this is not a "how-to" book. I am not qualified to tell the world how to decide to become an attorney, how to be an attorney, how to stop being an attorney, or how to use a law degree to become something other than an attorney in a law firm. There are many such books for sale, and I have consumed more than a few of those in my decades as a practicing attorney. It is not a book advising anyone to be – or avoid being – an attorney. Again, not qualified. I am only qualified to tell my story of what it has been like for me. Finally, this is not a tell-all book to call out specific attorneys and law firms. Not my style, and not how I feel about most of the attorneys with whom I worked or any of the law firms where I spent my career. For continuity, I have chosen to call the job "attorney," rather than lawyer, counselor, Juris Doctor, advocate, barrister, or counsel. I needed one word, and attorney fits the bill. With only a very few exceptions, I try to be gender-neutral.

The book is organized into five parts: six, short questions I have been asked frequently by friends and family as my book endeavor became more widely known, followed by writings on my life before the law, my decision to go to law school and the law school experience, my life as a practicing attorney, and my life since I stopped being an attorney. The compositions are presented in different formats throughout the book. Some are straightforward essays; some are presented in the form of short stories that are based on fact, but names and places have been fictionalized to protect the privacy of any particular person. And some are presented as fictionalized dialogues… think of these compositions as my law-related parables to express my view.

FREQUENTLY ASKED QUESTIONS

FAQ 1: Did you always want to be an attorney?

Heavens, no!

FAQ 2: How did you become an attorney?

Like so many things in my life, it just sort of happened. One day I drove a forklift, and the next day I found myself in law school and the next day I passed the bar exam and began life as an attorney at law. Just like that. Well, maybe not quite the very next day but after thirty-eight years of practicing bankruptcy law, time and space can sometimes get a little distorted and the continuum of the dimensions can warp.

FAQ 3: Did you like your life as an attorney?

Not always. Sometimes I hated it, and the world of the law firm; sometimes I tolerated it, and sometimes I may have even liked it. But mostly, as is true for so many attorneys, "like" was not typically the first word that crossed my mind when I pondered each day of my life as an attorney. I liked my life as an attorney more when I learned to accept the parts of the practice of law that drove me crazy and that I could not change. For that, I can thank the life as an attorney for helping me learn that I cannot control everything, and, at times, I can control nothing. At times, I was frustrated by the practice of law at a big law firm, and just as often, I was energized by it. Oftentimes, I made the people close to me miserable, and I believe I can attribute that unfortunate truth to the practice of law, rather than myself, although I can see how that is debatable. I sometimes frustrated my partners in the law firm; I believe they may have occasionally enjoyed having me around, just a little... but they don't have to admit it.

I did not always – perhaps even not often – really hate the practice of law. But, on balance, "like" was and still is a hard word for me to use in close proximity to the phrase "practice of law."

FAQ 4: What kind of book is this?

This is a just-the-way-I-see-it book. It is partly a memoir, so you know something about how I came to be an attorney and perhaps why I reacted the way I did to the practice of law; and it is a book of observations, each in a standalone essay that covers my view of the pertinent parts of the whole attorney-and-law-firm-thing. I am a believer in the notion that if you face the things you have lived through, it can help you get beyond them. This book faces up to some of those things and is my couch session – with you – to help me get beyond these things.

FAQ 5: Who is the audience?

I found myself at a Denver cocktail party, and the conversation turned to how I filled my days since retirement. I mentioned this book. My conversation partner asked, "Who is the book's audience?" A great question, and, since then, I have given this quite a bit of thought: who *is* the audience for this book? Who would ever want to read about the life and times of a respectable, midwestern attorney, not widely known throughout the country?

I have friends and some family. I am not sure I can count on them to read this book since they have largely lived through my life as an attorney, and have heard many of my views over the years.

Who is the audience? The most obvious answer, it seems, is attorneys, and those who hang around attorneys. After all, who but an attorney would relate to a book of essays about life before, during and after the practice of law? So, I did a bit of research, and I learned that as of 2014, there were more than 1.22 million attorneys in the United States. Wow. That is a whole lot of attorneys.

And, I thought, the book might be of interest to law students as well as attorneys. Law students are desperate to know what is in store for them in the wacky world of law firms. In 2012, there were approximately 149,000 law students in the United States. So 149,000 further potential readers, for a total of more than 1.3 million.

Then I thought, the audience could also include anyone who has an attorney friend. I figured even attorneys must have some friends (although not many), and attorneys always complain to their friends about being an attorney. The math suggests that even if every attorney and law student has an average of just one and a half friends, that would be a total of about 2,053,500 more readers, for a grand total of over 3.4 million readers.

Then I thought, the audience should also include spouses and significant others of the attorneys and law students. The latest census tells me that fifty-one percent of the United States adult population marries. That yields another 698,190 attorney spouses, taking my total readership over 4.1 million.

Then I thought, attorneys tend to drink more than the general population (and, sadly, all too often, have a drinking problem). Statistics collected by bar associations (the organizations that regulate attorneys) suggest that somewhere between eighteen and twenty-five percent of attorneys have a drinking problem. Even if we use the lower range of the scale, that means at any given time, 219,600 attorneys have struggles that lead them to alcohol abuse and to sit at bars – the drinking kind, not the legal profession regulatory kind (isn't it interesting, however, that attorney associations and liquor dispensaries have the same name?). If each of these attorneys drinking at a bar complains to two folks at the bar (I figure the bartender and the person on the next stool over), some portion of the bartenders and the poor person sitting next to the complaining attorney might want to read a thoughtful book of essays about the travails of attorneys. The math suggests that this could yield another 439,200 folks, for a staggering total potential audience of over 4.3 million readers.

Finally, I figure there are maybe five or ten others who could find the book on Amazon or Barnes and Noble, and read the book because it sounds interesting. Indeed, maybe those are the only ones who will read the book at all. So, I have concluded that a fair range of potential readership is between five people and 4,340,300 people.

FAQ 6: Why is the book called And... Just Like That?

The phrase, "Just Like That," connotes something that happens all of a sudden, and unexpectedly. I did not chase

becoming an attorney; I did not plan for it; and, in all truth-
fulness, I did not even see it coming. It just happened. Indeed,
much of my life happened, just like that, when one life plan
or another fizzled out. We will get to that later.

And, now for the essays...

PART ONE – BEFORE THE LAW

TIES THAT BIND

FOR THE ENTIRETY OF my law career, I sat behind a desk and wore a suit and a tie. I shaved every day. It was not always like that. Before the adventure began, I had nothing against people who sat behind desks. My dad spent his whole life behind a desk. He hated it. If he could not stand it, I had no chance, so why even try? I was going to do something for my whole life without a desk or a formal attire requirement. Something outdoors sounded good.

So before the law, I knew with conviction that I would never spend my whole life clean-shaven behind a desk wearing a suit and a tie. Then, just like that, I was starring in a late-night television B-movie nightmare, and I had become everything I always associated with desks and suits and ties and daily shaving rituals.

A desk! A suit! Oh my God, a tie! I had become the person I used to laugh at when I was a teen. In my younger days, when I knew everything, I swore I would never become that guy. But I did.

I tried, and thought about trying, many things to do before law school. When you are young, you can dream and plan, and I did. As a young kid from Queens, I read *Spiderman* comics and I dreamed that I would be bitten by a radioactive spider, stick to walls, swing between buildings, save New York City every night, and then in my alter ego, take photographs for a newspaper while I worked the crime beat. The required bite never happened, and there is no Spiderman without the bite. No bite meant no sticking, swinging, saving, and no crime beat photos. Bummer. It would have been fun.

I consumed baseball. I devoured the players, the literature, baseball cards, the folklore, the strategy, the essence. I was in love. It was the real thing. It was the perfect job, from what I could see. I could be famous, I would not have to wear a tie, and I could work outside each day. Of course, I needed significant talent to play – which I lacked – but, nevertheless, baseball helped me focus on the need for a career that was not work.

I played basketball and fell in love all over again. No ties. No suits. It was not an outside game, but there was no desk either. Nothing was as sweet as the sound of a ball tickling a net. Nothing as fine as the fantasies of a child thinking, dreaming, and becoming Walt Frazier for an hour; Barnett to Bradley to Frazier – swish; the imaginary crowd roared. No matter what community league I played in, I had to be number 10, because Walt Frazier was number 10. This was no childhood infatuation: I fell in love, hard. But that natty talent thing got in the way once more, as well as a certain vertical challenge diagnosis – no height and insufficient jump. I stopped growing. I considered hormones; I considered hanging from a chinning bar. I considered my fate; I considered it an undeserved, unwelcome sign. It is hard to be a basketball player of any magnitude from the under-six-foot perspective. I was pretty sure it was damn near impossible to do it from the five-foot-seven (okay, five-foot-six and a half) perspective.

I played the guitar. No tie, unless I wanted one. Idolizing teenagers screaming and crying and fainting. I could make social statements. I did not have George Harrison's hair, but I could improvise. And there was no desk. Each day I repeated

4

great inspirational thoughts like "something in the way she moves" and "baby you can drive my car." This guitar thing was not just any post-piano, childhood infatuation. I never came up with that great catchy lyric, that great original inspirational, quotable thought, but I was a respectable player and there were plenty of guitar players who did not write world-class lyrics. It just never happened, I guess. And my voice is an acquired taste, to say the least.

These dream careers that never happen are what happens to almost every kid. They are nothing more than the life-altering realizations of one's limitations. The dreams are necessary to winnow down the available life choices. I was — and still am — in love with each of my fantasies, but each one is a matter of the heart and none of them pay the bills.

Some of these fantasies, as well as others, gave me places to go when I needed to be somewhere other than a law career. I never could swing between Manhattan skyscrapers on a web, but I could play guitar late into the night if the law day had been hard to deal with. I could play basketball at a local neighborhood court until I became too old to do so. And, as you will discover, I had other places I could go when I needed a place to be other than the law.

But, as dreams faded, gradually, I started to move from fantasy to rationality as I considered my future and the need for food and shelter, as long as it was a future without the desk, tie, and suit. So, at the conclusion of each school year, I hunted for a summer job, sometimes with little or no success; and my dad (perhaps because he so hated sitting behind his desk or perhaps to help me realize that as bad as the desk was, there were worse things to do) helped find me outdoor jobs. Three stand out.

One year, through the good graces of the New Haven political machine, I was blessed with the opportunity to paint the lines on the highways of Connecticut – you know the ones, down the middle of the road and the crosswalks. No suit, no tie, no desk and a substantial chance for a great tan. When the crew and I painted the lines by a West Haven beach, it was also a good job for girl-watching. The state issued each line painting crew member a hard hat and a bright orange fluorescent vest. The vest was designed to catch the driver's eye so I would not be splattered all over the new freshly painted lines. The hard hat was apparently designed to save me from injury in the event a driver did not spy the reflective vest and splattered me. The vest seemed to work; I never tested the hard hat, but I had my doubts that it would work if put to the test.

As in everything I do, I learned something about myself that summer. In painting lines, I learned very quickly that I was not a Rembrandt of the open New England roads. I could not paint a straight line to save my life. Not to worry; Connecticut was a progressive state at the time, and if I could not paint a straight line, I could still work on the crew, scattering glass beads in the freshly painted lines. As the paint dried, the glass beads became embedded in the line and at night, reflected the headlights and helped the nighttime drivers see better and stay within the lines. I was a pretty good bead-scatterer, but after a summer of painting crooked lines, spilling paint on the shoes of other workers, and scattering beads, it just did not seem to me that I was cut out to be a line-painter for the state. No line-painting talent.

The next year, I could not find a job, but my dad came through in the clutch. This time, I had a real man's job. I was a septic tank troubleshooter at a mobile home park. I worked with another man who operated the backhoe. There was no written job description, but my job apparently was to get down into the hole he had dug and try to see what the problem was. The first few hours of my first day on the job went quite well. The other guy dug, and I hung out, occasionally peering into the hole to evaluate the situation in my capacity as troubleshooter. It was noisy work, so I typically just turned to my colleague and gave him the thumbs-up sign that his hole was coming along quite nicely.

The days of early summer in Connecticut are so fine, and made for hanging out, and I am sure they influenced my distaste for sitting behind a desk. The air smells so sweet out in the country and there always seems to be a breeze. While my colleague dug the hole, I had plenty of time to reflect on the air and the breeze, as well as the growing list of career choices I had left behind: Spiderman, baseball, basketball, rock and roll, and line painting.

Soon, the hole was finished, and it was my turn to go to work. I was offered no training class on how to be an effective troubleshooter. All I was told I had to do was to identify septic tank trouble and help fix it. Now, the key to this kind of work from what I could gather was to make sure that care was exercised in going down into the hole, and above all else, to make sure that the mobile homeowner under no circumstances flushed anything, especially the toilet, while I was in the hole. What I did not know was that it was not the backhoe operator's job to enforce this latter crucial requirement. I later found out that enforcing the anti-flushing rule was the responsibility of the troubleshooter – me. I do not think I will ever forget that day when I added the phrase septic tank troubleshooter to the list of careers that I could eliminate from my life plan.

We broke for lunch and found one of those maples growing its dense mop of leaves that later in the New England fall, make Connecticut so singularly and everlastingly memorable, and under the maple tree, we ate and talked about baseball and basketball and rock and roll and outdoor jobs and not being bound by any ties, whether the neck kind, or the female kind, or the life-shaping kind, and when we finished, down into the hole I descended.

I, of course, erroneously assumed the lady of the house, the woman of the mobile home, had been informed by the backhoe operator of the anti-flushing requirement. After all, he was the senior member of this two-man crew. The lady of the mobile home was uninformed, however, and so she did what homeowners do. She flushed. She chose to flush at just the moment that I found the pipe leading from her mobile home. I should be more specific. She flushed just as I grabbed the pipe with its end resting on my knee, the knee that was covered with my brand new pre-washed Levi's. It was not a long flush, but it was a long ride home that night. I was using my mom's Ford Pinto that summer. It was not air-conditioned, and just as well. There was no way I could have kept the windows rolled up. I did not think too much about the sweet air or the cool breeze and as I drove and tried very hard to hold my breath as much as possible, I was pretty sure I would be dead long before the maples along the road caught the fall fire. That night, the New England summers did not seem all that inviting. Lunch had long ago been lost (and not in a misplaced sort of way) and by the time I got home I had the further indignity of having to peel off my jeans by undressing at the front door of our apartment for everyone on our floor of the building to see.

The flush ruined my beloved Converse sneakers and the jeans of every rock and roll star's choice were beyond recognition. To say that my pants could have stood without the aid of an occupant did not begin to tell the story. Even my best friend, my guitar, could not help.

As I lay in my bed that night after what seemed like several hours of antiseptic and exhausting steam cleaning and showering, I thought about the great outdoors. Was I just cursed? Did my dad send me into the troubleshooting world and then down into the hole to make a point — to teach me something? No matter. My troubleshooting days ended with one eight-hour paycheck which bought me new Levi's, new Converse sneakers and left me some change, if not dignity, in my new pocket.

But my dad came through in the clutch again. He found me no outdoors job this time. This next employment endeavor was driving a forklift used to stack skids of frozen bagels twelve high in the basement cryogenic freezer of a famous frozen bagel bakery company. My shift — 10 p.m. to 6 a.m. No, it was not outdoors, but the freezer was so cold that the bakery issued a bright red ski parka to me to wear. With a little imagination, the freezer could have been mistaken for the great outdoors like a ski resort. Of course, there were some things missing, like the snow, the views, the mountains, the breeze, the endless blue skies, the fireplaces, and, well, you get the picture.

It was not a bad job at all. But there were a couple of problems. The primary issue was that I did not know how to operate a forklift. My instructor on the graveyard shift taught me by speaking to me in Portuguese and sadly, I didn't speak or understand a lick of the language and he did not do well with English. In all fairness, the entire crew gave me a crash course in forklift operations, and they were all nice guys, but, as I said, they did not speak much English, and I listened and sometimes said in Spanish "no comprendo" which may not even have been an approved phrase in Portuguese. There were other, lesser, problems — such as, in the freezer, icicles formed on my eyelashes so I could not see where I was going.

But that was surmountable. Most importantly, at the end of the training sessions, I did not know how to operate a forklift.

So on my first night on the job, having graduated from the training course, sort of, I donned my red parka and, with vision-impairing icicles hanging from my eyelashes, I drove the forklift I could not skillfully operate into the freezer with a skid of bagels that had to be fork-lifted on top of a tower of eleven previously stacked skids of bagels. Note to self – never drive a forklift while suffering from an incurable impediment to the performance of the appointed job duties, in this case, a severe lack of skill.

Two things went wrong. In retrospect, it was a miracle that only two things went wrong, but they were big things. I guess I had not yet mastered the "how to stop the forklift" lesson and I guess I did not get the "how to accurately raise a skid of bagels and deposit it atop eleven other skids" lesson. These two lessons were not pieces of cake in any language, at least not for me.

In any event, cutting to the chase, after a few attempts I successfully loaded the twelfth skid onto the forklift and drove into the huge freezer facility. But, sadly, my forklift (with me at the helm) crashed into the eleven-skid tower of bagels at about the same time that the twelfth skid did not get securely deposited directly atop the eleven skids. The result – the skids crashed down and there were cryogenically frozen bagels, hundreds (maybe thousands) of them rolling everywhere. They rolled around the freezer. They escaped and rolled around the bagel bakery plant. People on the shift were agitated, I suppose understandably, and they chattered nervously in Portuguese. One of them called the owner. To be expected.

At 3:13 a.m, the owner arrived to survey the scene, and to be honest, he had not tried to comb his hair and he looked like he had pulled a minimal amount of clothes over his pajamas. I guess that was also to be expected.

He began to talk to the crew, not in Portuguese, but in Yiddish. As I watched the whole thing unfold in slow motion, it struck me that people were talking to the boss in Portuguese, presumably explaining to him what happened, and he answered them in Yiddish, presumably barking some ethnic order to fix the problem. And, each seemed to understand the other. It was the damnedest thing.

Then it was my turn to talk. I apologized profusely and I suggested that since the bagels rolling around were frozen, they could be retrieved, repackaged, and restacked in the freezer. Of course, from a food safety perspective, that was not a viable idea, and the boss let me know as such in English – yay, finally a language I could understand.

I made it to the end of the shift, and I turned in my red parka, and I was sent packing. Another life lesson – freezer work with a forklift was not my calling.

Other eliminated careers based on work experiences included dishwashing in a dining center, waiting on tables in a restaurant, sandwich making at a submarine sandwich shop, lawn mowing, house painting, snow shoveling, bookkeeping, basketball refereeing, ticket-taker at a summer rock concert series, and beer tap renting, to name a few. All good life lessons to help focus on what might come next.

Many, many years later, after law school, I shaved every day, wore a suit and a tie and sat behind a desk. I often daydreamed and reflected: What did I learn from this pre-law school period? Life is so unfair. Who would have ever thought that I would be forced to join the clean-shaven, suit-wearing, tie-tying, desk-sitting throngs just because I could not hit, grow, lyricize, paint straight, troubleshoot, avoid a flush, and drive a forklift?

What else did I learn? This: it is darned hard to figure out what to do with a life. I often think back on the pre-law school times and reflect on whether I missed something. Did I have some other skills that I failed to identify and pursue? I have always thought I had some other skills, but they honestly never came to mind. So, just like that, one night I identified law school as my next potential calling, but I made a pact with myself that I would never practice law and I would never wear a tie. Little did I know.

What follows in this Part I is a little about me and my upbringing, and some lessons I learned that, whether I knew it or not at the time, seemed to begin to outline the path to law school and a life in law, even as I tried to resist mightily. Also, you will learn some more about the things I had in my arsenal to protect me from the law when the law became too much at times.

THE HEART AND THE HEAD

BY WAY OF PSYCHOLOGICAL overview and self-evaluation: I always felt like I was a heart guy, not a head guy. Marc Chagall observed: "If I create from the heart, nearly everything works; if from the head, almost nothing." But it is hard to earn a living as a heart guy and people rely on me to put food on the table. So somewhere along the way, I turned to the head which fit nicely with a life as an attorney... the ultimate head game. With that pivot, my life moved from Chagall's "Dance" to his "Wandering Jew" to Rene Magritte's "The Son of Man" depicting a meticulously dressed man wearing a bowler, but whose face is largely concealed by a large green apple. My law life as represented by art.

Magritte had a knack of making art out of the surreal and in doing so found his heart in what is strange. He observed: "Too often we tend to reduce what is strange to what is familiar. I intend to restore the familiar to the strange." For me, during my life as an attorney, the familiar was always strange but unlike Magritte, I could find no passion, no heart in the strange day-to-day routine that is the practice of law.

Now that I think of it, a good portion of my life before law was a bit strange as well. So, perhaps my path to a life of the law was strangely inevitable.

There are some important differences between heart people and head people. Heart people dream. Head people implement. I like to dream although I was able to learn to implement as well during my life as an attorney. At this point, I prefer to dream. It is so much more fun and rewarding and after a life of dreaming with, at best, mixed success, I am better at it now. Head people know the what. Heart people want to know the why. The why is very important to me.

A law career is not much of a heart endeavor at all. To borrow from Nathaniel Hawthorne's observation in *The House of the Seven Gables*, a pursuit of a life in the law is a "quest for mental food, not heart sustenance." I tended to fight this quest and turned to art and music to do so.

Nothing represents the heart in all of us more than art and music. My relationship with art is easy to explain. My relationship with music, however, is complicated so it will be addressed a little later. Some people jokingly question whether attorneys have hearts. I do. Art often got me through the dog days of courts and arguments. Art is the expression of emotional content created with the intent to evoke an emotional response. Van Gogh viewed art as a doorway to his soul and could lose the concept of self, created by the mind, in his artistic process. Let your head go free and feel the emotion in your art. Let your head go free? Not for attorneys. Lose the concept of self? Not after law school. This presented quite the conflict for me in my attorney world between freeing myself of my head in favor of my heart, and the need to have my head to appear in court.

For me, art is photography. "Camera" derives from the Latin "camera obscura" which means dark box, and "photography" derives from Greek origins meaning drawing with light. Light out of darkness. Almost biblical.

Until my junior year in high school, I knew nothing of cameras. The final high school I attended had an art requirement for graduation, which I ignored. I am colorblind and the prospect that I had to attend a class and create art freaked me out. Adults discovered my colorblindness in second grade in New Hyde Park. My classmates and I were all supposed to draw our teacher with our crayons, and I drew my teacher's dress with blue crayons. Apparently, everyone else thought she was wearing a pink dress and used a color-appropriate pink crayon.

Of course, some in the school thought I was being a smart aleck for drawing a blue dress that should have been pink, and I was hustled first to the principal's office for a confab and then to the nurse's office to make sure I had contracted no illness. It was that nurse, and I wish I knew her name, who took out a colorblindness test, gave it to me, and noted in her journal that I promptly flunked. When you are colorblind, the six to seven million cones in your eyes in the macula do not work properly.

In case you have never taken a color blindness test, they were invented by the Japanese and for people with normal cones in their eyes they are ingenious, and for those of us that are colorblind, they are insidious. The test is a palate of small, colored, dots, hundreds of them. Imbedded in the maze of dots is supposedly a number. If you have color skills, you can see the number. If you are colorblind, you cannot. Just that simple, and I have never seen a single number in the array of dots in my entire life.

At times, over the years, I convinced myself that there is no number hiding among the dots. It is a grand conspiracy perpetrated by billions of earthlings aimed to degrade the approximate 300 million people worldwide who have some degree of colorblindness. I am not paranoid; I am just saying.

Because of this minor affliction, there was no way I would voluntarily take a high school art class and subject myself to the usual rigmarole – what color does this look to you? Can you see the Florida orange? Of course, I can see the fruit – I am not blind. Do you see everything in black and white? Good question, but of course, no.

The best way to explain what I see and do not see is this. My dad purchased his first ever color television in 1971: A small screen Panasonic from Hallock's Appliance Store in New Haven. He was not great with set-ups and instruction booklets, so he handed me the assignment of tuning the television for him – in those days color televisions were manually tuned and the booklet said to find a football or baseball field and tune the greens. Once the greens were tuned correctly, all the other colors would fall in line. So, I tuned the greens. But, one of my biggest color problems is that to me, there is little to no difference between green and orange. For this reason, I tend to call my situation color confusion, not colorblindness.

Back to the Panasonic. I tuned the Panasonic, the greens looked great to me, and my dad came in and exclaimed: "The fuckin' thing is broken. Everything is orange!" A lesson to the wise, never have your colorblind son tinker with the television color.

It was with this background that I had informally declined the high school art requirement by simply ignoring it. But my compassionate principal pointed out that I had to take an art class anyway, and asked me, what would I think about a black and white photography class? Lee High School offered no photography class, but a non-profit organization had arranged for a test photography class and teacher at my school. Frank Martin. I said yes, fell in love with the class, Mr. Martin's Nikon, my used Minolta, and the darkroom, and the rest is history. So much so that I dreamed I would become a professional photographer and follow the New York Mets baseball team around the country as a *New York Times* photojournalist. It was not a bad plan, at least without the forethought of the modern-day death spiral of newspapers and the advent of a camera in every phone owner's hand.

I shot all kinds of stuff: New Haven Mayor Logue one summer; freelance for the *New Haven Register* and *New Haven Advocate*, the Haverford College weekly newspaper, and I decided that I would get a master's in journalism. So, after Haverford handed me my Bachelor of Arts degree, off I went to Northwestern University's Medill School of Journalism in suburban Chicago. But something got mixed up or lost in the translation, and instead of photojournalism, I found myself in the written word journalism program. Nothing against the written word, but I did not want to report about the Skokie, Illinois Nazi march of 1978; I wanted to photograph the conflict. So, I eventually left the master's program and headed back to New Haven to sort it all out.

Almost all of my photos from the era before digital images and jpg and raw formats were prints from my darkroom, or were slides. I had images of family, friends, places, things, and sports. I had images of my mom's chance meeting with Richard Nixon outside the Treasury Building in Washington D.C. as we exited from a Treasury tour and Nixon and his entourage made their way from Treasury back to the White House. My mom, with all the moxie in the world, walked past secret services agents, and right up to Nixon, who was answering questions posed by CBS reporter Dan Rather, and once she was upon them, she turned to me and demanded I take a picture of the three of them. I also had corralled many pictures of prior generations of our family. I kept all of the images on a high shelf in the closet in my second-floor room when I went off to college. In one move or another that came after I departed for college, somehow the images made their way from my second-floor bedroom closet of one house to the basement of another house.

From here, the story starts to get a little odd and the facts are, to say the least, just a little sketchy – the prints and slides all disappeared. The working story from the people of interest who owned the house – my parents – was that there was a flood, and everything in the basement was destroyed including all of my pictures as well as all of the family pictures. Just like that. Thousands of images, negatives, slides, all gone.

Truthfully, I have never been entirely comfortable with the story. It always seemed that it was a contrived story that had been practiced, and it always sounded to me as if the words uttered by the participants in the potential conspiracy were synced up. But it was never enough to prosecute. If you looked at my collection of images today, you would think I was born in 1978 when I married my wife Loren, and not in 1955, my actual birth year. And you might conclude that our family lacked prior generations because there is no record of older family members.

Since 1977, I have been on a mission to make all new images, better and better, more and more, and save them on hard drives in numerous secret and secure locations. I largely stay out of the cloud for storage because it reminds me of my high school days and the second-floor high shelf closet, and the basement storage area, and I don't trust it. In this manner, when I die, our son Zachary will not have a sketchy cloud flood to blame on a loss of historical imagery. I make images to this day and it is an integral part of my life. I shoot sports, portraits, landscapes, macros, places, things, music, politicians… pretty much anything. I have learned to wear earplugs at music concerts, and to get out of the way when there is a sweep in football and lots of large men are all running at top speed right at me.

As an attorney, I was able to turn to my heart and lose myself in photography when I seemed lost in the practice of law, and that helped me find myself, if that makes any sense. I survived many a horrible day as an attorney with my heart reminding me of the promise of a photography gig that evening, which provided me the will to go on... as an attorney. I am grateful I had photography during my law years. Every attorney needs a place to retreat when law and law firm life becomes overwhelming. I have several attorney photographer friends. I think they would concur.

A BRIEF FAMILY HISTORY:
THE ALWAYS ELUSIVE HOME

EARLY ON, I FOUND myself born in a hospital in New York City and I grew up in a high-rise, that might accurately be called a tenement, in Queens, New York. My parents were first-generation Americans, both born to Russian Jews who fled the homeland when they were asked by the Cossacks to leave one night, much like the storyline of *Fiddler on the Roof*. My four great-grandparents left their Russian homeland one night in a cart, made their way to a port, and sailed to the new world. My mom's family all ended up in the Bronx and my dad's family ended up in Brooklyn and Montreal. Both my mom's and my dad's families spoke Russian and English and used Russian to talk to each other when they thought that whatever they discussed should not be shared with the kids.

There is little to be found about either family before they arrived in the new world. My mom tried for years to find information about her ancestors and largely failed. I suspect Russian records of these departed Jews at the turn of the prior century are hard if not impossible to find. It is probably not high on President Putin's to-do list, I suspect.

My mom and her Bronx family were vocal Willie Mays, New York Giants fans, and my dad and his Brooklyn family were avid Jackie Robinson, Brooklyn Dodgers fans. When my folks married, there was only one way to address the obvious Giants / Dodgers conflict: they took their vows in Manhattan and moved to Queens – both designated as neutral baseball territory. Thus, baseball was in our DNA, and properly governed many life decisions. I was born in 1955 just a month after the Brooklyn Dodgers beat the New York Yankees in the seventh game of the World Series to win their first and only championship while the team was based in Brooklyn. I am told that during the World Series, my then-pregnant mom moved an ashtray in the living room and Dodgers star Duke Snider promptly struck out. My dad blamed my mom for jinxing the at-bat and did not talk to her for days. I probably heard their ashtray argument while I was in the womb. I am sure of it and I submit that it would surely have been the first dispute between a warring plaintiff and defendant of which I would be aware. Perhaps if my parents were both Dodger fans, and perhaps if my mom had not moved the ashtray resulting, according to my dad, in Duke's strikeout, I would never have become an attorney. Who knows?

My dad's family fed me homemade chicken soup and gefilte fish. My mom's family fed me homemade borscht and noodle kugel. I assumed these were dishes from their Russian past. Wherever they came from, they were memorable dishes. The secret recipes were not preserved.

When my brother arrived on the scene in 1960, there were four of us in the small one-bedroom apartment in Queens. Two beds and a crib squashed into one small bedroom. I went to P.S. 89 in Queens for a year, and then my parents moved to an old farmhouse that was falling apart in the middle of New Hyde Park, New York, Nassau County, on Long Island just east of Queens but outside the city. New Hyde Park was bliss for me. I had lots of friends, I walked to school every day with my best friend Ann, and as our old, decrepit house in New Hyde Park fell apart little by little, so it seemed did my parent's relationship, as they took on the persona of the battling Bickersons, a syndrome they would relish and take to new heights over the coming years.

My mom identified herself as a housewife. My dad identified himself as an accountant who never passed his CPA test. He worked for a small accounting firm on the eighty-something floor of the Empire State Building. When I got in my mom's hair, my dad took me to his office on Saturdays. I rode the Empire State Building elevator and thought it was an amazing ride to high atop where far below, people looked like a colony of ants who scurried around as they strove to give meaning to their Saturday lives.

In addition to the accounting firm, there were many law firms in the Empire State Building. So, I like to think these trips with my dad were my first experiences of what it would be like to commute to a law firm and ride the elevator in a skyscraper where I would provide legal services to clients from high atop one metropolis or another. I, of course, did not think of it as such at the time, but I can see how it was early training. I think my dad found solace in his daily existence in an office high atop Manhattan in a building that is so emblematic of the New York City existence. I would later have my chance to see if high-rise working provided me the same solace.

By contrast, my dad took the Long Island Railroad to work each day and found no solace in the commute. My folks had one car, a run-down 1950s Chevy, so we had to drive him to and from the train station each day. More than once, he fell asleep on the train ride home, missed his stop, and my mom, cursing like a sailor, drove east from town to town until he woke up and exited the train. Fun rides home as she told him off for the entire drive, with my brother and me in the back seat of the Chevy.

I went to the Polo Grounds with my New York Giants Grandpa to see the worst major league baseball team in history with crazy loyal fans lose to Jim Bunning and the Philadelphia Phillies. The Amazin' Mets of 1962. The Mets lost a record 120 games in 1962, but they had it all: a nutty team with nutty fans, a nutty mascot, a nutty theme song, and a nutty manager, and it was fun to be a kid and avidly root for such a nutty group.

I watched the Dodgers play the Minnesota Twins in the 1965 World Series with my Dodgers Grandpa on his black and white Motorola wood console television. By then, the Brooklyn Dodgers were the Los Angeles Dodgers, based on the move to the west coast to start the 1958 baseball season: The move that broke the hearts of my Grandpa and all of Brooklyn. But once a Dodgers fan, always a Dodgers fan. For some reason, I felt like I should root for the Twins. When I cheered for Harmon Killebrew, my Grandpa said to my dad: "Alfred, take him [me] outside on the stoop and talk to him." The talk was simple: no one roots against the Dodgers in Grandpa's house. Lesson learned. A good lesson for an attorney: No need to cheer out loud; less can be more.

My family passed down to me a love affair with baseball, and I built on that with my dream as a kid that I would play center field for my favorite childhood team – the world champion 1969 New York Mets. The dream of playing for the Mets morphed into a dream of following the Mets around the country with a camera shooting for the *New York Times* or the *New York Daily News* where I could record for posterity Tom Seaver or Jerry Koosman on the mound, pitching to

Jerry Grote behind the plate, and backed by an infield of Ed Charles at third, Bud Harrelson at short, Ken Boswell or Al Weiss at second, Ed Kranepool or Donn Clendenon at first, and an outfield of Cleon Jones in left, Tommy Agee in center, and Art Shamsky or Ron Swoboda in right. We baseball fans all remember the team of our youth as our very own field of dreams (for me, complete with the Rheingold Beer and Meet the Mets songs and I can still sing most of the words to each song to this day).

Like so many, I never played center field and never shot the Mets for the *Times* or the *Daily News*. It is OK to have an unfulfilled dream or three. It is the rare kid in America that dreams of playing for the Mets and then does. These unfulfilled dreams prepare you later in life for the eventuality that you do not always get what you want, and they most certainly prepare you for a life in the law where, despite best efforts, cases are lost, opposing counsel is unhappy with you, judges make rulings that are not what you hoped for, and law firms adjust your expectations of career and success.

I loved New Hyde Park or at least I have strong memories that lead me to remember and believe that I think I loved it. I played stickball in the street; I rode my Schwinn. I rooted for the Mets (approved and sanctioned by both Grandpas and both parents), I drank Yoohoo, I collected baseball cards, I liked *Car 54 Where Are You,* and Ricky Nelson on *Ozzie and Harriet,* and *Father Knows Best.* At my friend Brian's house, I met the Beatles for the first time on A.M. radio. I dreamed my dreams, and life was good.

My parents tried hard. But there can be no denying that they argued constantly and swore a lot. I never knew what to make of my parents. Perhaps most kids don't. My mom had a habit of imposing bans on contact with relatives. She fought often with her sister, her mother, and my dad's family. The ultimate result was no contact with grandparents, aunts, uncles, and cousins. Why my dad permitted the conduct has always been unclear to me. At times I figured he wanted to spend no time on the issue, trying to avoid another fight with my mom. At other times, he was absolutely a co-conspirator with my mom as he took down one relative or another with his own version of relative rants. I suppose that the warmth of love can be seen as the consequence of relationship friction, as one of my cousins once suggested. Maybe, but sometimes friction is no more than the byproduct of two cogs that do not fit well together. In any case, it was the law of the land that most relatives were no-goodniks and no contact was the household statutory requirement. One of the first laws I had to review, construe, and memorize.

We lived in New Hyde Park until Friday, December 10, 1965. I call December 10, 1965 "That Day." On That Day, my parents arrived at my grade school at 10 a.m., came to my classroom with the principal, whispered in my teacher's ear, and in front of all of my friends and fifth-grade classmates, my teacher and my principal, they escorted me out of the classroom, put me in the car, and drove me to New Haven, Connecticut where we would thereafter live. My dad, as it turned out, had secured employment in New Haven, and so off we went. Just like that.

I received no memo about the move, unfortunately, so the whole thing was more than a little surprising and traumatic. None of my classmates knew I was leaving so no one said goodbye to me. I had no idea I was leaving so I did not say goodbye to them. Long-distance phone calls were expensive, my parents said, so I never called any New Hyde Park friends once we moved to New Haven. Except for Ann, I never saw or talked to any of my New Hyde Park friends again. I did not see or talk to Ann for three years, and then I saw her in 1968 at my Bar Mitzvah, and then not again for decades. In our older age, we have now connected again and it is nice, although there is quite a gap of missing years. Brian and some of my other New Hyde Park friends went to the local Catholic grade school, and they did not even have the experience of at least seeing me walk out of the classroom. For these Catholic school friends, I was present on December 9, 1965, and missing the next day and forevermore. Brian must have thought someone beamed me up to the Starship Enterprise, and we were lost in a wormhole as we transported through a time warp to a different dimension.

Net, net, the names all stick with me today: Brian, Jimmy, Ann, Lance, Bruce, Charles, Roddy, Chet, George, and others. I often wonder where they all are. None became President – that I know. I don't think any became a governor. But beyond what they did not become, I would like to find out someday what they did, what they became, how they turned out, what kind of lives they lived. To all of these lost friends, I can only say, sorry mates. I did not run away to join the circus. I just did what I was told because that is what kids do.

That Day, more than anything, taught me that sometimes stuff happens just when you least expect it. That lesson did not soothe the pain of this move in any way whatsoever, and it probably changed me dramatically, to be suspicious when things seemed to be going well. As it turned out, the character trait of suspicion and the lesson of trying to expect the unexpected are good parts of an attorney's personality. That Day also taught me that not every ruling in life carries with it an appeal to a higher court. So, as much as I hate That Day to this day, perhaps my parents were just toughening me up for a law life?

My parents moved a lot. We moved, usually for no reason apparent to me. In my first eighteen years, we lived in nine different houses and apartments, and once we arrived in New Haven, we lived in seven different houses and apartments during the less than eight years I was there until I went off to college. It seemed like we were always packing and unpacking. Oftentimes, we did not even unpack all the boxes. Why bother? All of those moves back then make it difficult for me today to fill out the Facebook profile form which requires the identification of my hometown. I know that my towns and cities all had the word "New" in their names, and I thought of identifying my hometown as "New..." but that would only confuse the masses. I also thought of identifying my hometown as "here" because for me, home is here and here is wherever, and now, here is Denver, and home is now good, very good.

With each move came a different school as my parents felt no obligation to stay in one school district when they moved. I went to four different grade schools, one middle school, and two different high schools. All of the New Haven schools were very inner city, tough schools. With white flight in full swing in the 1960s, the politicians bussed me to inner-city high schools where I was in the minority. That was the point of bussing – to integrate otherwise segregated inner city schools. Bussing gave me the opportunity to learn a great deal about the plight of people of color and a great deal about the book and the cover syndrome; after all, it was the sixties. The Archie Bunkers of the world saw the cover in every person of color. I quickly learned not to and I think I am a better person because I try to focus on the book. All good lessons, that I try very hard to carry with me for my whole life.

For a good long while, I daydreamed that my parents were spies and all of the moves were dictated by a secret government agency whom they served. I figured that their assignment from the CIA was to live in places whose first name was always "New." Some kind of New World Op. I fantasized that they were the "New" spies. But eventually, I realized that they were not spies at all and there was no New Op; they were unhappy and perhaps moving gave them some hope that a new place or part of town would give them a chance to start over and find their happy place. They never found their happy place, but we can all dream, for sure.

Maybe all of the moves were instigated as an extended midlife crisis both parents were collectively experiencing. A midlife crisis can certainly make people do strange and unexpected things. But so many things? The sheer number of midlife crises meant we were always in a state of crisis. I certainly had numerous midlife crises during my law career and perhaps my experience as a bit player in my parents' numerous crises prepared me to handle the number of crises I seemed to have as a reluctant attorney. If the parental crises did not prepare me, they certainly helped develop crisis survival skills. Very important in the legal world.

In New Haven, my parents turned to politics, a very easy life path in the 1960s. They marched on Washington, let me stay up to watch the California primary results on television in 1968 only to see Bobby Kennedy assassinated, were delegates to a Democratic convention, and like everyone else, they lived through massive world changes that occurred, Just like that. Their home became campaign central for a small group of budding East Coast politicians including Joe Lieberman and Hank Parker, and they told the story that Bill and Hillary Clinton stuffed envelopes at our house for one cause or another during the Clintons' stay at Yale during their law school days. I remember Joe and Hank well and continued to write Joe over the years from time to time about one political issue or another, but I don't have a recollection of the Clintons. I stuffed envelopes and licked stamps with a team of stuffers and lickers and the Clintons were not on that team. As much as I admire the Clintons, I am just not sure they were dedicated stuffers or lickers. We all cried over the assassination of Martin Luther King and sympathized during the many riots in New Haven during 1968. We gathered on the New Haven Green to protest the Vietnam War with Yale students and the Reverend William Sloan Coffin and we sang "We Shall Overcome." I tossed my 1972 draft card in a trash can of burning draft cards on the New Haven Green and I hope that the statute of limitations has long since expired on that one.

All of the political activism led my mom to believe that she (or we) were on a secret list of dissidents kept by J. Edgar Hoover somewhere in the bowels of the FBI. Might be true; who knows? Hoover kept a lot of secret lists in his forty-plus years as the head of the FBI. Mom also believed that the FBI wire-tapped our phone. She felt that the wire-tap gave her a direct conduit to J. Edgar. So when the phone rang and she picked it up, here is what she said almost each time: "Fuck Hoover. Shaiken residence. How can I help you?" In her mind, she thought that J. Edgar himself listened to our calls, so I suppose this was the way she communicated directly with him.

As a high school kid in the age before mobile phones, I received phone calls at home from time to time and this type of greeting made many of my callers think I lived in some form of insane asylum. Can you imagine the effect of this greeting on a high school girl who might call me at home? Maybe my high school callers, boys and girls, thought that the apple doesn't fall far from the tree and if my mom was a bit crazy, maybe I was as well. Thank God I did not have many friends, girls or boys, after That Day, but what friends I had found the phone greeting bizarre and they let me know it. Fun times to walk between classes and have someone in the high school corridor say loudly: "Hey, you guys need to call Shaiken's house and hear his Mom answer the phone. What a looney toon!"

I am not sure what the phone greeting taught me or how it influenced my legal career. But, as an attorney, I joked on more than one occasion that I might file a Freedom of Information Act demand to see if there were any FBI files about my mom and if so, if they had yet been declassified. Maybe I would find a memo from a New Haven FBI field agent to J. Edgar yucking it up about this crazy housewife. But I never made the demand. If the files exist, wouldn't I feel stupid for doubting my mom? If the files don't exist, it would only serve to further confirm what I already knew – she was a bit bonkers.

Eventually, despite everything, I graduated from Richard C. Lee High School, and I had no contact thereafter with anyone I met in high school. Based on the "That Day" experience, I guess I thought that is what I was supposed to do – cut ties. Lately, I found a few of the high school friends on Facebook. Their question: where have you been all of these years? Good question. And an understandable area of inquiry based on my tendency to vanish into the ether. Their observation: not surprised you became an attorney. I was surprised by the comment. Maybe they saw a future law career in the teenage me that resulted from the conflicts of the sixties and the gypsy life and the friction and the unhappiness and the paranoia. Who knows?

Just before high school graduation, somehow Haverford College accepted me. Haverford is a small, liberal arts, Quaker college in suburban Philadelphia, where I met my Bryn Mawr College wife, I met my best friend, I grew up, and I learned a little on the side. My time at Haverford was special and so was Haverford. It gave me a much-needed degree of separation from the craziness back in New Haven. Miraculously, in 1977 after four years in the shelter of Haverford, I shook the college president's hand on a podium in front of Roberts Hall, in exchange for a Bachelor of Arts degree in American Studies and with that, I found myself deposited on the world's doorstep without a plan.

But, even though Haverford provided no help with the life plan, it gave me the tools to survive law school. Law school is nothing more than almost lethal doses of reading, writing, thinking, and speaking, and I can imagine no better preparation for law school than four years at Haverford to teach and hone those skills for a successful stint in law school. Haverford has opened all kinds of doors for me in life for which I am grateful. At the same time, the college provided me with my most feared recurring nightmare. I still dream of a call from the Dean of Student Affairs:

> *Mark, this is Dean Potter. In going over our records, we note an unfortunate mistake by our admissions department. We intended to admit a young man named, Mark Spataken from East Haven, Connecticut. His SAT scores were much better than yours and his application for admission was much more in keeping with Haverford's rigorous standards for admission. Very sorry, my friend, but could you please send back your diploma?*

In real life, Dean Potter was a decent guy. I graduated over forty years ago and Dean Potter is no longer with us. But this damned dream... it is always with me.

After my brother and I grew up and left home, my parents moved at least ten more times, spanning four cities and two New York City Boroughs. With these moves, they abandoned the requirement that they live someplace named "New." At one point, my dad dreamed of moving to Des Moines, Iowa, which he would have hated. That move never happened. Eventually, they each ended up in nursing homes, and eventually, of course, my mom and dad died. So, I guess two more moves each making the final, post-college number, twelve moves.

My mom always said she was a member of the Hemlock Society, a group that promoted rational, assisted suicides, inspired by Socrates' decision in 329 B.C.E. to drink Hemlock after spending hours in discussion with his colleagues about his choice between suicide, death sentence, and exile, occasioned by his alleged corruption of the youth of Athens. I never put much stock in her membership contention until I received a *Hallmark* birthday card from her that last year of her life in March (my birthday is in November). In the card, she wished me a happy birthday and wrote that she sent me the early card because she would not be alive when my birthday came around. She died days after I read the card. By her express wishes, she was immediately cremated so no one knows the cause of death. Was it just old age and illness, or could it have been the poison hemlock as Socrates ingested to take his life? If it was hemlock, how did she sneak it into the nursing home? There was little transparency in my mom's death and I can debate how rational she was, but she certainly was an interesting one... right until the end.

MY CHOSEN FAMILY

I HAVE MANAGED TO have a long and rewarding marriage to Loren, a veterinary radiologist with unending patience for me and a willingness to usually give me a pass for some of the fall-out from my past. Loren and I have a son, Zachary, who is a software engineer for a great company in Seattle. Too far away from me for my taste, but he provides me with a great deal of joy and satisfaction as I listen to his stories of his life and career. Nothing can be more rewarding for a parent than to watch an offspring launch, move from teenager to emerging adult, and beyond. It was a complicated process and it was not at all linear. There were lots of twists and turns but as Stephen Covey said: "The main thing is to keep the main thing the main thing." Loren and I tried very hard to follow Covey's main-thing adage.

Loren and Zac are not all I have, but they are all I need. Sometimes simplicity is the ultimate sophistication. Nevertheless, I decided to break with some personal tradition and publicly provide a few of the lyrics of songs I have written about them and our lives. There is no music, of course, in the printed word, so you will just have to read these as poems and know that melody, harmony, and occasionally other elements of music, go along with these words. But these will give you a bit of an idea of what I think of my chosen family. Not everything is peaches and cream all the time, but that is certainly a regular part of the law life, and indeed, a part of the human condition. Right?

Tenderly
(for Zac)

I sent you away
When I needed you most
Now you're back in my life
And the world should take note.
Can we still have love
After all we've been through?
I think that we can, and
I hope you do too.

Sometimes when we meet
We talk for those whiles;
We hug for a bit
Then say our goodbyes
Is this our true love?
Well it sure ain't the blues.
I think that it is,
And I hope that you do too.

It's easy now to feel this way
To see our love by light of day

OK to say yes
OK to say no
Just let the rest
Fly away slow
Nothing else matters
It will all be alright
Just tell me
you love me
softly tonight.

Play With Me
(For Loren)

Come play with me
On my playground,
Come play with me
And let's fool around.

I'm not yours
You're not mine
But we're here for all time.
So, play with me, come play.

Dance with me
On my dance floor,
Come dance with me
And let's dance forever more.

I'm not yours,
You're not mine,
But we're here for all time.
So, play with me, come play.

Cross winds change
So, I change as well;
Nature rearranges
She just doesn't tell.
But when we play,
And when we can dance,
Winds dissipating
So, come take our chance

and

Sing with me
Sweet harmonies
Come sing with me
And let's plant the seeds.

I'm not yours
You're not mine
But we're here for all time.
So, sing with me, come sing.

Takes My Love
(for us)

Takes my love,
Takes my heart,
Takes my soul,
And still we're apart.

What I know,
What I feel,
Hoping to dream
When I'm scared of what's real.

Hold me tonight,
Mean the embrace;
Squeeze 'till the tears, they
Run down my face.
Then, only then,
In this galaxy wide
Can all this make sense,
After Lord knows we've tried

Not happy with this,
But I don't like what's next:
Avoiding a train wreck
And all its affects.

I want to be up,
But right now, I'm down.
Sometimes our love's
Just romantic ghost towns.

It's that time of night
That I always dread,
When my head hits the pillow
And I'm lying in bed;
Waiting for darkness,
Waiting for dreams,
Waiting and waiting,
But nothing it seems…

Leads to that moment,
When todays fade away
And tomorrows don't come
Until the next day.

So, share when I win
And hug when I lose
Pentimento my scenes
To reveal all my blues.

Hold me tonight,
Mean the embrace;
Squeeze 'till the tears, they
Run down my face.
Then, only then,
In this galaxy wide
Can all this make sense?
After Lord knows we've tried.

Takes my love
She takes my heart
He takes my soul
And we each own our part.

THE NIGHT
THE BEATLES
DIDN'T PERFORM
IN MY HOUSE

FEBRUARY 9, 1964. I was an eight-year-old, third-grade boy, living at 1214 Terrace Blvd, New Hyde Park, Nassau County, New York, 11040, (516) Primrose 5-7919. President Kennedy's assassination only a little more than two months earlier weighed on everyone's mind as it began to shape the future of our country. The informed, progressive view is that we were a country in a collective depression. That night, seventy-three million Americans gathered around their small black and white televisions to watch *The Ed Sullivan Show* on CBS so they could experience the Beatles as they exploded into our lives, enchanted us, helped us move forward and out of our depression, and then enticed us through the 1960s and into a new world order.

Quite an extraordinary evening, I have since learned. I did not watch it; I desperately wanted to, and the next day at school I pretended I had – but I didn't. It was banned in our household. My mom forced me to watch Leonard Bernstein and his philharmonic orchestra on public television. I am sure Mr. Bernstein was a great guy, and I hear he was a wonderful composer and conductor, but he was a far cry from John, Paul, George, and Ringo.

Later, I learned Mr. Bernstein liked the Beatles, and I wonder if the Beatles ban would have taken effect in our household if my mom had learned that fact. Unclear. The power of research to support one's position is critical; the absence of timely research can doom one's case. Attorneys know this. I learned it, albeit a bit too late for *The Ed Sullivan Show*.

The days leading up to Leonard Bernstein Sunday went something like this: Friday, February 7, I began to mention to my mom my hope of watching *The Ed Sullivan Show* and the Beatles. Conflict, conflict, conflict, curse, curse, curse, and request denied. I tried again. Maybe my mom did not hear me. Everyone else would be watching, I said. Curse, curse, curse – and then it came without missing a beat. The verdict was read to the defendant in short, incomplete thoughts: ugly long hair, bad music, god damn British, not in this house, not on my television, not as long as I am breathing. I got the idea; I did the only thing I could and stopped listening. I heard enough of the judgment; I did not understand, but I got the essence – no, never, period.

Friday, February 7, 1964. After dinner, I snuck around the corner to my friend Brian's house to hear the Beatles. Brian, his three older brothers, and I listened to WABC Radio 770 on the AM dial and absorbed all the rock and roll we could. It was special. It made me feel grown-up and part of something big.

Saturday, February 8, 1964: during the day, I avoided my mom, and she avoided me.

At dinner, we had no discussion of the Beatles – what was the point?

After dinner, I was at Brian's house again for an hour or so in the evening and we listened to Murray the K, on WINS AM radio. Murray the K. The self-proclaimed fifth Beatle, and one of their first and most ardent supporters at the beginning of Beatlemania and the British invasion of the States. It was heaven. The talk in the room was all about watching *The Ed Sullivan Show* the next night. I lied. *I couldn't wait to watch*, I exclaimed. I was practicing the lie for Monday, at school. On the walk home from Brian's house, I hummed "I Want to Hold Your Hand" and considered who was my favorite Beatle. I was pretty sure it was Paul, even though I had never seen Paul, and did not know Paul from the others. It just seemed like the right Beatle for me to like the best, or at least I thought so. It seemed important in America on February 8, 1964, to have a favorite Beatle. As it turns out, it is still important to me today, and it is still Paul, but now that I am so worldly, I know that Paul is the right Beatle for me to like the best.

All of my dread for the impending night that the Beatles would not visit my home could not stop its arrival. And so Sunday, February 9, 1964, arrived. I looked at our little black-and-white television. I do not remember the brand; it might have been a Philco. It got seven stations, a cornucopia of choices afforded to those living in the tri-state area in those days: 2 (CBS, home of *The Ed Sullivan Show*), 4 (NBC), 5 (WNEW), 7 (ABC), 9 (WOR), 11 (WPIX), and 13 (W-something, something, something, the public television station). I used to remember the call letters for channel 13, but I banished them from my mind after that evening.

Sunday, February 9, 1964, at 7:50 pm Eastern time. It was coming: the end of life as I knew it. I focused so hard during the day to try to avoid thinking about the Beatles, and failed; instead of keeping them out of my thoughts, I dreamed that time would stand still at 7:45 pm, giving my mom more time to rethink her decision, and then when she finally came around, time could start up again. But time did not stand still, and just as I had heard the NASA countdown to lift-off, the Beatle's T-minus blah blah blah began, but without me.

I went to my room after dinner and waited. My mom came up and told me to get into my pajamas and then come downstairs. Could it be?? Finally, she had figured out that the Beatles were not Satan; she realized that they were The Word. So, I brushed my teeth, I put on my pajamas and flew down the stairs without seeming to touch a single step.

The television was on. My mom was sitting in front of it. There was a place for me next to her. I sat and then realized the dial was set to the reviled Channel 13 – New York Public Television. That night, no one held my hand or gave me their loving, and I saw no one standing anywhere. Not that night.

While seventy-three million Americans sat in front of their small black-and-white televisions and watched history – and the beginning of life as we would come to know it – being made; and while seventy-three million Americans sat and watched four guys from England with long(ish) hair sing (Set One: "All My Loving," "Till There Was You," "She Loves You," and Set Two: "I Saw Her Standing There," and "I Want to Hold Your Hand"); and while seventy-three million Americans watched the lads smile and laugh and look into the cameras and say to America, *follow us into the rest of the 1960s together and we can change the world and make history*; and while John and Paul and George and Ringo became household mates that night, I was not one of the seventy-three million. I was one of the four or five Americans who watched a classical music presentation on Channel 13.

Monday, February 10, 1964, a school day. I walked to school with my best friend Ann from 33 Evergreen Avenue. There was a slight fall of snow that day and it was 32 degrees. On the walk, I learned she watched *The Ed Sullivan Show*. I lied. Me too, I said. What did I think of it? Boss, I said. Me too, she said. Boss was the word of the times – shorthand for excellent and outstanding.

I arrived at school. Everyone was buzzing. Did you watch? Sure. What did you think? Boss, I said.

February 10, 1964, came and went as all days do, and life went on as life often does because life must. Because when you are a kid, that is what happens. Life goes on.

April 4, 1964: the Beatles had twelve songs in the Top 40. Shocking. I heard each one at Brian's house. I hummed them at bedtime with my face buried in my pillow so no one would hear me.

Years and years later, I read some remembrances of that night, offered by celebrities. Rosanne Cash, daughter of Johnny Cash, remembered that she loved the Beatles so much, it was physically painful. Of course, her mother allowed her to watch Ed Sullivan that night, and admonished her sisters to be quiet: "Shhhh, Rosanne is watching the Beatles."[1]

My dad liked and listened to Johnny Cash in the day. How ironic. I wish I had known Rosanne when she was growing up. Maybe she would have allowed me to sneak over in my pajamas and watch the Beatles with her. How cool would it have been if Rosanne's mother said, "Shhhh... Rosanne and Mark are watching the Beatles?" But I did not know Rosanne then (or now), and I could not sneak over.

On my sixtieth birthday, my wife took me to London so I could walk in the Abbey Road crosswalk (the one pictured

---

1   https://www.foxnews.com/entertainment/memories-from-those-who-were-there-for-the-beatles-debut-on-ed-sullivan-50-years-ago

on the front of the Abbey Road album). Afterward, we strolled through the St. John's Wood neighborhood, just a few blocks from the Abbey Road Studio. We walked in the rain for an hour waiting for Paul McCartney to come out of his townhouse to take his sheepdog for a walk. I had practiced what I would say to him: "Sorry, mate, that I didn't catch you guys on Ed Sullivan in 1964." But Paul did not walk the dog that day, and so I never got to tell him that in 1964, I was not there to greet the Beatles in my New Hyde Park house. But I like to think he knows why, and he would probably be OK with it. He's like that, I am sure.

So, what in the hell do my feelings about the Beatles have to do with the practice of law? Well, on some levels, everything. A good attorney should try to have an open mind. Without an open mind, maybe there is too much Leonard Bernstein on PBS and not enough "I Want To Hold Your Hand" on Ed Sullivan and, as a result, too much talking and not enough listening. Attorneys talk an awful lot; I am never sure if they are listening.

The last line on the last song of the last album ever recorded by the Beatles is: "And in the end, the love you take is equal to the love you make." An important notion on so many levels and good words to attempt to live by. Since at least February 1964, I have always tried to be keenly aware of the calculation of love taken and love made. Not something that many law firms keep in mind, and not something that I was able to keep in mind often enough in the heat of a law battle. But it is a spirited ideal that was critical to keep in the back of my consciousness as I struggled to survive in the law world.

Artists speak to the world in the artistic work they create. In the end, everyone needs a hero who speaks to them in those artistic creations. Attorneys are no exception. For me, the Beatles are my heroes and my artists, and their creations speak to me. Without those creations to turn to at night after a particularly unpleasant day in the law game, I am sure I would not have been as effective an attorney the next day.

I WANT THE MUSIC IN ME

As a kid, I played the piano. Or, more accurately, I played the piano because it was a nonnegotiable requirement. My mom grew up as something of a concert pianist and had designs for me to be the same.

One day, she decided that I had perfect pitch. There are two kinds of perfect pitch: active and passive. A person with active perfect pitch can sing or hum a specific note without first hearing any other note. Tell them to hum an F note, and they will. A person with passive perfect pitch can hear a note and tell everyone what that note is. Play an F note on the piano, and the passive perfect pitch person will be able to tell you it was an F note. I believe my mom meant I had passive perfect pitch. I believe I had neither.

Along with her decision that I had passive perfect pitch came the perfect pitch schtick and it turned into a type of vaudeville act. When her friends visited, out I came onto the living room floor in my pajamas to "prove" I was gifted with passive perfect pitch. Except, she (I guess *we*) cheated. I would know what the notes were that she would play and so I could dutifully tell the audience what note I heard based on the script. I was complicit. I am not so sure it was not a crime; I am sure it was rigged, it was weird, and it made me uncomfortable then and makes me uncomfortable still today. Back then, I feared that some Nassau County, New York district attorney would show up at our door during the schtick and arrest me for some form of criminal fraud. I worried a lot as a kid. Perhaps this was my first real brush with the law. Who would have thought my first brush would have been a violation, rather than enforcement, of the law?

As a child piano player, I performed from time to time at recitals. My last piano recital was to play Stephen Foster's "Beautiful Dreamer" at a fundraiser for our Cub Scout Pack No. 125 held not long before That Day (see "A Brief Family History – The Always Elusive Home"). That fundraiser show was a combination of comedy and musical performances. The Pack advertised the evening in the *New York Daily News*. The *Daily News* carried my picture as well. I manned the piano. For reasons I still have not figured out to this day, however, I decided to play "Beautiful Dreamer" in under a minute and instead of a lovely piece in 9/8 time, in *moderato*, I played the entire song in less than 50 seconds, as fast as my little hands would allow. Just like the pianist in *Reefer Madness*, I played like I was possessed. When I finished, I bowed to the audience of a couple of hundred people, and you could hear a pin drop. No one could figure out if I was part of the comedy or the musical portion of the show. The audience decided I was in the comedy troupe, so they laughed and then they applauded. My mom (and for that matter my piano teacher), sitting in the front row, glared and shrunk. For them, an early version of the modern day famous Southwest Airlines' series of television commercials that have the punch line: "Wanna Get Away?"

My mom did not talk to me for a week. When she finally did, I announced that was the last time I would play the piano – ever, and it was. I have often wondered if the "Beautiful Dreamer" piano recital was a direct protest to the February 9, 1964 Beatles incident. I have also wondered if That Day was as a direct result of "Beautiful Dreamer." Was my lesson for my mom that if I couldn't watch the Beatles on *The Ed Sullivan Show*, then I would not capitulate to properly playing "Beautiful Dreamer" on the piano in front of all of these people? Was my mom's lesson for me that if I wouldn't properly play "Beautiful Dreamer" the way Stephen Foster wrote the piece, then we would not stay in New Hyde Park? I would hope neither was the intended lesson, but you never know.

My takeaway was that I had much more power in the music negotiations than I ever realized. My first brush with dictating the course of negotiations based on my assessment of leverage. Who knew Stephen Foster could lead to such negotiation sophistication in a ten-year-old?

Once in New Haven, I found a second-hand Harmony brand guitar, fell in love with it, and have played guitar ever since, although the Harmony did not last very long before I upgraded with my summer job money. I am pretty sure my mom never wanted to hear me play guitar, except perhaps through the walls, hearing the muffled sounds with a bit of disdain, and I am completely sure she never asked to hear me play. I don't think she looked at the guitar as a musical instrument, opting to view it simply as not a piano; a long-necked piece of wood with six metal strings.

Music has always been important to me. For that, I have my mom to thank. So, thanks, Mom. Music is also very personal to me. I write music but I don't perform. I guess I am not willing to risk another "Beautiful Dreamer" incident. Indeed, I don't usually play for others. It is mine and mine alone. During my law life, it was the place to go to escape. Every attorney needs a solid, reliable, and accessible place to go to escape. So again, thanks, Mom. Maybe someday,

I will show up on a corner on the Sixteenth Street Mall in Denver with my guitar. Maybe someday, I will show up at an open mike night at the Last Chance Bar and Grill on South Broadway. I doubt it, but who knows? My hour of music a day is a truly great hour for me, every time, each and every day. And it is mine – just like that.

ALL THERE IS TO DO IS DREAM

I HAVE ALWAYS DREAMED. At early points in my life, it was an escape from whatever might have been going on and whatever parental fight was unfolding. At other points, the dreams were substitutes for a viable life plan. At still other points in my life, dreaming was a way to plan; I would call it the initial outline phase of a plan. OK, that is not correct. I want this book to pass any authenticity litmus test and my family will call me out if I leave the statement as I wrote it. So I need to correct it: by and large, my dreams were not outlines of anything. Mostly, they were random ideas that I hoped might lead to an outline and then perhaps a rough plan and then maybe a more formal outline from which there could be plan implementation. Most of my dreams never made it out of the idea stage; stuck in a dark corner of my mind's eye where ideas get formed, considered, and then cut and dropped to the floor like rejected frames in a film editing room, only to be swept off the floor each night by the cleaning crew.

I like dreaming. In my view, attorneys don't dream enough. You will see discussions of dreaming in this book because I have done a lot of dreaming during my tenure on planet Earth. Kobi Yamata said, "Follow your dreams. They know the way." I would beg to differ. Mine did not always know the way, or any way for that matter. Maybe there was no way. Anyway, it was hard to follow them or even keep track of them. Bobby Kennedy borrowed from George Bernard Shaw and famously said: "Some men see things as they are and ask why. I dream of things that never were, and ask why not." I love that quote, and I loved Bobby. I am sure I never dreamed as lofty and important a dream as either Bobby's or George's, but I have worked through a goodly volume of dreams; they are still coming, and it is a good way to go through life and a necessary way for me to survive the law life. Dreaming was and is critical to survive.

Certainly, the things I have dreamed about throughout my life mostly never came true, and even when I asked why not, as Bobby advocated, they largely still did not materialize. After NASA set up shop in Houston in the 1960s, the city became a place that dared to dream big, very big. When Loren and I moved to Houston in 1984, we were struck by how much of a "can-do" city it was, probably as a result of dreaming big. Perhaps that is why we loved our years in Houston. I don't necessarily dream big, but I dream often and maybe that is big for me. I wanted you to know early on in the book that I can get lost in dreams. I also thought this was a good time to observe that my law life first fueled, then interfered with, and finally capitulated to, my dreams. I never thought the law life would capitulate to anything, so it was a real "can-do" moment when the law life finally gave way, ceded the road, and stepped aside for a dream. But I am getting ahead of myself.

STRANGELY INEVITABLE

THIS ATTORNEY THING. WHO would have thought? It sure wasn't planned. To this day, I am not sure exactly how it happened. All I seem to remember, other than my job training, is that I know I had a childhood, I went to college, I graduated, and then things get fuzzy.

Somewhere along the way, I bought the *Yale Insider's Guide to Colleges* and planned which college to attend. I picked out some likely candidates, planned an excursion with my dad to visit the campuses, and made a rational informed decision, based on objective "quality of education" criteria, about the school someday I hoped would be my alma mater.

I was a pretty typical college student. Nothing remarkable. I planned which classes to take to afford me ten hours of sleep each night. I planned my major, which room on campus to live in, which teams to play on, which beer to drink, which cliques to join, which girls to date, which classes to skip, which causes to patronize, which records to buy, and I kind of got my education on the side. I learned not to let my studies get in the way of my education.

But I was not a great planner. It seemed I always had an 8:30 a.m. class, never slept in double figures, picked American Studies as my major because I was in college for an education, not a job, never won a decent campus room in room draw, never played on an intramural championship team, drank Yuengling ('nuff said), never joined any cliques, dated exclusively Bryn Mawr women, skipped classes occasionally, and patronized the cause of coeducating Haverford.

All of a sudden, one day the sky turned dark, angry thunder clouds rolled in and time and space distorted. I had to plan my future.

My inclination was to take chances on this one but to avoid screwing up. A lot was riding on the plan. I finally had to decide what I would be when I grew up. I had little experience in the growing-up exercise and even less experience in identifying something I was good at that interested me. I just did not know how to plan, identify, and select a suitable life option. Hell, I didn't know then, and for the next forty-one years, I still did not know.

Think about this for a moment. There should be some kind of test before you are allowed to go forth and construct this life plan. The test should determine if you are qualified to select a path for your future, or if you need to have some remedial training.

Deep down, I knew I was not qualified; I had already bombed out on several promising career choices. But with a liberal arts degree in American Studies, a glut of schoolteachers on the market in the post-Vietnam war era, a Bachelor of Arts diploma with calligraphied Latin and "power invested" words in black ink still not quite dry, all the world in front of me (and arguably the best years behind me), I developed my simple plan: I would need some more time... to plan.

So, in December 1977, after graduating from college seven months before, failing at finding a life course to pursue, and crapping out on the journalism school gig, I did some nifty research and I discovered I could go to law school, thereby delaying the planning process for three more years. Hell of a deal.

Law school was thus inevitable. It was not a dream of mine, but a convenient way to continue to work on my dreams, or at least so I thought. Indeed, law school may be a dream for very few people. For me, whatever else it was, it was my means to delay. And the storm cleared and off I went. As Walter Cronkite said every night, that's the way it is.

Just like that.

PART TWO – LAW SCHOOL

SOCRATES, WHAT DO YOU THINK?

LAW SCHOOL, IN MY experience, is three years of classrooms in which answers are never given. What a long, strange trip. All the answers to all the questions can be found in the cases that the students read – or so they say. The teacher, however, never divulges an answer, but rather prods the students into realizing and discovering the answer on their own. Questions are returned with, "Well, what do you think?" In effect, the teacher seems to deny the knowledge necessary to answer the question and relies on the students to figure it out. Students don't rely on the teachers; teachers rely on the students. Welcome to the world of Socratic-method teaching. Welcome to law school.

The point of the Socratic method is to teach the students not only the law, but also how an attorney is supposed to think, reason, and operate. While not always obvious, law school is not actually about the answers; it is all about the method to solve problems. After law school, when a client calls with a problem, no one will be around then to tell the attorney the answer, if there is even an answer. So, the Socratic method teaches the student to figure out the answer without too much assistance.

It is much too frustrating, however, for a student to be denied a hard-and-fast answer to a straightforward question. So, there are places to go to find the answer other than the cases. For example, in Constitutional Law, law students read case after case decided by the United States Supreme Court since this country was founded, not only to learn the rules of law but also to learn how the law evolved. It can be confusing. It is always time-consuming. The confusion is not always resolved in the classroom, because the teacher is using the Socratic method. If you missed the legal principles when you read the case, there is a decent chance you will still have no understanding to help you when you ask a question and the teacher replies, "What do you think?"

But the wonders of modern science have reached even the ivy-covered walls of the law school tenement halls. Rather than read dated cases with hidden, dusty rules of law to discover the history and the occasional rule, you can buy prepackaged guides, fancy study aids, or turn to online searches. You do not even have to read the cases, and many do not. They just read their aids. All the answers are there in black-and-white. The aids tell you what is important to know, and what is important to forget. The aids give you the outline to memorize at the end of the class to prepare for the final exam. The aids largely skip the facts and get straight to the rule of law. The aids have nothing to do with Socrates and his ancient methods.

There are all kinds of aids. Some aids follow the course textbook exactly and provide a short statement of each case, including facts and law and reasoning. These aids save the law student the time and hassle of having to read the law. Other aids provide an overview of the whole course subject with an index to guide the student through especially troubling areas of the law. Still other aids are long outlines that give the student the final examination tool – the outline – which, if memorized and regurgitated on the final examination, will ensure a passing grade.

I went through law school, however, the old-fashioned way. I practiced safe law – so, no aids. I read all the cases, I took notes in a notebook, I identified the issue, rule of law and rationale for the rule, I wrote my outlines, developed my anagrams when I studied to help me recall the rules of law, exercised my short-term memory, and I passed my exams. I tried not to ask for an answer and so was not disappointed when an answer was not forthcoming in the classroom. I would have made Socrates proud.

After the last test in the last class in the last semester of law school was over, however, the big daddy of them all loomed just over the horizon. The bar exam! This is not a test for any disciples of Socrates. This is a test where everyone, both worshippers and detractors of Socrates, screams, "Give me outlines! Give me aids!" I was no different. You see, the Socratic method is a creature of law school that becomes extinct the minute the last law school exam ends.

For the bar exam, I acquired hundreds and hundreds of pages outlining the majority and minority rules of law in virtually every subject I had studied Socratically for three years. I had no Socrates to guide me, but rather unadulterated answers by the pound, bound in two neat books that I kept for thirty-eight years after law school ended. I had indices to the outlines and cross-references to different topics. I had suggested shortcuts to cram as much of the outline material in my short-term memory as was humanly possible.

I was left to wonder, if it was all in the outlines, why did I have to go to law school? Why did I have to spend three years in a classroom where no answers were ever given? The bar exam materials were all the law and all the answers I could ever want or need. So I asked a law school teacher of mine, "Why go to law school if it's all in the bar exam outlines?" And do you know what he said? "What do you think?"

Very funny. If I knew the answer, there would be no need to ask the question. Sometimes the Socratic method lets a teacher hide behind a sarcastic reply to a legitimate, answerable question. Sometimes, a teacher's reply in the Socratic method of teaching is nothing more than a euphemism for "You mean you do not know? Harrumph."

I thought about my question, unanswered by my teacher, for some time, and I finally came up with an answer for the law students of this country. The problem with the books and aids and outlines is that they create a false environment where there appears to be an answer to every question. Socrates knew better. There is often no answer that is any better than what you critically think. On the other hand, I sure wish I had had the aids in law school. Socrates is all well and good, but you can take a good thing too far sometimes. I mean, what do you think?

LOOKING FOR THAT FIRST LAW JOB

As LAW SCHOOL WOUND to a close, I began the process of finding that first job. For me, this was the beginning of the end of the three-year planning extension afforded by law school, during which I had thought I would figure out what I would do with the rest of my life. Normally, I would have dreamed a lot during the three years, because that is what the heart is for, and that is how I lived and supposedly planned. And it was my hope (and plan) that I could remain a heart guy and that one of those dreams would be the answer to the riddle of the rest of my life. But law school is all-consuming and did what law school does – it kind of took over and left precious little time for dreaming. This was my first experience with the law's insidious habit of getting in the way of a good dream session. So, as the three years started to draw to a close, I was no closer to realizing any viable dream. Bummer. Still a heart person, but in need of money and quickly finding out that the head would take over.

I decided to give the law job location process a try. Who knows, I thought. Maybe a law job would not be all that bad and it likely would be much better than law school. And what a process it was. Remember, this occurred back in the dark ages where three by five note cards of possible jobs were posted on a bulletin board in the basement of the law school building. First come, first served.

The notecards were tempting, so I read them and the intrigue of a job in the law set in. Instead of listening to that little voice in my head that said, *wait, slow down, think this through, dream a little*, instead I started to interview for a job in the law. Much to my surprise, a coveted clerkship for a federal bankruptcy judge in Kansas came my way, but not without some bumps in the interview highway, discussed a little later.

The judge was impressive and had a stellar reputation among the bankruptcy practitioners, and I thought, *take the clerkship, learn bankruptcy law inside and out from an expert, work for a great guy, and delay, again, the final decision of what to do with the rest of my life.*

I went through my normal thought process – delay again – but this time, I settled on the plan of delay without a great deal of hand-wringing. I was becoming quite comfortable with the figure-it-out-later methodology of formulating a life plan: easy to employ, and low stress. So, just like that, I signed on to be a law clerk for a federal bankruptcy judge. But first, I had to pass the dreaded bar examination.

BAR EXAM

IT IS THE MID-SUMMER ritual for which all law school graduates live and die – the Bar Examination, affectionately called the Bar (I assume no pun intended by the ancients of the law business). Examinees do not take the exam; they sit for it. I am unclear about the origins of the notion that the examinee sits for the exam, but I am also unclear about what alternatives to sitting in a chair on the days of the exam are available. Apparently, it originally meant to take an exam in a formal setting. But, in that case, it is redundant. The exam is relentlessly formal and unimaginably stressful. No need to double up on the formality.

The exam is the great demarcation between those who pass and are licensed to practice law and those who are stigmatized by failing the exam and relegated to the need-to-find-another-job-for-the-time-being, law school graduates.

Within minutes of graduation, the grim reality sets in for the newly matriculated. Law school is over, summer associations have ended, a permanent position may await, but a state license is needed. The schooling, the association, and the degree are nice, but they are all of little value without the license, the authorization from some state, somewhere, to research, render advice to clients, draft documents, negotiate, appear in court, to advocate, and to hold oneself out as an attorney at law. States issue a license to practice law based on the results of the bar exam given by the state, usually twice a year: once in February, and once in July. So, after graduation, the immediate, short-term post-graduation future is simple. Two months of cramming followed by days of testing, in a two-, three-, or four-part, too-bad-if-you-flunk exam. It is a lonely, introspective, secluded time of abject and ever-increasing fear: what happens to graduates who flunk the bar? *Don't ask, but don't worry*, I was told when I posed the question to one of my former professors. I took half of his advice – I decided not to ask.

Most law school graduates choose not to face these two months without a crutch. The modern crutch is a review class. This is how the two months of review class, studying, fearing, paranoid-ing and sitting for the exam collectively work.

<u>Review Classes.</u> The bar exam is outrageous. There is no other word to describe it. It is so outrageous that most graduates need help. They need help preparing, cramming, sorting through the legal principles, memorizing, analyzing, staying calm, visualizing sanity, and developing a strategy for attacking the test questions. They need help to pass.

As it turns out, law school provides an insufficient amount of preparation for the graduate to become a licensed attorney. Remember, law school teaches the law student a process – how to think and analyze, often with the luxury of time as the students of Socrates had in the ancient days. Law school, however, is a cakewalk compared to the bar exam.

Not too long ago, there were no review classes. Then a smart attorney-to-be graduated from law school, sacrificed all semblance of normal daily activities for two months, passed a bar exam somewhere without any outside help, realized that law school is little help with passing the bar exam, had a few beers, and came up with the idea that the process of passing the bar exam could be taught in two months. And in that experience, this law graduate developed and began to teach a bar exam review class, billing it as the all-purpose, be-all and end-all, hand-holding exam prep. Law school graduates signed up in droves and classes popped up throughout the entire country. In every state, graduating law students were encouraged to sign up for a bar review class, and how could they refuse? They could never look in the mirror if they had a chance to increase their odds of passing but declined the opportunity.

There's money in them there review classes. Imagine, every year, thousands of test-fearing law students graduating and paying big money to garner every advantage they can possibly think of in the hopes of passing the bar exam in the state of their choice. That is thousands of money-bearing, weakened, vulnerable, impressionable, volition-less, anxiety-ridden (did I say money-bearing?), emerging adults, who will do almost anything to pass. Sitting ducks.

Hence, the review classes. Filling a need. Graduates want help. Graduates want hand-holding. Graduates want outlines with all the law there ever was, and ever will be, right there at their fingertips. The review classes give it to them... for a fee. A large fee. Are the classes worth the fee? No graduate is brave enough to risk taking such a test without the benefit of the review class, so we may never know.

After graduation, the student selects a review class and enters the pre-test training, cramming as much law as humanly, but not *humanely*, possible, and hoping upon hope to be able to regurgitate the learning and the memorizing during the test. Typically, review class teachers give three-hour lectures each night starting at six o'clock, covering lengthy outlines the examinees supposedly reviewed that afternoon. Constitutional law, fifty-page outline. Six hours of solitary review. Three-hour lecture. Criminal law, fifty-page outline. Five hours of solitary review. Three-hour lecture. Torts, eighty-page outline. Torts is very dry; maybe only four hours of solitary review. Maybe attend the lecture. Contracts, sixty-page outline. You get the rhythm.

The key to the class is the outlines. The solitary, consistent, repetitive, commitment to reviewing the outlines, dry or otherwise. Never-ending, all-encompassing, comprehensive outlines of everything and more an examinee ever needs to know to pass a bar exam if the examinee could memorize the content and recall it at will when presented with the bar exam questions.

The review class provides sample essay questions from years past, with suggested correct answers. The answers are often lengthy, and well beyond what any human could possibly write in the time allotted by the bar examiners. But the sample questions and answers give the examinee an idea of what the test will be like. The sample questions and answers also give the examinee a sense of futility. All part of the game. All part of the review class racket. Make the examinees feel helpless, then take them by the hand and lead them out of the valley of doom. The examinees tell all their friends about the miracles performed by the review class. Testimonials: water to wine. More graduates sign up. Say hallelujah.

The review class also provides volumes and volumes of practice and sample multiple-choice questions and answers. Thousands of sample questions; thousands of explanations of why "A" was the correct answer and not "C." Hundreds of suggestions of recent trends in bar examination multiple-choice question topics. Common law (how things were in England in the olden days) and uncommon law. General rules and exceptions. Helpful hints. Memory tricks. Anagrams.

I have often thought that the process of developing ana-grams could be a career in itself. For example, a common law school anagram to help remember the elements of owning land by adverse possession is OCEAN: Possession must be **O**pen, **C**ontinuous, **E**xclusive, **A**dverse and **N**otorious. The prospect of developing one long anagram to cover all the law, like supercalifragilisticexpialidocious, has always intrigued me. But I am sure that having reduced the law to a single anagram, I would likely forget what the letters stood for, and no matter what the question was, I would be forced to print the anagram, and hope for a bar examiner who corrected my exam with a sense of humor or pity.

I took and passed five bar exams (or parts thereof) in my thirty-eight-year career, as we moved around from state to state, and I have taken more than five review classes to pre-pare for the tests. Like so many of my fellow test-takers, I did not have the will to take the exams without the review classes. And I passed; so, the classes certainly did not hurt.

<u>My Pre-Test System</u>. The bar exam is largely an exercise of mind over matter. Study enough, and try to achieve that moment of a belief that you will pass the test; try to arrive at that point where you have done everything possible to pass. Some describe this state of mind as the moment when the exam-inee no longer worries. The examinee's moment of testing enlightenment. Most examinees begin studying and then slowly lose all sense of control and ultimately, sanity. While an absence of worry is an aspiration, it is not something the examinee ever achieves. They can try not to worry, but what they really have to do is to attempt to manage the fear.

I developed a bar exam system over the years that I sub-jected myself to as we moved around the county. I designed my system to try to manage the fear and study, but I never copyrighted the system or sought inclusion in any of the self-betterment recordings found in various "life can be great" audiobook catalogs or on *YouTube*.

My system worked like this: I was very rigid in my study plan. I counted the days I had to study, multiplied the days by the projected number of hours per day I thought I would be able to endure (usually eight or nine or ten), divided that product by the number of subjects upon which I would be tested (usually ten to twelve), and arrived at the number of hours per subject I would have to study to pass. I operated on the assumption that this was exactly what the examiners expected the examinees to do. I presumed that most examiners believed that if the examinees studied, they would pass. So the only way to pass was to determine how much study time there was, and then divide it equally among the various subjects. Usually, there were twenty-five hours per subject that were available for cramming.

It was my little endearing way of substituting immediate mental illness for the slow burn of constantly worrying. This kind of rigor, however, had its price. In my system, I quickly lost my ability to utter, speak, and even communicate. As time progressed, I first became a babbling idiot and then I could not talk at all. I knew the law was stuffed into my brain because it must simply have been in there after all the hours of reading outlines over and over and over. When I finally could no longer communicate, when I could no longer utter a single word of what I had learned, I achieved testing enlightenment and then I knew I was ready for the bar exam.

The toll was even greater. For example, typically, I never lost sleep over anything. Occasionally, however, in the middle of the two months of terror, I lost a night or two of sleep and panicked. "What if I never sleep again until the test?" I yelped at my wife (this was while I could still talk). If I could no longer talk, I wrote her a note and underlined the "what if" several times for emphasis, as if she could fix the problem. She always tried to calm me down, sometimes succeeded, and I drifted off to a restless sleep featuring another of my recurring nightmares where I take a final examination in a college class I never attended and about which I knew absolutely nothing. Nothing like sleep to invigorate and control any inclination to worry.

As the test day approached, I became irrational. Two days before I took my first bar exam, I cooked spaghetti, and for reasons to this day I cannot explain, I became disgusted with the pasta (or my life), drained the pot of its water, and threw the entire pot of pasta against the kitchen wall where much of the spaghetti stuck. I guess it was cooked past *al dente*. The night before the last bar exam I took, thirty-three years after my first experience, I sat quietly on the couch, and then for no reason at all, I howled to my wife: "What in God's name am I doing?" Not a question that begs an answer. By this point in my law life and the many years of inhumane testing, she had learned not to respond to such a question.

The last week before the test, things got weirder and weirder. I usually tried to read a book during the last week, and traditionally, it was *Fear and Loathing in Las Vegas*, by Hunter S. Thompson. It just seemed appropriate. Once, I also read *On the Road* by Jack Kerouac, but I usually shot for only one nouveau picaresque novel per exam.

This was my system. It was a great system; at least, for me.

Test Time Rules. Finally, thankfully, test time arrived. By now, the examinee was convinced that flunking would be better than one more week, one more hour, one more minute, of studying. Fatalism set in. It would all soon be over. Flunking would not be so bad. There had to be other careers: maybe business school; maybe an English teaching gig at a private school somewhere in New England. Maybe a management trainee position at the local burger-and-shake shop. More career dreaming. But before changing careers, first the exam. One more cup of coffee, sharpened number two pencils in hand (enough to rewrite Moby Dick by hand), extra erasers, a kiss from the wife, and off I went to do battle in the hall of doom. The wise examinee left plenty of time to drive to the test, to account for any unexpected traffic jams, detours, nuclear disasters, or highly-trafficked deer or elephant crossings that might be encountered along the way. The wise examinee mapped out several routes to the exam to account for such experiences.

Like everything else in my life, I had my own special concoction of rituals and rules I followed and found comfort in. I usually arrived early – Sign-in was usually thirty minutes before the test began – showed my driver's license to prove I was who I said I was, and took a seat to get the lay of the land. Seating was regulated: only every other seat could be occupied, so no one could cheat. Perhaps it went without saying, but the testers said it anyway. More tradition: by test time, I had not shaved for at least a week. The growth gave me something to rub, and assisted me in looking thoughtful when I had no idea what to write or which answer to choose. I noticed that many people had growth to rub. It goes without saying that I always wore my lucky-everything: shorts, socks, jeans, ring, shirt, belt. During the Texas bar exam, I adopted an old, beat-up Kansas City Royals hat as my lucky hat. Hell, I would have worn my lucky bra if I had one and if I thought it would get me through the test.

There was always a bathroom just down the hall. I never sat near it (one of my more important rules of bar exam taking). The examiners thoughtfully provided the bathroom for the conventional kind of relief and to accommodate the statistical number of examinees who, upon opening the test book and reviewing the questions, had an uncontrollable need to relieve themselves of breakfast while hanging over the toilet and vomiting, loudly. Consequently, I never, never sat in the back of the testing hall near the door to the bathroom.

There oftentimes was a large window in the testing room, and another rule of mine was to avoid sitting near that, too. I was not in the testing room for a view. And the test was usually given in a hotel in a not-so-great part of downtown, Some City, America. There was nothing more distracting when choosing an answer than having some guy gaze in from the other side of the window and shake his head from side to side, seemingly in response to my last multiple-choice answer I selected on the test, while he drank from a brown paper bag that hid a bottle of who knows what. Windows were distracting – too much real world on the other side to contend with. Or perhaps he was sent by my guardian angel, and I should have considered his hint? Who knows?

After an eternity of seat-choosing and milling about, proctors distributed the tests, and they reviewed rules and regulations with the examinees. I always listened to them with the same attention I give to the stewardess discussing what would happen in the unlikely event of a loss of cabin pressure – I had read the rules many times in the study materials. Like in the air, my thought was, let's get going. Proctors and examinees synchronized their watches. The clock struck nine, and the proctor said, "You may begin." For whatever reason, my ears always got hot and tingly when the proctors uttered those words. Examinees opened the exam booklets. A statistical number of people excused themselves immediately and headed for the toilet to throw up, and the examinees were off to the races. Tally ho.

<u>Part One – The Essay Questions</u>. Part One of the bar exam is a written essay test. It is supposed to test both knowledge and legal analysis. Some states give Part One on day one. Some give it on day two. No matter. The correct answer is important; the method, the logic, and the legal analysis the examinee uses to arrive at an answer, right, wrong, or otherwise, is *more* important – the culmination of three years of Socrates.

The essay test lasts six hours, three in the morning and three in the afternoon. It is six hours of writing in a blue book, with a number two pencil, or, perhaps in the modern era, on a laptop that is locked out of the internet. It is six hours of making short, scribble outlines of points to cover, issues to mention, rules to state, exceptions to note. It requires the test-taker to have semi-legible handwriting. The examiners cannot pass what they cannot read.

I always found the written essays to be fair. If I knew the answer, I wrote it down, explained it and moved on. If I did not know the answer, I turned to creativity, explained my creative views that had no grounding in law or proper analysis, and I moved on. One review class professor suggested that if a question was outside of my knowledge base – meaning I didn't know the answer – invent a statute, quote it, and apply it to the facts. Simple enough, just like law school. The essay test gives the examinee the opportunity to pontificate and, if need be, make it up – just like law school. But many states do not even review, correct, or grade the essays if the examinee obtains a sufficient score on the multiple-choice test. These states rely on Part Two of the test to determine who is qualified to be an attorney. It makes you wonder about the essays.

<u>Part Two – Multiple-Choice</u>. The second part of the test is called the Multistate exam, the "Multistate" for short. It purports

to be a standardized, multiple-choice test by the folks from Princeton who brought us such golden oldies as the SAT's, LSAT's, GRE's, and MEDCAT's. Multiple-choice questions are these people's specialty. The Multistate may very well be their most glorious achievement.

Part Two is a six-hour test, three in the morning, and three in the afternoon. There are one hundred questions in the morning and one hundred more in the afternoon. The questions are usually between one-hundred and three-hundred-word fact patterns, followed by a series of questions. For the truly anal, that amounts to 1.8 minutes (108 seconds) per question. 1.8 minutes (108 seconds), to read and digest the fact pattern, the question, the four possible answers, and to select the obvious winner before moving on to the next 1.8-minute-question.

The key to the Multistate is that the questions test nuances. They test the ability to pick the *most* correct answer out of four choices and they also test the ability to pick the *least* correct answer out of four choices. It is not enough for the examinee to recognize that no answer is correct. The examinee must be able to identify an answer that is almost correct, or, even worse, that is the most wrong. Can you imagine? It is a test where the examiners tell the examinees that for a significant number of the questions, none of the answers are completely correct.

It is nuance without any opportunity for pontification. No express analysis is permitted. The examinee earns the brass ring by selecting the correct answer, and the examinee selects the correct answer by thinking like a Multistate examiner.

The only way to share a bit of the fabulous, inspired Multistate experience is to share a typical question. I made up the following question because I could never remember the actual questions from any of the many Multistate tests I have taken over the years. And, remember, you only have 1.8 minutes (108 seconds) to select your answer. The answer will appear at the end.

> *It is a dark and stormy night. Bill is very upset. He has discovered that someone, he thinks Bob, has been telling people that he is a criminal. Bill may very well be, but he does not want anyone to know. So Bill is not just mad at Bob, he is enraged. Bill knows where Bob lives. He sets out to teach Bob a lesson. He will rough up Bob. It is late. Very late.*

Are you following the story so far? Time is ticking. Remember, you only have 1.8 minutes (108 seconds). Make sure your reading comprehension is finely honed. You will need it. Back to our question.

> *Bill arrives at Bob's house and knows Bob's bedroom is upstairs, on the east side of the house. There is no moon tonight, so it is very dark. No one sees Bill. Bill begins to silently climb the trellis on the east side of Bob's house that passes directly next to Bob's bedroom window. He arrives at the window, which is cracked an inch, raises it the rest of the way, carefully enters the bedroom, and sees a sleeping Bob. Tiptoeing across the bedroom floor, Bill reaches the waterbed where Bob lays snoring. Just as Bill reaches for Bob, Bob coughs and awakens. Bob is confused. Bill takes care of his confusion. Just as he planned, Bill punches Bob in the eye and breaks his cheekbone. Bill exclaims, "Keep your mouth shut from now on, and mind your own business!" Bill then leaves, feeling very satisfied that he has taught a loudmouth a lesson. On the way out, Bill sees an antique silver shaving stand on Bob's dresser but decides*

he cannot carry it down the trellis with him. He makes a mental note to return some night for the shaving stand. Bob is terrified, so much so that he does not call a doctor and ends up bleeding to death.

Now, wasn't that fact pattern fun? I am sure you only used a few precious seconds to read and absorb the sordid tale of Bob and Bill. Remember, the object is not just to read the question, but also to answer the question in the same 1.8 minutes (108 seconds):

Question: If the Police make a mold of Bill's sneaker print in the mud near the trellis, arrest Bill as a result, and the district attorney's office prosecutes him for burglary, is it most likely that Bill will be found:

     (A) guilty, since his blow to Bob resulted in Bob's death;

     (B) guilty, since he broke into Bob's house without permission and intended to commit a felony within;

     (C) not guilty, since he only intended to shut Bob up, and not kill him; or

     (D) not guilty, since at the time Bob broke in and entered, he didn't intend to commit a felony?

What are the important facts? The trellis; the time of day; the sneaker print; Bob's death; Bill's state of mind; the silver shaving stand? Remember, they prosecuted him for burglary, not murder. Drum roll, please. Remember, do not just pick a correct answer: pick the *most* correct answer. The most correct answer is "D." And now, the explanation. In old England (attorneys call it "at common law"), a criminal committed burglary by breaking and entering another person's dwelling house at night *with the intent to commit a felony*. Assault and battery at common law was a misdemeanor, not a felony. So, Bill did not intend to commit a felony; he only intended to commit a misdemeanor when he broke and entered. Foolish district attorney's office; it should not have prosecuted Bill for burglary.

Remember, you had 1.8 minutes (108 seconds) to answer that one Multistate question. How did you do? Piece of cake, times one hundred in the morning and one hundred in the afternoon.

Please do not ask, "What is the point?" The point is you have to pass the Multistate to get a license. The point is not that the Multistate tests any skill an attorney is expected to have or to develop, or any method of testing that is used in law schools, and no one ever suggested otherwise. In practice, attorneys do not have to be speed-readers; attorneys do not typically face multiple-choice questions; attorneys do not even usually deal with old English crimes. The Multistate is the quintessential modern-day doublespeak. There is no sense to the Multistate. There are only units of 1.8 (or 108), and a need to conform to the format, because... well, just because.

<u>Post-Test</u>. When the examinees finish the test, none of them ever know if they passed. How could they? Most people pass, and in time, solace can be found in this statistic. Several months later, anticlimactically, after the test and all the short-term knowledge have passed from recollection, the test results come. By that time, some law firm has the associate/soon-to-be-licensed attorney in the library until late at night researching god-knows-what for who-knows-what reason, with an unreasonable deadline established by who-knows-which law firm partner, who has gone home to be with the family. The fear of unemployment and flunking have passed;

the shock of employment and research deadlines has set in. And the score comes, and it is a passing grade, and the licensee decides between (A) celebrating with the spouse, (B) calling the parents, (C) telling the boss, or (D) finishing the research in the library. And the answer is "D." The other choices are correct, but "D" is the *most* correct answer. The licensee can celebrate later... later, when there is a moment.

PART THREE – LIFE IN THE LAW

AND SO IT BEGINS

WITH THE BAR EXAM behind me, I started my gig as a bankruptcy law clerk just as the agricultural economy fell on hard times. The judge (and I) were very busy with failing farmers and stressed agricultural lenders and a relatively new bankruptcy code with which to contend. Very unfortunate for the farmers and lenders, but what a great environment in which to learn bankruptcy; a new code for the judge to interpret and construe. What a truly exciting time to be a new bankruptcy attorney.

In fact, I admired the judge immensely, and found myself intrigued by bankruptcy law almost as much, so that when the clerkship ended, I thought I had finally identified my life plan: to pursue a career as a bankruptcy attorney. I seemed quickly to be morphing away from being a heart-guy and the head-guy-thing was taking over. I decided that I needed to find a job at a firm with a good bankruptcy practice. The judge had a non-interventionist approach, and said little about my decision. Over lunch one day, however, he let slip some astute advice that I ignored. He said that the practice of law was not all it is cracked up to be. He was the little thoughtful voice in my head that I heard clearly, but would ignore.

Instead, off to Houston Loren and I went to learn how to talk Texan, eat Texas barbeque, and to experience the effects of under-ten-dollars-a-barrel oil and the demise of the oil and gas industry. Again, an economic tragedy for the oilmen and the lenders, but what a great environment to be a young bankruptcy attorney at a law firm – or, at least, so I naively thought.

I always figured I would continue to explore the dream world of things I could do besides hanging out with lots of attorneys in large firms. I was not in the law firm gig for the long haul, I told myself. I jokingly said that I did not know what I wanted to do when I grew up. I am not sure how emotionally healthy it was to perpetually deny that I was an attorney in a law firm for life, but it made for good conversations at cocktail parties. I left more than a few people entertained and confused by my view that I could check out of the law firm world any time I wanted.

As I got deeper and deeper into the law firm system, it was such a foreign experience for me that I found that I expended many, many hours and a great deal of energy trying to think of a way to get out, dreaming of other possibilities. I am living proof that getting out is harder than getting in. It is like the Eagles' "Hotel California": you can check in, but you can never check out. I think this problem pops up for most attorneys from time to time. Whether it pops up for them as often as it did for me, I cannot say. We attorneys are generally a discontented bunch at various points in our careers, and sometimes, there seem to be as many of those moments of discontent as there are stars in the sky.

Through it all, however, it was mostly a good career – not perfect and not great, and sometimes quite imperfect and disagreeable; but, on balance, mostly an acceptably good career. Yes. I hear myself say that now, and I surprise myself when I say it. Today, I am mostly comfortable with my feelings about my career most of the time; it is the product of an evolution that occurred over thirty-eight years in the trenches, but it is not how I always felt. There were many times in my career that I could be very black-and-white about law – it was either good or evil, positive or negative, and for so much of my career, the practice of law was hard on my health, rough on my relationships, a negative influence on my psychological well-being, a constriction on my ability to be creative, and a consumer of my time that I could otherwise have used to dream. In other words, a tough way to go through life. But even liberal-arts-major lawyers evolve and find more gray than black and white and indeed, maybe that is a sign of the process of aging regardless of the profession. As my evolution occurred, the statement, that I had a mostly good career, has come to fit my current thinking. This is not gospel, though; I don't even know if I can say it is typical or a widely-held belief by liberal arts majors/former law clerks/bankruptcy attorneys. I have taken no survey to determine the data and statistics for typicality and breadth of beliefs in the industry. I can only say with certainty that I am not the only one who felt like the practice of law was a tough way to go through life, and then evolved to more positive thinking. Just like that.

Wow. Such mental verbosity. Lawyers sure think and over-think a lot, don't they?

THE INTERVIEW

YOU CANNOT BE AN attorney at a law firm without first enduring the interview process. To change jobs, to improve your station in life, you have to interview. It is part and parcel of the attorney experience. It is not an easy process; it is not a natural process, and you have to learn by doing. I feel like I must be one of the most knowledgeable – experience breeds expertise.

It is hard to say how many interviews I had in my life as I explored options, tried to improve my station in life, dreamed, and moved around. It is even harder to say how many times I fended off questions about my life, my career, my job requirements, my wife and her career. I cannot begin to recollect how many times I discussed the weather, wine, the local football teams, the front page of the newspaper, the back page of the newspaper, veterinary medicine, or any other silence-avoiding, time-filling topics that come to the mind of the person across the desk from me.

Now that I am out of the law business, and not exploring paying jobs anymore, I do not expect too many more interviews. Good riddance. The age of enlightenment has begun – no more probing inquiries. As I enter that new age, however, here are my thoughts on the interview process. I expect my views differ ever so slightly from those of the life coach teaching a client how to interview.

The process is simple: they (the firm) have the money. I (the interviewee) need it. To get it, I must put my wares on display and permit the firm's representatives (the interviewers) to inquire. I have to let them know I want the money, but I know I will not get the money unless I make the exploration enjoyable for them. I have to give them pleasure. I am like a whore standing under a dimly lit corner streetlight. My body, my presence, the way I carry myself, my air, have to say, "buy me; buy me;" my words have to say, "I can't be easily bought." I have to create the chase, the pursuit. Then I have to let them have their way with me. I suppose another analogy for the modern-day interview is as an art form – the questions are the canvas and the answers are the brushes and paint used by the interviewee to create a masterpiece or a print to be sold at a flea market. Interviewing is an amalgamation of nuances and inflections. Say the right thing at the right time in the right way to the right person. Give them something they want and that they are willing to pay for. Bond. Give them the warm and fuzzies.

Interviews are live and learn. No two are exactly alike.

My first round of professional interviews began in my senior year of college. I struggled with the age-old problem – what to do with a liberal arts degree. I had a sports column in the college newspaper, I photographed for the newspaper, and I liked the "Oscar Madison" way of life, even experimenting with smoking cigars. Photojournalism seemed to be the answer; sports photojournalism, to be exact. I wrote to every newspaper and magazine in a thirty-state area. I called, and begged, and cajoled, and hung out, and my reward was two interviews. They were short and very unsatisfying. At each paper, I arrived on time with my portfolio of editorial articles and pictures under my arm and searched for the managing editor. Each time, I anxiously hoped that I found myself on the brink of my new career instead of the edge of a sheer cliff. The managing editors each strolled out of their Lou Grant-like glassed-in offices.

"Son, you can't work here without professional experience," each of them said.

"But how do I get the experience?" I asked.

"We don't know," they replied, "but we only hire experienced folks."

Simple. I looked unattractive to them under the dimly-lit corner streetlight. No warm and fuzzies; no bonding; no sale. I did not fight it, I left quietly and quickly and without a job.

I tried so many newspapers. I inquired; they ignored. I wrote; they rejected. I typed by hand; they sent "to whom it may concern" photocopied replies.

Many nights, I pondered. I was just not selling. Maybe it was the eerie glow thrown off on that dim-lit corner. I probably needed a new corner, but I was not certain. I hung out on that corner for a few more months selling and strutting and enticing and offering and saying, "buy me." I even started an in-person door-to-door campaign. "Hey, Joe. Want a good time? Are you interested?" Eventually, the bulb in the corner streetlight burned out and I was forced to find a new corner. That new location was the corner of contracts and constitutional law – law school.

In my third year of law school, I began my second round of professional interviews. I was in Kansas at the time, waiting for Loren to graduate from veterinary school.

Early in the process, I met one person, a bankruptcy judge, who seemed to care. Maybe he took pity. I don't know, and I've never asked. He called me in for an interview, we talked about Social Security, of all things, and we both had the warm and fuzzies. There was some initial bonding; he hired me, I accepted, and I was his law clerk for just over two years.

My first real job. I guess I sold him something he wanted. It felt good.

When I finished my clerkship, I needed a real attorney's job, presumably at a law firm. The Kansas City firms were not ready for a transplanted easterner with a bankruptcy law background. The eastern firms were not ready for a Kansas law clerk. "I could be midwestern," I told the Kansas Citians. "I could be eastern again," I told the easterners. "I can be whatever you want me to be," I told anyone who would listen. I found myself abandoning one of my life tenets: You have to be what you are – the human version of *it is what it is*.

I had interviews; lots of interviews. The eastern firms thought my background was too farm-oriented and asked me what I had learned in the many pig farmer bankruptcy cases I had undoubtedly seen during my clerkship tenure. How should I respond? I had not prepared for this question. Should I say, "I learned that the average sow has two-and-one-half litters per year and eight piglets per litter?" It was true – I had listened to testimony from pig farm experts time and time again. The truth was always reliable and safe. But it was also small talk, which had no place in the interview. Avoid sarcastic small talk in an interview, at least if you want the job. Should I emphasize my eastern roots? Maybe those eastern roots had died, and I could no longer use my eastern ties. I was stumped, and I never answered the question. I went home to Kansas without a job.

So, I tried Kansas, but the Kansas firms thought I was too big eastern city-oriented. All the attorneys knew me because I was the Judge's law clerk, but I was still the easterner. One firm showed some interest, sort of. They had me in for the interview, and seven of the partners formed a semi-circle around me. Imagine: before anyone sat down, there were seven chairs and one in the middle. This seemed either like a bad taping of "Meet the Press" or the rehearsal dinner for a next day execution. It was hard to prepare for such a forum, and near impossible to bond with seven people at once.

Eventually, I learned quite a bit about the interview process as I exhausted the Midwest and several areas of the northeast, each interview culminating with a letter expressing the firm's thanks for my time. I decided that someday I might paper my bathroom with the letters. Then guests who came to my home and found themselves in my bathroom could familiarize themselves with the many ways to say no while they attended to their needs: "We will keep your resume on file" (translation: "We will be tossing it into our wire mesh trash can any second now"); "We had many excellent and qualified candidates" (question: were some of the candidates qualified but not excellent, or excellent and not qualified? And in which group did they place me?); "The decision was a very difficult one" (translation: "It took some time to get the committee together to vote because of the holiday season, so we are sorry if the delay caused you any consternation during this time of good cheer"); "It is with deep regret that I write to inform you" (not quite as deep as the regret I had when I read the letter); "The committee was very impressed with your credentials" (translation: "But there was something you said or did during one of the interviews that pissed somebody off"); "We were looking for someone with more experience," or, "We were looking for someone with less experience" (then why the hell did you waste my time and yours with the interview process? You knew how much experience I had before I even walked in the door).

I felt that the letters would make the bathroom truly memorable. But first I needed a bathroom, and to get a bathroom, I needed a house, and to get a house I needed money, and to get money I needed a job. So, I headed south to someplace where they didn't care as much where I was from. Houston: a melting pot, and the reigning bankruptcy capital of the world at the time.

In Houston, I worked for a large Chicago firm's satellite office. Before the firm made the offer of employment, I had to fly to the Chicago office to meet with the head bankruptcy partner. This interview, as it turns out, was a masterpiece of mood and subliminal artifice. The firm's recruiting officer let me into the partner's office. There was precious little light: the overhead light was off, the desk lamp was on low, and he had the shades drawn. I could hardly see him behind the desk. The low wattage was certainly environmentally sound, but it also made the interview setting feel much as I have always imagined confessional must be for Catholics, just dim lights and a disembodied voice. Even with my 20/20 vision, I could see nothing behind the desk. I could hear him, though, and I knew he was there, ready to pull whatever strings needed to be pulled and push whatever buttons needed to be pushed, like the Wizard of Oz, ready to make whatever needed to happen, happen. Very impressive.

"Sit down," he said quietly, and of course I did. *Unlike* the Wizard, his voice was normal, and soft-spoken. Thankfully, my eyes adjusted to the dark and in a few short minutes, I could make out the outline of a small side chair, barely.

"I've read your resume," he stated. "I have to be honest. You have a lot of downsides. But I wanted to meet you. Do you have any questions about our firm?" Was that it? Had he already decided? No sale? He seemed to give me the chance to ask questions only out of deference for the process. It was expected; a recognition that there cannot be an interview without the interviewee speaking. But I had no questions about the firm, only about his "honest" comment.

"Downsides" I asked? I had not planned for an aggressive approach, but I did not know what else to do. I was confused. "There's an upside, too, or I suppose you wouldn't have flown me here to meet and talk to you." I had to figure out a way to take control, but not offend him. I wasn't sure this was the way.

"You're right. You went to the same college as I did. But that's not a reason to hire you." The old college alma mater coming through in the clutch again, even though it was so dark I could not even see anything framed on his wall, let alone make out the alma mater on the sheepskin. But it did not matter if it wasn't a reason to hire me.

"Well, what is a reason you would hire me?"

"Look, I'm never going to win an award from the EEOC."

I said, "I want to be a bankruptcy attorney, not an EEOC investigator. I need a job. I thought you needed a body. Am I mistaken?" Total *ad-lib*; very dangerous.

And so on. No light. No direction to the conversation. No chit chat about the old school. No substance. I had no idea, and I felt like I had no chance. I was painting the canvas by doing no more than drizzling paint randomly on the surface. Not a pretty picture, and not a typical interview. But what is typical? I thought, *No sale.* He did everything except give the perseverance test – he did not ask me to open a window that he had already nailed shut (I heard they did that at Harvard Law School interviews).

And yet, somehow, he heard what he wanted or needed to hear. I am not so sure that we bonded, but whatever his impression, it seemed to be enough. Surprisingly, it *was* a sale. Who would have guessed? Within days, he offered me the job. Why? I have no idea; interviews can be weird. When he was my boss, he was beyond great. I was altogether very lucky, although after the interview I always remained a little once-bitten-twice-shy and when we worked together, I preferred to talk to him in bright light.

After Houston, I next worked in Philadelphia. My parents' proclivity to move often made me wary of moves, but Loren's residency was in Philadelphia, so off we went.

To get a job in Philadelphia, I had to drag out the corner streetlight attire again. And the games and the exploration and the enticing and strutting began again. "Buy me." Handshakes exchanged. "Buy me." Coffee and soft drinks offered. My suit jacket on. His off. His hands clasped behind his head in relaxed repose. My hands folded in my lap in controlled nervousness. Give them what they want, but this time, no questions, just silence. Another weird interview in the making.

Interviewers hate silence. It drives them crazy. They feel they have to fill the void. Textbook questions were the rage at the time, and perfect void fillers. You know, like, "If you could be anything, what would you be?" (I have often wondered that myself. After all, the attorney thing just happened and was still very much a work-in-process. Something to do with rock and roll, I am sure, I said; if I was only a better guitar player, I thought.)

To break the silence, the interviewer reached into his textbook and pulled out, "What periodicals do you read?"

I smiled on the outside as I grimaced inside. What a crazy question. What does it matter, I wondered? Are there periodicals that would disqualify me from getting the job? What do you read? What do you expect me to read? Several eternal seconds ticked off the clock as I struggled to find the right thing to say in the right way at the right time. Finally, I had to fill the silence. Interviewees also hate silence. So I answered, "I don't read too many magazines. Gloom and doom, you know. But I always read *Rolling Stone*." Did that make him want me?

Click! "Gee. I haven't read that since college. I loved it. What about the *Journal?*" I assumed he meant the *Wall Street Journal*.

"I'm afraid not. No sports page in the *Journal*. But I read the *Inquirer*." Hopefully he assumed I meant the *Philadelphia Inquirer*.

Now all this media lore did not appear truly relevant to whether I was qualified to work in this law firm. But it was filled with nuance and inflection. The only problem was I couldn't tell if I was bonding or bombing. No matter; sometimes in interviews, you just have to go with the flow... a little bit of a what-the-fuck mentality.

And on and on. Warm and fuzzies, bonding. Why? Who knows? Nothing to do with the law or attorneying, but bonding. Lesson = interviews are weird. You just never know what will click. But he hired me and as my boss, he was outstanding.

From Philadelphia on to Kansas City when Loren's residency ended. A return to the Midwest, and a new start. I interviewed with the managing partner of a law firm. He smoked a pipe and had a really nice office. As his secretary led me in, he reached under his desk and pushed a button. The door to his office magically closed behind me. Unnerving, although it did not creak like in horror movies. He was a very nice guy and, from all I could tell, the sale had been made before he met me, and he simply wanted to make sure we should proceed.

So, by now, I had heard all the questions. I gave all the answers, or at least all the answers I could think of. I had sat through silence and endured it. I had been surrounded, and farmered, and yankeed, and ganged, and weirded, and confused, and alma-matered, and I survived. I guess I was officially a skilled interviewee. This is not a marketable skill at all. No one pays for someone to stand on the dimly-lit street corner forever, enticing and strutting and trying to bond and sell the warm and fuzzies. The skills, however, proved useful. I used them when I became the interviewer. I made a few modifications in the techniques I used when I interviewed candidates. I had the lights fully on in my office, the shades up, and the door open. I never interviewed in the round. I never asked about magazines or the *Wall Street Journal*. I did not care whether the interviewee was from either coast or somewhere in the middle of the country. I did not care whether the interviewee liked rock and roll. Well... truth be told I did care about *that*. Hard to trust someone who does not like rock and roll. But I never asked that question.

THE SUMMER ASSOCIATE SYSTEM

LARGE LAW FIRMS AROUND the country operate a very strange system called the summer associate system. A law student interviews with a virtual gaggle of law firms for a summer position as an attorney-in-training, and the lucky twenty-six-year-old candidate will get the job of their young life for the summer.

During year two of law school, law firms arrive at the law school campus in early fall and interview law students for summer positions. Each interview, during which the student and the law firm representative will form a lasting impression of each other, may take fifteen minutes, kind of like a speed dating session, and the following rules and regulations apply:

The interviewer may ask several probing questions about the student's aspirations and goals, using the "Handbook of How Not to Conduct an Effective Interview In Three Easy Lessons" (written by the same people who write the "Miss America" contest questions and answers, and supplied at no extra charge before the interview begins) as a guide.

The student may ask several incisive questions about the kind of law the prospective firm practices, using the "Handbook of How Not to Make an Impression in Fifteen Minutes or Less" as a guide.

Some famous questions from the student interviewee hand-book will include "How formal is your law firm?" (translation: "Do I have to wear a suit and tie, and does this firm place form over substance?") and "What new areas of practice does your firm have?" (translation: "I already know I am only interested in being a transnational intergalactic comparative satellite law attorney").

In the end, neither side will learn a great deal and the initial process may very well be as uncomfortable and unenlightening as a failed Tinder blind date.

The lucky student who makes this first cut of campus interviews will be invited to visit the law firm in an all-expenses-paid trip to (hopefully) the city of their choice for more interviews, food, and perhaps to see the firm in action. No expense will be spared, no amenity will be forgotten. She or he will be wined and dined, shepherded and flocked. The student expects the firm to provide a stay at the Ritz or the Mansion on Turtle Creek or the Four Seasons for a memorable hospitality experience. There may be a limousine ride from the hotel to the firm office. There will be at least one French dinner at a *Zagat*-approved, 5.0-rated restaurant served at a table surrounded by partners and associates, like fishermen around a fishing hole stocked with trout.

After a dinner – testing poise, character, attire, coordination, attention span, etiquette and the limits of cholesterol tolerance – the summer associate will be witness to the traditional guffaw-ing over true, semi-true, and outright fictional war stories of recent or not-so-recent legal triumphs, all designed to bait and hook the prospective summer associate and to leave a lasting impression that this firm is the one where she or he should practice law. The fish cannot be caught without the bait, and the savvy fish will not strike the hook unless it is baited just right. So, make the hotel suite reservations. Practice guffawing.

Next, the lucky student who is chosen from this final group of candidates will be offered a position as a summer associate. A proper letter will be written on a partner's letterhead extending the summer offer and telling the student how much the firm looks forward to her or his arrival after the second year of law school ends. The partner will use a form available in *The Pocket Guide to Extending An Employment Offer*. The offer letter will be nonnegotiable. A proper reply letter will be expected from the twenty-six-year-old telling the firm how much she or he looks forward to spending an exciting and stimulating summer learning how to be an attorney. A form letter from *The Pocket Guide to Accepting An Employment Offer* is recommended. Those Miss America people are amazing.

The position is called a summer associate position. In the not-too-distant past, it was called a law clerk position, but as firms all have other clerks, the more professional, "summer associate" title was born. Since new attorneys in law firms are called associates, "summer associate" implies being just one step away from that coveted first job as an attorney.

The lucky summer associate will be paid handsomely, usually enough money in a twelve-week summer to live quite comfortably during the school year without the need to work at a paying job. Salaries can exceed the equivalent of $150,000.00 per annum. Not bad for a twenty-six-year-old.

Once at the law firm, the summer associate will be exposed to a variety of attorney-like experiences to impart a feeling for what it is like to be an attorney. Almost every night, there will either be a firm-sponsored event – maybe a party, or a baseball game, or an opera for cultural spice, or an exotic soiree, put on and chaperoned by a summer associate committee typically called the R & R committee. Each day at lunch, there will be more dining and flocking, and the firm will pick up the tab. Each morning, the summer associates will congregate and discuss the previous night's happenings and occasionally reflect that, "Hey! life as an attorney is not all bad."

Of course, there is work to be done. After all, it is a law firm where the summer associate works. Research is the backbone of a young attorney's life, and much of the research projects will be passed down the pecking order to the summer associate, who will be expected to grab onto a research project like a swollen cow teat and milk it for all it is worth. This will be the summer associate's chance to shine, to show what she or he is made of. Pull and squeeze. The law firm will moo. The more milk, the better. It is all in the technique.

There will be library time during which the summer associate will be expected to solve the unsolvable mysteries of the everyday practice of law without care or regard for the amount of time spent. Amass the cases; synthesize the legal principles; ultimately, draft a memo. In the memo, include all the issues, all the law, all the arguments, all the rationales of a thousand cons of summer associates past. The memo will be a sacrificial testament to the summer associate's ability to think like an attorney. Use the process. Include all the citations recorded perfectly in the memo. Labor over the grammar so it is impeccable. No passive voice; no hanging prepositions. No run-on sentences.

And, after a trying six hours at work, one and a half of which was spent dining, the summer associate will hit the nightlife trail, dine, flock, spectate, and party, and when the morning arrives as it always does, she or he will get up and do it again.

At the end of the summer, the lucky summer associate will receive a permanent employment offer to join the firm after completing the senior year of law school and passing the bar examination. With the memories of the summer association still warm and vivid, the lucky summer associate will be reeled in by the expert fishermen. One more catch, and one less fish in the stocked fishing hole.

A summer associate who has received the coveted offer from the law firm for employment after graduation might be tempted with other career options – public service, the business world, not for profit service, politics; and a little voice in the summer associate's head might cry out, "Pick something else besides the law firm!!" But most will not bite on the alternate options. After all, how can most twenty-six-year-olds with significant student loan debt turn down the prospect of large compensation so soon after law school poverty?

And the summer associate will think, "Wow, what a great way to make a living! Six hours of work and six figures of income!" Ahem, not so fast.

It is not the most honest way for a law firm to teach students of the law what life as an attorney is like. But no one ever said fishing was especially fair for the trout. You can imagine the shock of the affable student when law school and the bar exam are over and she or he shows up at work for the first days as a real attorney only to discover for the first time what a new greenhorn attorney really does for a living. Review documents. Carry bags. Crawl home for a shower and an hour of sleep at three in the morning. "Ahhh, sleep. I knew it well." It is not a pretty sight. Many a new attorney has been heard to say, "Hey, where's the nightlife? Where's the good life full of champagne and fun?"

It is all about money and earthly wealth. No one works for free, and fewer and fewer attorneys are in it for the glory. There is a quickly diminishing amount of idealistic righting of wrongs anymore; many people do not go to law school anymore to help the needy, or to take up a cause or to learn a system on which the foundation of a nation was constructed.

They go to law school for a career and the big house and the fancy car. Many law students seek no visit from Ralph Nader. They want to be courted by Mr. Green, and Dollar Bill, and Buck. And it starts these days at the ripe old age of twenty-six or so. Make no mistake – the competition to hire the top law school graduates is fierce among law firms. The stakes are high, and growing higher. A law firm is only as good as the quality of the new attorneys it hires, and it cannot hire quality new attorneys without participating in the summer associate system.

Law students and new graduates know this; they are promised the sun, paid enough to travel to the moon, shown a beachfront illusion, baited, hooked and then for the first time, after they have been reeled in, introduced to what they thought was a luxury resort but was really an inferno of late hours, stress, and very hard work.

Of course, I did not seek a courtship with the almighty dollar. I was not in law school for the privilege of a law career so I was never wined and dined and, at least as a law student, I never signed a pact with a large firm. I suppose that was a benefit of my plan to stay in law school while I continued to dream of what I would do with my life, this time, after law school ended.

There is a not-so-old joke about the man who is approached by the devil to sell his soul in exchange for earthly wealth and power, and before selling his soul, the man asks to see Hell. The devil complies with the request and escorts the prospective seller down to Hell where everything looks like a high-end beach resort. Thinking that an eternity in Hell will be a gas, the man signs the sales contract, the transaction is consummated, and the soul is sold. Wealth and power immediately follow, but in due course, the devil returns and says the time has come to claim the soul. The unsuspecting seller – bathing suit and bottle of sunscreen in hand – willingly submits, and the devil takes him to Hell, where, upon crossing the River Styx, the seller is confronted with an unbearable inferno of fire and brimstone. The beach resort life is nowhere to be seen. "But what happened to the resort?" cries the bewildered seller. "Oh," says the devil. "You must have been in our summer associate program."

THE SKILLS OF THE ATTORNEY

OFTENTIMES, WHEN AN ATTORNEY looks in a mirror, they think they see a highly-skilled professional staring back. At a cocktail party, they may portray themselves as a highly-skilled professional. That is their identity. They certainly are professionals. Lest they forget, however, it is worth the reminder that most attorneys had no marketable skills when they graduated from college. They decided to go to law school because what else can a college graduate with a degree in history or English or sociology or philosophy or religious studies do for a living? That was me. That, and the chance to delay the life plan as many times and as often as possible.

What are those exact skills that attorneys see in the mirror and exude at the party? Attorneys read, write, speak and think for a living. These are the tools of the trade. But a skill is something that one employs that other people cannot. Many people know how to use each of these tools without going to law school. For that matter, most attorneys may be no more skilled at using the tools of their trade than the next guy on the street corner. Is it really a skill to read, write, think, and speak?

Consider other career professionals. Plumbers install and fix plumbing and heating systems. They use wrenches and pipe threaders. Electricians install and fix electrical systems splicing wires and read schematic diagrams. Engineers do whatever engineers do and use whatever engineers use (I am sure it involves more than reading, writing, speaking and thinking), and doctors and veterinarians heal living beings through surgical, diagnostic, and applied medicine techniques and use scalpels, retractors, x-rays and ultrasound machines. The average person knows diddley-squat about plumbing, electricity, engineering, medicine, wrenches, threaders, schematics, scalpels, retractors, x-rays or ultrasound. Thus, plumbers, electricians, engineers, doctors, and veterinarians have unique talents. Therefore, they are skilled. They do things most people cannot.

Let's examine the four basic attorney skills. As we do, please be aware that during my law life, I was guilty of all of the following.

Attorneys read. I learned to read when I was three or four years old; in any event, long before I attended law school. I have been reading ever since. I read alternative publications such as *Rolling Stone*, and I read cheap dime-store mysteries dating back to a love for *Ellery Queen* mysteries. From time to time, I read something that is socially redeeming or a biography of one rock-and-roll star or another, or I read about an article that is socially redeeming and think to myself that maybe I ought to read the article.

Law school did not refine my reading skills. If anything, law school made them sloppy.

In law school, there is a substantial amount of reading every night, but it is virtually all one genre – reality show in black-and-white print. There is case after case to read in a given topic from which the student extracts a legal rule. After reading 1500 pages of cases in a single topic, the law student amasses at least 1500 rules of law and then puts them together in an outline, which they study, reduce to an anagram, memorize, and with any luck, this forms the basis to answer hypothetical essay questions in a three- to five-hour final exam in which the student selects, regurgitates and applies some of the 1500 legal rules.

Facts are largely unimportant. It is not as important to remember that the army doctor amputated the right leg of a victim whose left leg needed amputation, as it is to remember the rule of law that the doctor was negligent because he violated his duty to the patient to act as a reasonably prudent surgical doctor would act under like circumstances. It is not as important to remember whether the accused rapist could maintain an erection, as it is to remember the rule of law that any penetration, no matter how slight and even if by a dead weapon,[2] is sufficient to constitute rape. Some facts are more memorable than others and help as a memory prompt, but it is the legal rule and not the facts that are important.

As interesting as the facts may be, law school teaches you to be a sloppy reader. Damn the facts: get that rule! I think that is why I like dime-store mysteries. The facts are so important. If they were not, I could just read the first and last chapters, find out who did it and who solved it, and skip the story.

Law school may have taught me a process and a way to think and how to extract a rule of law to apply to a situation. But, as you can plainly see, law school did not teach me to read. While attorneys almost certainly can read, they probably do not do it any better than the rest of the world.

<u>**Attorneys write**</u>. In the practice of law, attorneys write *motions* – a fancy word for a request made of a court; a proposed

---

2   This example of rape is exactly how my criminal law professor explained it during my first year of law school. I guess he was trying to keep us interested in an otherwise horrifying topic.

form of the *order* to be entered by the judge – a fancy word for the court's decision granting or denying the motion; and *briefs* – a fancy word for an essay that promotes the legal rules that entitle an attorney to have the motion granted. Each is a very stylized form of writing and offers no cause for the Shakespeares of the world to fear competition.

In the old days in England, attorneys were paid by the word, so they developed a writing style designed to say what needed to be said in as many words as possible. The reward was for endless edification, not efficiency. Wills began with the famous phrase "being of sound mind and body," even though the phrase was largely unnecessary because everyone was presumed to be of sound mind and body. But attorneys threw it in a will because it was six more words, based upon which they would be paid.

Today, attorneys do not get paid by the word, but they continue to find ways to complicate simple things and communicate with all the clarity of a thick Cape Cod fog, partially to maintain the mystery, and partially because they are taught to write in a bizarre, stylized fashion in law school. For example, when an attorney sets out a group of facts chronologically, an attorney will often write, "subsequent thereto." Why not just write "next" or "afterward?" Attorneys "aver" or "indicate" instead of just getting right to whatever is on their minds. Attorneys describe things as "clear," when there is a hurricane of clouds on the horizon and no visibility. When an attorney describes something as clear and lucid, watch out: what follows will be unclear and opaque. Attorneys describe the case on which they currently work as "the instant case," or the "case at bar," or "the *case sub judice*." Why not just "this case?"

In court, attorneys object to a witness' testimony about a contract and say, "Your Honor, the document speaks for itself."

Meaning, "Judge, stop this witness from explaining what the document says because we can all read what it says." But documents do not speak. I have listened. Documents make no sounds. If you do not believe me, move this page up to your ear. Do you hear anything? Of course not.

When attorneys attach a copy of a document, they write, "a true, correct, and accurate copy of which is attached hereto and marked as Exhibit A." Are there any correct but untrue copies? Are there any true but incorrect copies? And, how could the printed word be inaccurate? Inaccurate copies produced by a photocopier manufacturer's photocopy machine would undoubtedly be bad for sales. And why mark it as anything? Isn't it just Exhibit A? When attorneys send a document along with a letter, they write, "Enclosed please find." Is that supposed to be courteous? Why not just "Enclosed is?" Attorneys conclude an argument by saying "accordingly" or "thus" or "hence." Why not just say "therefore?" Sometimes they end their argument by saying, "In closing." Is that to give a heads-up to the judge that the argument is finally near its end?

What about all this Latin that attorneys include in their writing? For example: *a fortiori* (by stronger reason), *ipso facto* (by the fact itself), *res ipsa loquitur* (the thing speaks for itself – as if inanimate things speak), *res judicata* (the thing has been decided), *ipse dixit* (his own statement not made on the authority of any precedent – hip shooting) and the once-very-popular *quae ad unum finem loquuta sunt, non debent alium detorqueri* (those things which have been said for one purpose ought not to be twisted into another). More words for dollars, but not words to live by. More muddy water.

Often there is some written statute or regulation on the books. Attorneys, however, do not just report the contents of the legislation. Things are the way they are "pursuant to" this section of a statute or another. Most people do not hear "pursuant to" in the average day:

> *Well, dear, pursuant to that lamb stew recipe, I aver that*
> *subsequent to adding thyme and rosemary, you should roast*
> *for one hour and accordingly produce a delicious dinner.*

That would be nutty, right?

I had an attorney friend who described the act of carrying papers to the courthouse for filing as "effectuate filing of papers." Why not just "filing papers?" At the end of an affidavit, attorneys sometimes write "Further Affiant Sayeth Naught." Really. Come on.

Attorneys live for double negatives. Positions are "not inconsistent." Opposing counsel is "not incorrect." Amounts in dispute are "not insubstantial." Constitutional laws are "not invalid." Why not consistent, correct, substantial and valid? Double negatives are commonplace because in attorney land, no one is too positive for fear of raising suspicion.

When an attorney wants to make a point, the point is stated twice for emphasis. A warning in a contract says, "if and only if." Time is identified as "then and only then." Following a long explanation, an attorney will summarize by saying "simply put," usually after saying the same thing in very complicated terms. Why not stick to the use of "if," and "then," and why not just say it in simple terms in the first place?

Attorneys make announcements by stating "know all men by these presents." Attorneys end motions by stating "Wherefore, premises considered." Don't even ask; I have no idea.

Briefs are rarely... brief. Briefs – what a misleading name to give a long, analytical, argumentative document. Some judges insist that attorneys must write briefs of no more than ten pages; anything more than ten pages lands in the trash. Yet, attorneys struggle to write their names in ten pages, and briefs usually run twenty pages at a minimum. Where else but in the law world would a twenty-page document be called brief? No matter how short a brief could be, an attorney will be inclined to write it twice as long because attorneys instinctively are wordy, long-winded, and in their heart, may still have the "bill by the word" trait in their DNA.

Between the words used, the length, the quality and style of the written communication, and the dubious beginnings of billing by the word, it is hard to carry an argument at a cocktail party that attorneys write better than other people. Like reading, attorneys just write more, not better.

Attorneys Speak. Some attorneys are great orators, but most are not. Most do not really speak: they lecture, they pontificate. They can be ponderous. They expound *ad nauseum*. They drone on; wail, whine and argue. They dogmatize, moralize, and even evangelize their position. They love to hear themselves; they may be the only ones.

But have you ever heard attorneys speak? I mean, *really* listened. They do not sound like a television attorney with a perfect vocal timbre and a delivery that was... well, perfectly scripted. Oh, some real-life attorneys have a wonderful delivery, ripe with emotion, laced with persuasion, dusted with credibility, and with the beautiful timbre of a baritone opera star. But, no, most attorneys are not great orators, and often write better than they speak; and you know how well they write. It is hard enough to write "pursuant to" and "effectuate" and "sayeth naught," let alone utter such words in public.

Law school does not teach attorneys to speak. The Socratic method was not designed for classes of over 100 students, and the wily student can use the size of the classroom and the Socratic method of teaching to avoid the need to speak in class for months at a time. No one tests attorneys for their speaking skills, and no state requires that attorneys prove their competence in oral communication before they renew a license to practice law. The bar exam has no oration component.

By contrast, baseball players can be wonderful orators because they have practiced and honed the skill for years before arriving in the major leagues. In furtherance of my childhood dreaming of playing center field for the New York Mets, I granted imaginary interviews to Ralph Kiner, the color commentator for the Mets during my youth:

> *Well, I'll tell you, Ralph, I was just trying to go with the pitch and drive it through the infield.*
> — or —
> *Well, I'll tell you, Ralph, I never gave up on that wicked sinking line drive.*
> — or —
> *Well, I'll tell you, Ralph, I'm just taking it one game at a time.*

I have never heard an attorney give a great interview, and although there are certainly exceptions, my general rule is that attorneys are mostly boring orators and do not speak with any greater skill than the general masses.

I did know one attorney who regularly responded to a question from the judge by saying, "Well, I'll tell you, Judge..." and it certainly was folksy, but I have my doubts about whether it made him any more effective. I give him credit, however, for trying out a different way of speaking in court. When we were in Texas, there was a whole different vernacular:

"Judge, he's running with the rabbits while he's hunting with the hounds," (translation: he is inconsistent in the things he is saying). "Judge, you can count the seeds in an apple, but you can't count the apples in the seed," (translation: the proposition is speculative – you can't count the apples that will be produced from a seed). Texas was certainly colorful, but the Texas attorneys were no better at Texanisms than mere mortal Texans.

Attorneys Think. Yes, they do, but so what? Attorneys have no monopoly on the thought market. The plumber, electrician, engineer, doctor, veterinarian, and even the baseball player each also think. Attorneys will tell you they think logically and critically. I guess they are trying to distinguish themselves from the illogical masses?

The dictionary says that logic is a system of reasoning, whether correct or incorrect; it is not the thought that counts, but rather the way you get to the thought. It is kind of like the new math – the formula used to solve the problem is more important than the answer.

In most trades, the thought itself is paramount, not the process followed in arriving at the thought. How long will you continue to go to your accountant if he logically, but incorrectly, prepares your tax returns? How many audits will you withstand before you return the accountant to the streets? How long will you continue to seek medical advice from a doctor who logically but incorrectly diagnoses your ailment, time and time again?

I suppose the point of law school's emphasis on the thought process is that eventually, the attorney will learn to not only think correctly but also to arrive at the correct answer. Three years of law school confirms otherwise, however, as a student can do quite well in law school with sound arguments even if the arguments lead to the wrong answer. Some of this anomaly bleeds into the practice of law. In a lawsuit, usually, only one side wins. That does not mean the attorney representing the losing side was not logical in his or her thoughts. Probably, she or he was very logical, but perhaps just not correct; or perhaps the attorney was correct, and the judge got it wrong. Some attorneys make a career from representing clients in lawsuits who never win. This attorney still has to think logically, but no matter how logical she or he is, she or he will usually be incorrect. Some attorneys are so good at thinking logical, yet incorrect, thoughts that sometimes they win a lawsuit, not based on the correctness of their client's position, but by accentuating the system of thinking and subjugating the correctness of the thoughts. For them, that is the ultimate intellectual orgasm. In any case, unlike baseball pitchers, there are no statistics published about attorney thinking and their win-loss records. It is hard to argue with a straight face that attorneys are great thinkers when the legal system accepts incorrect conclusions as being as valid as correct ones, as long as the attorney used the correct process.

So, while attorneys indeed read, write, speak, and think, so do many of the humans on our planet. With just those skills in mind, attorneys may not be able to escape the ranks of unskilled laborers.

Should we therefore conclude that attorneys lack skills? Of course not. Do they have other skills? Yes, of course. We all know them: they argue and persuade and construe and distinguish and distort, and sometimes they even prevail. If the law is on their side, they argue the law. If it is not, they argue the facts. If they have neither the law nor the facts on their side... well, it happens, and then they pound the table and try to mitigate the damage from the impending train wreck. Those are the real skills they have: the ability to argue endlessly and concede nothing – to zealously advocate, as the ethics experts would say. That is what clients actually pay for, but those skills don't sell well over drinks. Most non-attorney drinkers at the get-togethers are not there for an argument, so with drink in hand, attorneys just say they are attorneys and leave it at that.

The mirror reflection, however, reveals a different story. Let the reflection reveal, in the lines on the face and the bags under the eyes and curve of the spine and the fading sparkle in the eyes, the endless argument that is the life of an attorney.

DEAL OF THE DECADE

SOME OF MY BEST attorney friends over the years were transaction attorneys. They did deals. They negotiated and wrote agreements. Their world had its own language. I always found it fascinating, and I learned a great deal from them. Here are some of the things I learned.

Deals: they heat up, they crater, they blow up. The language of a deal is unusual. The attorney working on a deal may be "doing a deal" that is "heating up," negotiating "deal breakers," "caving" on points, trying to prevent a deal from "going south" or "tanking," or trying to save a deal that is "cratering" or "blowing up."

The deal attorney may work in fits and starts – drafting documents feverishly, then waiting for opposing counsel to review the documents and provide comments. The deal attorney may be "slow" while waiting for comments, then "slammed" when the comments require redrafting of the documents. The deal attorney is a reflection of the client; deal attorneys often represent unusual clients. So many clients want to do a deal, just for the sake of doing a deal. It is insane. To understand the deal attorney, you have to understand both the deal and the client doing the deal.

Deals. In its simplest form, a deal is nothing more than two sides, each wanting something, and ultimately coming to an agreement. Let's suppose...

I am a visiting businessman from Wamego, Kansas. I travel around the country with my entourage of attorneys and accountants and investment bankers and assorted other advisors and hangers-on, and I buy things – sometimes assets, sometimes companies. I buy low and sell high. I provide no service to the citizens of this country. I manufacture no product to better people's lives. In inventing nothing, I add no jobs to the economy, I add no value. I have no allegiance to any particular set of morals. I have no religious beliefs. I have no children. My assets are my offspring. I have no political beliefs. I don't like politicians. They get in the way of my quest to acquire.

I used to be charming and engaging. Several hundred deals, battles, and conquests later, my hair is mostly thinning, and now people say I was never charming, just disarming. I am not a nice person; I abuse, I bully. I am fine with that. My style is one I developed at Harvard, or Yale, or Wharton. And in the end, I usually get what I want. I am short on friends, but big on ego. My attorneys like to think they are a lot like me. Sometimes I pay them. Sometimes I do not and hire new ones. Whether I pay them or not, they all want to work for me.

I have always wanted to own a bridge, a little piece of Americana. I met you on the footpath of the Brooklyn Bridge one day while I admired the view and told you I would not mind owning the Brooklyn Bridge. You told me you would not mind selling it to me. After our talk, my deal attorney contacts your deal attorney; your deal attorney tells my deal attorney you might be interested in selling it to me at the right price. The two attorneys negotiate a price, and an understanding is reached. When the understanding is reached, the "deal" is defined. In this case, the "deal" is the sale of the Brooklyn Bridge by you to me.

<u>Doing the Deal</u>. Once the "deal" is defined, the goal is to "do the deal." We direct our efforts to the creation of written agreements that you can sign, and I can sign, and our deal attorneys can recommend that we each sign, not that I necessarily listen to my deal attorneys, mind you. While we are directing our efforts in this way we are "doing the deal." When we are ready to sign these agreements, we will "do the deal." Once we have signed these agreements, we will have "done the deal." This is known as conjugating the deal, or at least that is what I call it: my homage to my Bachelor of Arts in English.

<u>Heating up</u>. Our understandings are usually only the framework for the actual agreements. To sell the bridge to me, there are a million little points that have to be hammered out. Often, what is agreed to late at night around a large oval weathered oak table in a conference room, that in the older days was smoked-filled, may be different from what is written down.

For example, what is the condition of the bridge? When I met you on the footpath, you told me it was in wonderful shape and would last well into the twenty-second century. Now, however, you seem reluctant to sign a document saying that the bridge will last until tomorrow, let alone into the next two centuries.

Do you own it? You spoke lovingly of the bridge and gave me a brief history of the famous people who had walked across it and jumped off it throughout the years. I told you I was swimming in oil and natural gas back home and I had more head of cattle than I knew what to do with. You said, "Why not invest in New York real estate, like this bridge?" I said, "It sounds like a great idea. I'll have my deal attorneys call your deal attorneys." Now, however, you are unwilling to sign anything that says you actually own it. Your deal attorneys give my deal attorneys some story about New York title laws.

How much is the bridge? Well, I thought we had agreed on the number, but now, you want more money. You say something about the cost of living and inflation in New York.

When will I have to pay the full purchase price? On the bridge footpath, as we gazed out over western civilization, you said I could pay you in installments. Now you want the full purchase price in cash up front at the closing. You are hard to pin down, but I am used to your kind. You will be pinned. Of that I am confident.

So, you can see, there are lots of points to hammer out before we write the agreements and sign them.

The negotiation of each little point usually comes in waves. It is a process in which we wear each other down, like two boxers caught in a round-after-round clinch – expending energy but avoiding damaging body blows. You have a view of the world from where you sit, which I cannot see from where I sit. Over time, I begin to understand your view and maybe even steal a look at the world from your negotiating room chair. It is not even that complicated. I know you are trying to screw me; you know I am trying to screw you... the screw me, screw you blues that George Harrison evoked when the Beatles were breaking up (although he was more proper and called the confounding process, the "Sue Me, Sue You Blues"). We both know we will not be able to completely screw the other, but we try while we are in the deal clinch until we tire of the effort.

Over a three-month period, our deal attorneys may spend only a few hours a day working on the deal, and may only negotiate one or two points. All of a sudden, you or I may decide that the time has come to finish agreeing to each little point. We are worn out and screwed, blued and tattooed. I am getting fed up. Do you or don't you own the bridge? Will it or won't it last? Word is sent down from on high that all points must be negotiated and agreed upon. Almost instantly, the deal attorneys go from working a few hours each day to non-stop negotiation and writing. The deal has "heated up." It never gets too hot in the kitchen, however, for a deal attorney. Of course, it never gets too hot in Hell for the devil either.

<u>Cratering</u>. While a deal has heated up, substantial friction can develop between the deal attorneys on each side. And one of the million little agreements that have to be reached may turn out to be an insurmountable obstacle to "doing the deal." If there is a point on which we cannot agree, it may become a "deal-breaker."

For example, I become concerned when a friend of mine in Carteret Rahway, New Jersey mails me an article from the New Jersey edition of the New York Times with the head-line: *OWNERSHIP OF BRIDGE QUESTIONED. ANCIENT MOHAWKS CLAIM BRIDGE AS SACRED GROUND.* I call you and tell you that I need proof that you own the bridge. You assure me that you do, but you offer no proof. I tell you that I have checked but there is no record that you ever bought it, inherited it, or own it. You tell me not to worry because New York bridge records are notoriously poor. Turns out, you say, that the original Dutch settlers of Manhattan Island who paid the Native Americans next to nothing for the land were so giddy about their deal that they never set up a reliable bridge keeping record system. I do not believe you. I have developed a sixth sense in my years as a Wamego businessman, and I am starting to sense there is something amiss about this whole investment, Dutch settlors notwithstanding.

This point of bridge ownership is a "deal-breaker." Unless we agree that you will provide me proof of ownership, I will not do the deal.

When a deal-breaker is discovered and it is not immediately resolved, the deal begins to grow old and to wither. It begins to die. Deals do not die instantaneously, but they do die quickly. The process of a deal dying is called "cratering," from the neo-Anglo "to crater." The bridge deal is cratering because I insist that you show me proof that you own the bridge, and you only assure me that you do. I don't trust you.

<u>Caving</u>. After several late nights of intense negotiation, however, I am convinced that the Mohawk descendants have absolutely no claim to the bridge and that even if they did, you are a direct descendant of an ancient Mohawk chief yourself, and their claim of ownership does not affect your claim of ownership. I will no longer require proof of ownership. Instead, you will give me title insurance and you agree. I have partially given in and you have partially given in. To a degree, we have both "caved" on this point. We have negotiated. We have caved in on a point for which we said we would never cave in. Caving.

<u>Going South</u>. With the ownership issue behind us, I turn my attention to what I am going to do with this bridge when I own it. My accountants and advisors have studied and projected and reviewed and formulated a plan to charge a toll for people who walk over the bridge to generate revenues. With the projected increased cash flow from the bridge, it will be worth thirty-five percent more than I paid for it in a matter of a few months and I can then sell the bridge to someone

else at a nice profit. You see, as much as I have always wanted to own a little piece of Americana, this is just business, an investment from which I will make money.

Two days after I caved on the ownership issue, however, the *New York Daily News* runs a banner headline that says: *CITY TO TAX FOOTBRIDGE TOLLS.* The *News* reports that city council was inspired by *Taxman* as written by George Harrison on *Revolver*. This tax will change all the projections, all the studies, all the formulas. If there is a tax, the cash flow will not increase; it will decrease, and the bridge will be worth less than I am paying. This is a disaster! I may lose money on my investment. When a once-profitable investment becomes a money loser, the investment "goes south." I am apoplectic when I am involved in a deal that goes south. My bridge investment is "going south." I have to dig in and fight this tax or back out of the deal.

<u>Tanking</u>. Usually, when I buy a new toy, I borrow money from my favorite bank, the Wamego First Bank and Trust Co. ("WBTCo") and as security for the loan I give WBTCo a mortgage on the toy. As far as the toy is concerned, it has pledged itself for the privilege of being owned by someone else, me. What does the toy get out of this? Why, a new owner. A better owner? That is what I think, and my critics and I can at least find some common ground that the owner is new. I say I am a better owner and because I am so smart, I will bring my superior intellect and therefore value to the bridge project. Like I said, my critics and I can agree that the owner is new. The point is, I don't usually pay for the toy; I have the toy pay for itself. So, I never have to dip into savings. I am proud that I make money without spending money. Isn't America great? In this case, however, WBTCo was not real sure about the bridge idea, so to make the deal

happen, I decided to buy this bridge using cash in the bank rather than a bank loan. I am not real happy with WBTCo but that is a different story. If I am not successful in blocking the tax, I will lose real cash. My cash. If I lose real cash, the investment will "tank." "Tanking" is when an investment that is going south drops below the Mason-Dixon Line and actual money, my money, is lost.

I don't like to lose money, actual or imaginary. Losing cash, my cash, is unacceptable.

To avoid this possibility, I direct my deal attorneys to block the tax, no matter what it takes. They hire consultants and lobbyists and other even lower forms of bottom-swimming dark alley inhabitants with whom I am acquainted, and after a week of some behind-the-scenes, between-the-sheets, and under-the-table work – the details of which I do not need to know and I do not want to know – the *Daily News* runs the following headline: *FOOTBRIDGE TAX MYSTERIOUSLY ABANDONED.*

Blowing Up. Time is of the essence now, so our deal attorneys negotiate all day and draft the agreements all night. When they work this hard, they are "slammed." We are both spending a fortune on teams of deal attorneys to finalize the deal. When we spend this much money to do a deal, we are both unhappy. In this unhappiness, we have common ground. You and I have read more drafts of agreements than we ever thought possible and I have finally approved all your language and you have finally approved all my language.

We set closing for Tuesday morning at nine-thirty a.m., and we decide to sign all the documents and do the deal on the bridge footpath. Our deal attorneys and their staff of assistants arrive early and set up the tables with the many documents to be signed and initialed in quadruplicate. There are Asset Purchase Agreements, and Bills of Sale, and Memos of Intent, and Closing Sheets and Statements and Releases and indemnity agreements, and letter agreements and other documents, the names of which I cannot even remember, that in the end will be shipped to a bindery and made into a book with the name of the acquisition/conquest printed in gold leaf on the spine, to be displayed on my shelf and my deal attorneys' shelves. The binder will be my version of a now-endangered wild animal head trophy mounted in a cloistered game room of a great white hunter. My penthouse corner office is filled with such bound volumes. My deals; my head trophies. After I acquire these trophies, I can think about becoming a naturalist. Is there money in that pursuit?

We set up a conveyer belt of sorts. You sign a document and pass it to me, and I sign it and pass it to witnesses who sign it and pass it to notaries, who notarize it and pass it to paralegals and young attorneys who check off the executed document on a closing sheet listing all documents to be signed.

Just as we get to the second document to sign, there is a huge roar from the far end of the bridge. A group of Native Americans is marching across the bridge straight toward us. Right behind them is a CBS television news crew in a mobile van. The Native Americans stop right in front of us and present a decree from one federal bureau or another that they own the bridge. The decree appears to have been signed by some fed at 11 p.m. last night. The news crew jumps out of the van and begins to film the whole tawdry episode, with Josh Mankiewicz reporting, "We are here at the scene of a memorable deal closing."

Josh continues, "An ancient group of Mohawk descendants has just interrupted one of the biggest sham purchases in New York history. A Kansas oil-and-cattleman was seconds away from consummating a deal to purchase the Brooklyn Bridge from a now-fleeing unemployed former New York hot dog street vendor masquerading as a big city deal maker." These New York newsmen are amazing. Who gave this one the lead?

This deal just "blew up." A deal blows up when an unexpected event makes it impossible to ever do the deal.

Your deal attorneys and our deal attorneys are exasperated. They point fingers at each other and accuse each other of being responsible for the deal blowing up. Josh shoves a microphone under my nose, but I have no comment. I never comment. I don't like microphones under my nose so I push it away... aggressively, for emphasis. So Josh turns his attention to the professional way my deal attorneys are dealing with your deal attorneys. He does not need my comment; the public social interaction of the deal attorneys is enough. Finally, after ten minutes of finger-pointing and runaway machismo, my deal attorneys say to your deal attorneys, fuck you – our trial attorneys will be calling your trial attorneys and we will see you in court. No attempt is made to use a more creative way to make the point. Three years of law school and that is the only way they have to express themselves?

Most deal attorneys have never been in a courtroom in their life, and those that have, have never spoken a word in court. But when a deal goes sour, they nevertheless know how to threaten the other side with the last straw, the lawsuit. In their minds, their job ends when they release the raw-meat-fed trial attorneys who they keep in cages in case a deal blows up.

Josh goes home. I go home. The deal attorneys go home with their papers and pens and lists and tables. The bridge remains. That night, in the airport bar, Josh is on the six-foot screen and reports: "Deal Demise. Blah, blah, blah...." Journalistic alliteration: catchy.

<u>The Afterglow</u>. On my way back to Wamego, I wonder how my deal attorneys could have let this deal go so far? My deal attorneys; I made them what they are. I gave them life. "Give me electricity, Igor. Throw the switch. The monster lives!" They like to think they are just like me. They are not. They are mere mortals with a law license regulated by the state's highest court. I am a deal guy; I am unregulated, and I didn't need this bridge anyway. There are other transactions, other acquisitions, other conquests, other toys. Anyway, I heard there was a bridge for sale in San Francisco.

BILLABLE HOURS

AS A LAW CLERK, I reviewed billing attorney statements but I never wrote down my time for each project on which I worked. My first law firm taught me how to record my time. In most law firms, each hour or fraction of an hour must be recorded. So, if I reviewed documents for a client and I spent two hours and fifteen minutes performing my task, I wrote down in a diary (or, these days, in an electronic time recorder program), the name of the client, the task performed, and the time I spent performing the task. My diary entry might look like this:

ABC, Inc.: review documents regarding possible action against XYZ, Inc. – 2.20.

Sometimes my life as an attorney seemed like nothing more than a series of billable hours strung together. It was a hard way to go through life. I am glad I don't do that anymore; there is nothing about billing my time and living my life by the point ones that I miss. The system works something like this:

Most law firms have a benchmark of billing hours that they expect each associate to meet, typically 1800-2000 hours annually. If an associate takes a two-week vacation each year, that means there are fifty weeks in a year to bill 2000 hours; thus, the associate has to bill forty hours per week. Associates tend to measure the day not by the standard Greenwich time, but rather by hours recorded and hours to go. Requisite hours. The magic quota. The legal pot of gold at the end of the jurisprudential rainbow is filled with increments of time.

It is almost impossible to bill each and every hour of the day to some client. Most associates eat, go to the bathroom, daydream, send a statistically verifiable number of personal emails and texts, lose time when things get hectic, interact with many of the administrative heads of the law firm's departments, attend continuing legal education classes, consult with other attorneys, visit with their legal assistant, and the like. But throughout all of these diversions, the associate must still bill eight hours that day. My point is simple, if you have to bill eight hours in a day, you will be at work substantially more than eight hours that day. It is a given of the practice of law.

Many, if not most, law firms now bill in increments of six-minute blocks; .1 hours. Having to account for your life by the point-ones: painful. In an eight-hour day, there are eighty point-ones that come and go. In a ten-hour day, there are one hundred. In a five-day week, there are at least five hundred. Think about the psychological effect of having to account for eighty to one hundred units of your day, each day dragging on, one-tenth of an increment at a time. It is staggering, oppressive: point-one billing. Plumbers, electricians, and engineers do not do it. Doctors don't do it, but if they did, it might look something like this. Picture the proctologist that had to bill by point-ones. His entries might look like this:

.1 – scrub re Mr. Jones exam.
.1 – don lubricated gloves re same.
.2 – o/c w/ Mr. Jones re status of membranes and life
in general.

.1 – insert
.1 – conduct exam
.1 – withdraw, remove gloves and scrub
.1 – o/c with Mr. Jones re results
.2 – dictate memo to patient file re exam results.

If you received this narrative with your proctology bill, what would you think? And imagine how much time the doctor would lose recording each movement, each preparatory step, each examination technique.

To make matters worse, billing hours are one of the important measures of the attorney. If an associate bills more hours, she or he is responsible for more revenues, makes more money for the firm, is more readily loved by the partners, and may more quickly be admitted to the partnership club. Billing hours usually mean a bigger bonus. It could mean the difference between a BMW and a Hyundai, between fuel injectors and fuel efficiency, between Brooks Brothers and Men's Warehouse, between one hundred percent virgin wool and one hundred percent recycled polyester, or between a private, four-year liberal arts education for those soon-to-be-born children and a state land grant university degree.

Serve the client and bill the client. Record time. Bill the client and serve the client. Record time. Bill the client. Record time. Bill.

And when an attorney dies and makes it to the pearly gates, she or he, like everyone else, will be met by St. Peter, who conducts the initial check-in for all heaven applicants. Attorneys do not usually easily or quickly make it past St. Peter, however, because there is always a discrepancy about their age. St. Peter tends to compare the birth age to the billing records. Based on billable hours, it may be difficult, even for a Saint, to determine the actual age of the attorney.

And no one passes through the pearly gates until all I's are dotted and all T's are crossed. No T's are crossed without the billable hour reconciliation.

In attorney death, like in attorney life, it is nothing more than billable hours.

SECRETARIES

In this piece, I refer to this important law firm cog as a secretary. In many firms, the crucial cog of the law firm workforce is now referred to as a legal administrative assistant, but for the bulk of my career, that phrase did not exist. I mean no disrespect by opting for the word secretary. I just grew up calling them secretaries, just as they called themselves. I sincerely hope that this moniker offends none of my secretaries of days gone by. Finally, all of my secretaries were women so I write from that perspective.

SECRETARIES, NOW CALLED LEGAL administrative assistants, or LAAs for short, run the world. In the not-so-older days, every attorney had a secretary for two reasons. First, to type, file, attend, answer the phone, and catapult the attorney through the day. Second, to teach the attorney interpersonal skills, a topic not addressed in law school. Today, with the advent of voice mail, direct dial phone lines, mobile phones, and word processing programs, LAAs type less, file less, and answer the phone less, but they still attend to attorneys, catapult them through the day, and definitely teach them interpersonal skills. No attorney could survive without one. Most attorneys need interpersonal skills lessons from someone who is not an attorney.

During my career, I believe I had a total of twenty-two secretaries. I remember most of their quirks, many of their faces, some of their names. Some were part of the solution to the problem of being an attorney; a few were part of the problem. Many of them refined my interpersonal skills. It is not that I had trouble keeping a secretary or getting along with my secretary. Some of them might beg to differ, but I wasn't an ogre or a prima donna, at least not in my opinion. It is just the way it worked out.

My secretaries ranged in age from a low of twenty to a high of sixty-six years old. They were single, married, divorced, separated. Some had kids and some did not. I had African American ones, white ones, Latino ones, and ones whose heritage I did not know. I had quiet secretaries, loud secretaries, friendly secretaries, surly secretaries, uninformed secretaries, opinionated secretaries, smart secretaries, not-so-smart secretaries, skilled secretaries, unskilled secretaries, highly-educated secretaries, and not so highly-educated secretaries. I had secretaries who painted their nails, and some who painted the town, almost every night.

I had secretaries who left at five and secretaries who would not leave until I left the office. I had secretaries who ate lunch and those who would not. I had secretaries who wanted to stay overtime so they could make extra money, and those who would rise up out of their chair and raise the loudest Cain ever heard this side of the Mississippi at the mere suggestion that some overtime might be necessary tonight.

Some were motherly; some sisterly. Some were socially adroit, and others obviously took their people-skills training from attorneys and therefore were the antithesis of Emily Post etiquette and possessed all the social graces of a charging rhinoceros. I had secretaries who ran a tight ship, secretaries whose hero was Captain Bligh, and secretaries whose idea of order was the chaos found only in a complete state-of-nature. I had secretaries who could take dictation and secretaries who could barely type. I had secretaries who could read my handwriting and many who could not, and secretaries who would try to decipher my chicken-scratch and those who would not even put in the time or effort to learn my system. I had secretaries who could make a decent plane reservation and many who made flying the friendly skies not just a job, but an adventure in "which-city-will-I-be-visiting-today" aviation?

I had all kinds. A true American melting pot.

Perhaps incredibly, at one point in my career, I had ten secretaries in a seven-month period. What an ordeal. During this record-breaking string – spanning several snowstorms, Thanksgiving, untold secretary-related disasters, two seasons of discontent, one partridge in a pear tree, and my growing concern that some secret star chamber club of secretaries had fingered me as their annual target – in all fairness, at least one or two pieces of correspondence arrived at their intended destination, a smattering of things were filed where even today they can be retrieved, and I myself occasionally arrived at the correct courthouse at the correct courtroom at the correct time and, of course, on the correct day in the correct city for the correct client. One of the magic ten said that if I had the courthouse, courtroom, time, day and client nailed down, the city was a mere technicality that eventually would work itself out, and I should have nothing to complain about. Maybe she was right.

Some law firms realize that an attorney is only as good and as sane as the secretary is competent. Other law firms only realize this as it is explained to them by an attorney standing on the ledge outside a thirty-fifth-floor window. It took my last law firm thirteen tries before it got the message, lured me off the ledge, and got it right. When they got it right, though, they really got it right, and my secretary and I were together for more than twenty years. Twenty great years where, just like that, all of the chaos ended, and life was grand, or at least that part of my life that was organized by my secretary.

In my view, I demanded little from my secretaries. I did not ask for coffee, or for my laundry to be done, or for them to attend to my personal problems. I did not ask my secretary to do my bills, balance my checkbook, or prepare my taxes. I did not want to be called Mister anything. My parents gave me a first name, didn't they? I did not ask my secretary to do anything I haven't done at some time in my career, including filing papers, pleadings, and correspondence. I did not yell. I tried not to stamp my feet. I don't sexually harass or sexually discriminate, although it is a stark fact that all of my secretaries were women, and some had been harassed or were the subject of discrimination at some point or points in their careers. If I could, I would smack (or worse) every one of the attorneys who mistreated a secretary.

At times during the hiring process, I would be granted the privilege of outlining what characteristics I wanted in a secretary. I asked for a secretary who would not share my snide remarks about others with anyone, especially other secretaries, and who would make an effort to enter my billable hours relatively timely, so the firm did not charge me money for late-entered time. I asked for a secretary with a modicum of loyalty, a pinch of personality, a sprinkling of humor, a modicum of maturity, and an unlimited supply of patience. And they had to teach me and guide me back to the life lane where civilization traveled. Interpersonal skills: I had them, but they abandoned me at times, for which I am not proud. The perfect secretary guided me back.

Loyalty, humor and personality, and life skills lessons. All very important. Many years ago, when I was a young pup,

I had a secretary; let's call her Judy, although her name is changed to protect the somewhat-innocent, me. Judy was an excellent typist. She was short on other things, but she could crank out the documents and rarely made a mistake. We were together for one month. She did not want to be *my* secretary, viewing it as a demotion because her primary assignment was the firm's head litigator. To show how much she did not want to be the secretary of a lowly associate, she started our time together with a lack of loyalty, and she rarely smiled, and in our month together, I never learned much about her personality. One month is hardly enough time to get to know someone.

Judy presented me, however, with one of my most enduring and powerful life lessons. She was a truly great teacher, albeit more than a bit cruel. The story goes something like this. One particularly difficult, stress-filled day, I found myself with three hours of dictation to generate, and only two hours left. So, I had to utilize every precious moment. Dictation is one of those attorney skills that has fallen out of favor. Back in the day, attorneys had little hand-held recording machines into which they dictated their words. Then the attorney dropped off the recorded media with the secretary for transcription; my media was usually a micro-cassette. The secretary donned her headphones, listened to the cassette, and typed the words and thereby created a document for an attorney to edit and finalize. These days, a substantial number of attorneys just create the document draft themselves in a word-processing program and the dictation machines of the world sit on a law firm shelf gathering law firm dust. I was always a heavy dictation generator. Even as the age of word-processing bloomed, I liked the idea that my secretary would type one document while I dictated another. I know I date myself by this admission, but it is a Monday-morning-throwback-truth.

When I walked in the halls, I dictated. When I rode down in the elevator, I dictated. On the way back from a client's office, I dictated in the car, through the parking garage, and back up the elevator. I don't think anyone saw me, but I cannot be sure. I did not eat lunch so there was no need to dictate my way through a cheeseburger and a cola. But that day, I did drink an uncharacteristically substantial amount of coffee, the nectar of the gods when there is a deadline pressing and dictation to crank out.

Coffee definitely affects me. That day, like most, it got me up and going, especially because I did not ordinarily drink too much of the stuff. With my coffee high, my mind got to processing information faster, my mouth got to dictating quicker, my hands got to editing swifter, and my kidneys got to filling up sooner. Filled kidneys meant more bathroom runs.

After spending the day dictating no matter where I went and no matter what I did, I was running out of time and I really had to relieve myself in the bathroom. Here is where it all started to unravel.

Off to the bathroom I hurried with my trusty Lanier micro-cassette dictating machine clutched in the sweaty palm of my over-caffeinated hand. My thumb mashed the record button while I dictated my way through the halls. I dictated through left turns and right turns, around several office corners, out the office's back door, into the floor's common area, and right into the men's room. I entered the stall, still dictating ("attached hereto and marked as... blah, blah, blah...") and stood over the bowl, assumed the position, and yes, dear reader, I urinated. Unfortunately, it only takes one hand to urinate (no need to go into the details with a short primer on methods of urinating, but at least for most of us, it can be a one-handed activity). So, my other hand, with its fingers still grasping the Lanier dictaphone, ascended to my mouth area, record button depressed, and a letter of confirmation and information transmission to an opposing counsel was completed. I flushed, dictated who was to receive copies, and who was to receive blind copies, and headed back to my desk. As I passed Judy's desk, I finished the tape, and I dropped off the micro-cassette for her to transcribe.

Ten minutes later, she brought me the draft. She was quick anyway, and as I learned, this particular microcassette inspired her to type *very* quickly. I began reading the draft letter and it said, word for word:

> *Attached hereto and marked as Exhibit A is a document [water-related sound begins. Sounds like a stream running into a larger pool of water] to the previous group of docu-ments [loud rush of water. Sounds like several gallons of water forcibly escaping a porcelain receptacle] you should have already [door slamming] received.*

In the privacy of my office, my face got very red. Oh, no. I had dictated my way through a very private bodily function. What was I thinking? What had it come to? Would I next dictate my way through a shower? In my sleep? Through sex? I shook my head to myself and thought how lucky I was that no one else in the firm would ever find out about this small, embarrassing indiscretion. Thank god for the bond of loyalty between a secretary and an attorney.

And then I realized the awful truth. This was Judy. She was like the six o'clock news, and she did not want to be my secretary because I was nothing more than a lowly associate. She wanted to ditch me and I had given her the ammuni-tion to begin the clean-break process. This incident would be broadcast all over the firm like the lead story delivered by Katie Couric. I had to talk to her. Surely, she would have some compassion? And then I thought, Judy? No way. What was I thinking? She hates me. She doesn't respect me. She has no loyalty. She wouldn't give up this bit of juicy gossip for anything in the world. I could offer her money, a piece of my salary check every week for... forever. I could appeal to her sense of fair play and dignity. Judy? No way!

Instead of talking, I decided to play it cool. I stepped out of my office and calmly walked over to her desk. But she was not there. End cool; start fear. It was her break time. She would be in the coffee room with four or five other secretaries, chatting, about this and that, and him and her, about ME! End fear; start panic attack. I ran through the halls. I didn't realize until later that I still had that stupid Lanier dictaphone in my hand, like a relay race baton that the runner cannot pass, in a recurring nightmare. I arrived at the coffee room, burst in, stopped, caught my breath, and tried to coolly survey the situation. Be cool. There was giggling. No guffawing, just giggling. Did it sound like bathroom-related giggling, I thought? Is that how loud I would laugh if I were a secretary and heard a story about someone's boss peeing in the men's room as it is recorded? I had no idea. No more cool. Nothing like this had ever happened to me, or anyone else before, as far as I knew.

Was that my name? I heard my name! They were giggling about me. It was all over. My career was ruined. Shakespeare was wrong; I didn't care if all the lawyers were killed, but first, the secretaries had to go. Where was the loyalty, the confidential relationship, the trust? It was down the toilet, that's where it was. Flushed, like my career.

There was no reason to have a heart-to-heart talk with Judy. I could barely look her in the eye. What had I ever done to her to deserve this? I don't know. So, I told the office manager that I felt Judy was incompatible with me. We just weren't working out. Was that the hint of a smile on the manager's face? Did she know? Oh God, she knew! Judy was quick. Who else knew? It might be easier to figure out who didn't know. I couldn't bear to think about it. No matter; we were incompatible, we needed a divorce, quick. Judy didn't object – in fact, that was her plan. Very sophisticated in its development and its implementation.

She taught me a good lesson, complete with thought-provoking interpersonal skills homework. After a brief time on the thirty-fifth-floor ledge again, the firm came through with a replacement secretary, and I moved on to Linda (her real name). Linda was, and is, great; tied for best I have ever worked with. Just a wonderful person, who taught me that with every screwup, there can be a new beginning, and she gave me a chance to redeem and prove myself. Of course, I never tested Linda's loyalty with a dictation indiscretion.

But I am scarred for life. Shot down in the prime of my dictating life by a disloyal, questionably-humored secretary. Important lesson in interpersonal relations learned: secretaries run the world. They make you or break you. Oh, and also… don't dictate in the men's room.

LEARNING NOT TO SAY FUCK YOU

IN MY YEARS AS an associate, I learned several lessons. An important one I learned was not to say "fuck you," at the end of a conversation. There were opportunities – many of them. I don't think the opportunities presented themselves because of anything unique or particular about me, most were just the product of life in a large firm in the modern era practice of law.

For example, it is 6 p.m. on a Friday and you are collecting your papers, jamming them into your briefcase, rolling down your sleeves, pulling up your tie, grabbing your suit jacket, reaching for the light switch and making your way to the door and the elevator bank beyond for the ride down thirty-five flights to catch the 6:10 p.m. express to freedom.

Just as you get to the door, a partner catches up with you and hands you a research project that will take you all weekend to understand, let alone find the answer (if one even exists). You think, *how the hell do I know whether it is illegal in northern Lithuania to set up a franchise to sell silk long johns?* You consider saying, *I haven't seen my family in three weekends; I'm sure you understand.* If you say this, however, you are sure the partner will *not* understand. You consider that accepting work projects is kind of like an addiction to cocaine, and maybe you should "just say no." But you know you will not. This particular drug is not a controlled substance. This partner seems to take great pleasure in hunting you down as the weekend arrives. This particular partner seems to hold onto research projects before assigning them at the last second. So, you consider saying the only thing a sophisticated, educated, frustrated, anything-but-placated, philosophical professional thinks of at a time like this: "Fuck you."

As all these thoughts are running through your mind, however, you hear yourself meekly say something like, "I've always been interested in Lithuanian silk franchises," and you accept the weekend exile in the library, again. What a wimp.

Another example: a client calls up and complains about a law, validly enacted by Congress, that he says he has no intention of following. He wants to fight it, he says, but upon hearing how much it will cost, he screams about how only attorneys get rich. You, of course, know your client is a multimillionaire. He rails on about how it is all the fault of attorneys. He unwittingly quotes Shakespeare and suggests all the attorneys should be killed. He asks you to explain the reason for the law, and then interrupts you and tells you he does not want to hear it. He knows better, he tells you. He squeals and rants and raves like the grownup he is. You are sure he will not pay for this phone call; that's not how he got to where he is today. What can you say? Not much; not what you want to say. This particular client believes that part of the reason for hiring an attorney is to abuse the attorney. Who knows? Maybe he is right.

Example: a classmate of yours in law school is extolling the virtues of one legal principle or another, at a cocktail party designed to help you forget about the law. *Drink*, you think. *Drink, you fool: That's what we're all here for.* But your classmate chooses not to drink, and forces you to listen to his overly-zealous dribble about the sanctity of whatever position he is advocating until you want to put your hands over your ears and issue a primal scream of those two words from the depth of your soul. But, you don't. What *do* you say? Not much. It's hard to talk with the narrow end of a beer bottle in your mouth, and legal dribble, especially at a "let's forget about the law party," usually leaves you dehydrated and in need of carbonated fluids.

Example: an associate at the firm, who never sees the light of day and has a reputation for never smiling, sets his jaw, narrows his eyes, and tells you he is "this close" to the designation of a "number one" rated attorney. It is unclear if that is worldwide, nationwide, at the firm, or just in his mind. Your firm rates attorneys on a scale of one to seven, so you assume it is just at the firm. A "seven" is usually fired and a "one" is usually the equivalent of legal royalty. When he says "number one" he narrows his eyes, raises his chin ever so slightly, elevates his left hand twelve inches in front of his nose, and presses the pointer and thumb ever so close together, to provide you with the visual aid he knows you need to fully understand just how close "close" really is. You are not sure why he is telling you this. All you asked as you passed him in the hall was whether the men's room on the thirty-third floor was working again. You heard there was a plumbing problem. What do you think? You guessed it. What do you say? Oh, you mumble something about how nice that is and try to get as far away from the suspended thumb and pointer as possible. As you begin to retreat from his visual aid, you notice that his fingernails need to be trimmed and you wonder about his aversion to the daylight, his pale, almost bloodless, complexion, the icy chill in the air as he leaves the room, and why he never smiles.

Example: an attorney representing an opposing party calls you on the telephone for the late afternoon brushback. In baseball, if a hitter is standing too close to the plate it is fair game for the pitcher to throw a fastball high and inside to force the hitter to back away from the plate. It is called a brushback pitch. In the practice of law, it is common to receive a brushback from the other side in the form of a particularly unpleasant phone call explaining why your position is without merit and how bad things will be for your career if you continue to take such nonsensical stands. You better duck. This is the attorney equivalent of a high, hard one.

Like in baseball, some high, hard ones are more threatening than others. It depends who is throwing the pitch. Did you ever try to read the lips of the batter as he picks himself up off the ground and removes the sand from inside his belt line after dodging a high hard one? The law is the same way. You think about telling this Nolan Ryan attorney to read your lips as you utter the magic words. Do you? No. What do you do? Not much. You probably sarcastically tell him to have a nice day and that you will see him in court.

Example: you have planned this vacation for months, and you purchased nonrefundable airline tickets to Albuquerque to visit and commune with the Acoma Native American tribe. Tomorrow morning, you have a seven o'clock flight to solace and retreat. A partner stops by your office, and you naïvely think he is visiting to wish you well on your first vacation in a year and a half. After all, when they hired you, they told you all associates were entitled to four weeks off each year. You weren't asking for all eight accumulated weeks in a row; you only wanted one week of solitude.

But this isn't a social call. A case you have been handling is "heating up." Even though there are hundreds and hundreds of attorneys in the firm, you – and only you – can handle it.

You cannot believe your ears: you think he just suggested that you should cancel your vacation. You want to say the magic words. You really do. If you could speak, you might actually utter the sacred phrase. But your body's natural defense systems have taken over; you are so upset that your vocal cords have constricted. You cannot say anything. You cannot breathe either, for that matter. You can only smile. If you are smart, you smile, and you get on that plane the next morning. If you are not smart... well, the ancient Indian pueblos have been there since the twelfth century and probably will still be there next year.

I think Woody Allen described each of these responses as punching your assailant in the fist with your eye.

As often as I wanted to flip someone the verbal bird, to shoot them the great punctuation mark, to give them that middle digit visual symbol of animosity and disdain I know they deserve, and as hard as it may be for friends who know me well to believe this, I usually restrained myself. It is a harsh ending to a conversation. It does not add much to my position. It loses its impact the more that it is uttered. I am fully aware that it seldom changes the outcome. And, most importantly, I always had the fear that the person to whom I contemplated delivering the seven-letter message would be immune to its intended impact. Remember, it was usually an attorney, a colleague, or a law school classmate to whom I contemplated delivering the message, they had heard it before and tended to discount the force of the message. Also, they are not words easily uttered. They are harsh, and mean, and charged and impactful... overly impactful. Those two little words also conjure up visions of unemployment, disbarment, and physical pain.

But I did use the words after each of these incidents. I did take the opportunity to say, "Fuck you..." but only to myself in the mirror after each encounter. Each time, I was mad at myself for not speaking my mind and for being in a position where I wanted to say the words, but couldn't. So, I developed other ways, maybe much more sophisticated ways to say, "Fuck you."

For example, you are negotiating late into the night on some securities deal. Opposing counsel is a real peach. As the clock strikes two, he leans across the table and with a terse smile – revealing a very poor capping job by his dentist – he says, "Look, this could go a lot faster, but you're obviously not a securities attorney." You *could* say the magic words. But you do not. Instead, you look him in the eye (you cannot bear to look at his teeth) and say, "Look, you're right. I'm not a securities attorney. On the other hand, I'm not a proctologist, but I know an asshole when I see one."

Another example: a first-year associate tells you he cannot help you find the answers to five questions because the case is too small, and he only wants to work on large, sophisticated mergers and acquisitions transactions. He gratuitously tells you that he disagrees with your analysis of the questions, and points out totally irrelevant issues he suggests you should consider, and with which he believes you should be concerned. He tells you he only thinks there are two questions of importance. He will not be able to help, he reminds you, but he is sure his off-the-cuff view of the problem, based on his experience developed over the three months he has been a "big case" licensed attorney, has been helpful.

You need research, however, not a consultation. You need answers, not irrelevant considerations and suggestions. You *could* flip him the verbal bird. But you do not. Instead, you agree with him and tell him sarcastically, "I thought this *was* a big case worthy of even *your* time and effort." You assure him that there are five questions because last night when you were in court until nine o'clock, the judge recited these very five questions as the points the judge wanted the parties to address. "It must be nice to be a 'big picture person' so early in your career," you say, but you agree there is no harm in starting to train to be a head partner or chairman of a board now rather than developing your skills as a mere member of the tribe. You smile (always smile when sarcasm is used), and you set off to find someone else with a little less knowledge, a little narrower view of the big picture, a few more social skills, and someone who does not fancy himself a direct descendant of a chairman.

Sarcasm with a smile is one of the most often-used substitutes for the magic words. Often, the recipient of the sarcastic communication is unaware that it was sarcastic. Perfect.

One final example: you just received an angry phone call from an attorney who always barks, bites, scratches, and screams. You've listened to this so much that you usually just hold the receiver twelve inches from your ear. Today, however, you take the offensive and in the middle of an especially barbed remark by your caller, you grab the receiver like a hammer handle and bash the mouthpiece quickly three times on the desk, pause, and then bash it again three more times. Of course, most law firm phones have been tested for this kind of abuse. Your verbal assailant may now be experiencing a temporary loss of hearing, but you do not care. You bring the receiver back to your mouth and yell, almost apologetically, "It must be a bad connection, so I'll have to hang up." And you do. Never offer to call back.

Insincere apologies coupled with loud noises are another often-used substitute for the magic words.

The point is, when you graduate from law school and join this austere and learned legal profession, you are expected to be more creative with your "fuck yous." You have to work much harder to end the conversation on an intellectual substitute for that famous conversation-ending word-duo. Perhaps you could do the equivalent of flipping someone the bird, with an Aesop's Fable about proctologists. Sarcasm works sometimes. Insincere apologies coupled with temporary noise are a favorite of mine. I do not know all the possibilities; I kept learning these alternatives up until my last day as an attorney, and I also learned that at some point, in every attorney's career, they find themselves dedicated to creating a new, ultimate conversation-ender. Their individual donation to the worthy cause.

RITES OF SPRING

WE SAT AT LUNCH. It was our traditional spring meal at the traditional spring bar and grill that made the best traditional burgers around. It was partnership time at the law firm – time to chart who was up for partnership, and who would make it. Entry into the ranks of law firm ownership; making partner, for short.

We analyzed this process each year and untold times before. Every spring since we joined the law firm, we snuck off to this godforsaken dimly-lit greasy pub – with an old Motorola color T.V. and a pock-holed dartboard from the eighties, each mounted on a wall – for the privacy of a worn, vinyl-covered booth that your slacks stuck to, and a bartender who doubled as a waiter and who knew how to leave his customers alone. We were both partial to the familiar smell of grilling onions, and the indescribable tang that years of private conversations, stale cigarette smoke (before the city fathers and mothers banned cigs), beer, whiskey and lonely companionship left in the air.

Each year as the azaleas bloomed, we publicly led our colleagues to believe we did not care who made partner and that we were above the whole process; privately, we were partnership junkies, as caught up in the process as anyone, and we had our annual laugh as we observed the quest for partnership take its moral, physical, emotional, and spiritual toll on the hopefuls, faithfuls, wishfuls, and "no-way"-fuls.

Early on, we learned about the two classes of attorney citizens in law firms: associates and partners. Associates – the attorney employees of law firms who do not own an interest in the firm and who spend eight to ten years learning their trade, sharpening pencils, carrying bags, pleasing their employers, placating their clients, always on call answering emails and texts until all hours of the night, smiling, agreeing, sacrificing, repressing emotions, and avoiding telling their employers just how awful the associate existence truly is. In other words, highly-educated, highly-trained, highly-paid, highly-motivated, highly-stressed, highly-troubled, professional emotion-suppressors. Some eked out this existence with more verve, panache, feeling, and with less need for therapy, than others.

We learned about partners: the attorney owners of law firms; the former associates who, after eight to ten years of sharpening pencils so pointedly, bag carrying, learning, pleasing, placating, smiling, agreeing, repressing, avoiding, and responding, were admitted to the ranks of owner. More on the ins and outs of that exalted status later.

We both knew the game of making partner. Truth be told, it was a fun process to observe. We discussed it a thousand times before. But Robert was a couple of years ahead of me and he was up for partner this year. Somehow, things were different. He didn't seem hopeful or faithful. He wasn't laughing or praying either. But, tradition required that our ritual be followed to the T, so I asked him as the burgers were delivered by the all-knowing, keeper-of-confidences bartender, "Robert, do you know how many people are up for partner this year?" Over the years, I had asked him this a hundred times before, and he always knew.

"I guess I don't," he said. "I try not to think about it. If it happens, it happens. If it doesn't, well, at least I didn't get an ulcer over it." This was new; this was unbecoming of our tradition; this was disrespectful of our years at the firm together; fatalism didn't suit him. I knew full well that he didn't believe in providence, divine or otherwise. When he spoke, he had a distant look. He later told me that when he gazed at someone who was talking, he did not decipher what they said and saw a jabbering camel.

Something was very wrong, so as a highly-trained attorney, skilled in the art of observation and inquiry, I asked: "What's the matter?"

"You know, in college, I discovered the observance of an ancient pagan ritual at Bryn Mawr College. I'll never forget it. Every May 1, the students carried a maypole, secretly stored all year in the basement of a college dorm, out to the lawn in the wee hours of dawn and righted it so it pointed straight into the heavens. There were crepe paper streamers attached to the top of the pole and the college women grabbed the streamers and danced around the pole in a traditional pagan fertility dance. In ancient times, the dancers were called merrymakers. It was a strange custom at a school where every other day of the year, fertility and paganism are shunned in favor of independence, equality, and education."

This was serious. But before I could stop him, he continued. "After encountering the maypole and the pagan fertility ritual, I was pretty convinced that highly-educated women who danced around in a fertility ceremony at an all-women's school where the motto was "our failures only marry" was by far and away the most bizarre spring ritual I would likely encounter in my life." He stopped, nibbled on a burger and continued, "I was wrong. Law firms have their own dance around a symbolic pagan law pole. It's the pagan ritual of who will make partner. It's many times more bizarre than virgin coed merrymakers innocently dancing around a twenty-foot pole. Each spring, a partnership maypole is carried out of the dusty basement storage area of the law firm and is righted in the lobby for each associate to see every morning as a symbol of power and legal fertility."

He was cracking and needed help. And, I was pretty sure I had no idea what he was talking about. "But... Robert—" I pleaded.

He ignored me. "Look. The partner gods announce 'Associate merrymakers, come gather around the pole to dance and lay ceremonial offerings to us. Chant and bow and pray.' And the associates do in the hopes of pleasing the gods. But these are very difficult gods to please, and there is often thunder and lighting and earthquakes. When they're not pleased, some associates are sacrificed. It's that simple. But I guess we're supposed to be willing to risk sacrifice for a chance at admission to god-dom."

Now I knew I had no idea what he was talking about. We had never had this type of discussion before. Every time I mentioned partner, he thought of a twenty-foot pole and associate sacrifice at some symbolic alter. It couldn't have been the food, though. These burgers were the best in town, even if the lights and the booth and the vinyl and the T.V. and the dartboard were not.

"Come on, Robert! Look, I've charted the whole thing. We've done this before, but this year it matters. There are 170 associates in the firm, give or take. Of the 170, twenty-eight graduated from law school at least eight years ago. They are eligible—"

"I know, I know. But only five people made partner last year. *Five*, out of twenty-eight. Last year, the chances were less than one in five. This year will be more of the same, or worse. Like I said, it's not worth thinking about, let alone charting. I used to think spring was reserved for crocuses, and grapefruit leagues, and the end of the college basketball season, and rites of spring. It used to be fun to chart this stuff. But I was wrong. It's not." He was trying to distance himself from our tradition; his heart was not in it. I was losing him.

I said: "But not all of the twenty-eight have a chance."

He observed: "None of the twenty-eight may have a chance."

I said: "Look, three of these folks are out for sure. They've pissed off too many partners over the years and it's payback time. That leaves twenty-five. Out of the twenty-five, six graduated only eight years ago. They don't have a realistic chance because no one ever makes partner after eight years. The firm just says that to hook you."

He said: "You're not going to go through all twenty-eight, are you?"

But I had to. It was tradition. So, I continued: "That leaves nineteen. Of the nineteen, seven have been passed over before. They're damaged goods. They'll never get it. They're permanent associates. If they had a conscience or a soul, they'd move on."

He countered: "Why should they? They have a good job with a steady check. Maybe being a permanent associate wouldn't be so bad. Not everyone can be a partner god. Someone has to be the flock." Very rational, very true, and very much not part of the annual ritual. Robert was obviously bone-weary; tired of his years at the firm. Not everyone is cut out for the years of long-term abuse.

"Robert, Robert! What are you saying? You can't lose your edge. You have to go the distance. That leaves twelve associates. If they make six of those partners, the odds are one in two. You're in, man."

"Are they laying odds around the coffee machine?"

"I got ten bucks on you buddy."

"Wha— ?"

"Just kidding. But the thought has crossed my mind. There is some money to be made here. It's like a sporting spectacle. Maybe I should sell beer."

He said, "The whole thing is crazy. Maybe we should sell beer and game-day programs in front of the law pole. 'Get your programs here.' You can't tell your merrymakers without a program."

I had to ask. "So, what would the program say about you?"

Finally, he smiled. The distant gaze faded. He wasn't having a pole-vision, or a camel-vision for that matter. Clarity descended and took over his being.

"What would this game-day program say about me? I guess it would say 'he used to ride his bike in the wind with a friend trying to go as fast as he could, and when he was in high gear and the wind was blowing his hair straight back, he felt free. He heard and smelled and felt the sound of the air rushing by. It was a time to clear his mind and let it wander into dreamland. Then he went to law school, graduated, got a great job at the firm, was sold the plan, and played the game... and played it well. But he didn't ride his bike anymore and the dreams stopped one night without warning. He fell into the great chasm of blind belief that there was something worth having at the other end of the law firm rainbow that made it all worthwhile. But he found out there wasn't, and it wasn't. He didn't dance, and he isn't much of a dancer anyway. He just hung out and watched.'"

I stared. There it was. The clarity of resignation and a shift in the cosmic universe of a life plan. It wouldn't say that in any game day program I sold. This was his distorted vision. All of a sudden it was like I found myself in someone else's dream, and a strange one at that. But he snapped me out of it.

"You know, I bought a new bicycle last weekend. We both did, Gen and me. I haven't had a bike since I was in college. It's pretty cool. You should buy one too."

"Look, Robert. I don't want a bike. I don't want to dance around a pole at Bryn Mawr or anywhere for that matter. All I want to know is – what are you talking about?"

"It's all a question of perspective. It just took me a long time to get it. Kind of like a born-again philosopher. It's like Groucho said; I'm just not sure I want to be a member of any club that would have me as a member. At least not this club."

"Why?"

"I'm not ready to trade in my brand-new bicycle. I'm having a hard time smelling the forest or the trees or the air rushing by. I don't smell the coffee anymore. I am tired. I don't breathe in enough oxygen as the firm seems to always suck all of the air out of my room. I want to get back to dreaming. No, I need to get back to dreaming. All of the above."

I looked at him and he looked at me. He said it and I heard it, but I didn't understand, and I don't think he expected me to. There was nothing else to say. So, we ate the rest of the burgers in silence. They were good. They were always good. The firm offered Robert partnership status two weeks later, and almost immediately he said *no thanks*. He convinced the partners to give him a sabbatical and he left quietly one night. The office still had his nameplate beside the door, but inside, it was empty. Half the firm was abuzz about his courage; the other half was abuzz and appalled by his foolhardy decision. After all the charting and laughing and burgers, I guess I did not know him all that well.

Robert's sabbatical was officially for one year but was extended, and I didn't think he would come back. Meanwhile, every once in a while, I got a letter from him. The last one was postmarked from Montana, and he made some joke about buying some land and raising dental floss – he always liked Frank Zappa.

I was up for partner the following spring. Just before the partners met to decide my fate, I had a weird dream. I was dressed like a court jester in medieval England. I was holding a crepe paper streamer in my hand as I skipped around a twenty-foot pole. Someone else on an eighteen-speed bicycle had hold of another streamer and was riding in circles around the pole. Groucho Marx had a club in one hand and a program in the other and was buying a drink from a lawyer dressed in a suit, button-down shirt, and a tie.

They say dreams take your thoughts, your hopes, your fears, your little corner of reality and reorder them. And, when you wake up, you have to put everything you dreamed about back in the right order. First, though, you have to figure out the right order. When I awoke I was not enlightened. I made partner but I spent a great deal of time during my career thinking about Robert and my last-minute dream. Was Robert right to head to Montana and find the open road wind in his face? Or was I right to accept the partnership offer? Or… was there *no* right answer?

MY PLATE IS FULL

Associates, please gather 'round.

We all know there are things that associates will say to try to get out of a work assignment. We all know that there are things partners will say in response, to make sure the associates stay occupied round the clock. This is the constant tension between the two groups, right? Who gets to decide how much work is enough? Who gets to decide what kind and how much of an outside life is sufficient? I guess the partners think they do... and that's probably true.

I was an associate for many years, at several firms in different parts of the country until I made partner. I, therefore, consider myself to be a card-carrying member of the Associate Alumni Association of America, and I write this piece for all of the associates of the world. It is based on an amalgamation of my real experiences and interactions.

Most associates have to decide whether to try to fend off the late-Friday-afternoon partner assignment, not so much out of laziness, but rather out of self-preservation. To do so, there is a whole underground language of cute little phrases associates use as a first defense. And, of course, there is also a set of approved partner responses designed to circumvent attempted self-preservation. Most partners trained under Mr. Spock – the Vulcan, not the baby guru – and dogmatically believe that the needs of the many outweigh the needs of the few.

Make no mistake: the partner response usually prevails over any associate excuse to try to avoid a work assignment, and *always* prevails over any weak or unsubstantiated attempt to fend off work. An associate might say she is swamped, slammed with work, cranking for other partners, up to her ass in alligators, or busier than a mosquito in a nudist colony. Or the associate might say she has so much work, she is fearful of malpractice, or is beginning to burn out, or is so tired that she is running and practicing on impulse power. All are tried and true, some are cute, some are thoughtful, and most are quite ineffective. If the associate has any chance at all, she must reach deep and appeal to the partner's sense of creativity and their dormant sense of fair play. Yes, some partners do have that dormant sense. Some can (fleetingly) remember their times at the firm before they made partner. Associates, you have to stir something in the deep, dark recesses of the partner's mind to trigger the self-preservation recollection. It is your only hope.

Associates, as we communicate out of the purview of all partners, I am going to share with you a line to use, my favorite phrase, passed down to me in secrecy during the dark ages of the practice of law from associate to associate. I am sure you may have heard it; you may have even used it. It may form a part of your defensive strategy in your interactions with partners, but perhaps you failed to analyze it in detail or to consider the likely victorious response from the partner.

The story is true – it really happened to me, and maybe it will ring true for you. The associate author of the phrase and the partner creator of the response is long forgotten, and I consider the phrase (and response) to be in the public domain, probably posted on one associate listserv or another. Folklore has it that the phrase I am about to give you worked at least once, but I can offer and if the assignment sticks, if self-preservation fails, do not call me.

This is how it usually comes up: a partner approaches you, and says there is a project for you to work on. You ask how much time is involved in it, and the partner responds, "It should be largely completed in a week or two."

First, remember: nothing in a law firm is over in a week or two. I have friends and colleagues who unwittingly entered the "in a week or two" black hole of work assignments, never to be heard from again. The "week or two" turned into something approaching a lifetime. Second, "largely completed" is a world away from completely completed. So, if you are a normal red-blooded associate, any time a partner tells you it is only "a week or two assignment," you must try to fend it off unless you are prepared to commit yourself to the cause for an eon of law firm purgatory. Indeed, this type of work assignment is a red flag that should send powerful waves of warning tingles down the typical associate spine, already challenged for its strength by service in the law firm world.

One way to fend work off is to use other work assignments as a defense. To the non-attorneys reading this, imagine that working in a law firm is like eating in a cafeteria-style restaurant. Work assignments are food items selected from behind the counter and placed on a plate, then passed from the salad counter staff to the vegetable counter staff to the entree counter staff to the dessert counter staff. As items are selected, and the plate is passed from staff member to staff member, it fills up until there is just no room left.

In a law firm, the partners choose what items fill the associate's plate. The problem with partners is two-fold (just two?). First, partners are not very good at estimating how much one associate's plate can hold. Often, they hand the associate a plate stacked with food that is all commingled, spilling over the edges. There are so many items on the plate, and it is piled so high, that it is almost impossible to separate one item from another.

Second, many partners do not care what other partners put on the plate; not their problem. The associate has a full plate when the plate is piled so high with food that there is just no way that another thing can be placed on top. So when the partner approaches this overloaded associate, and asks if the associate can undertake one more short assignment, the associate tries to fend off the work and replies, "I really can't, my plate is full."

That's the line – my plate is full. Four words: concise; to the point.

As a warning, often when a partner asks an associate to undertake an assignment, the partner has the food scooper in hand and is in the process of depositing a hefty portion of a work assignment (that resembles runny mash potatoes and off-colored gelatinous gravy) on the associate's plate before the associate can even construct an answer.

Once it hits the plate, it is too late to even suggest that your plate is full; there is no mechanism for returning what's already on your plate. So the associate has to be prepared to get right in the partner's face when the scooper is in view, and calmly, but firmly, say "My plate is full." The associate should not feel guilty. While there are many associates with their plates piled high, it is also a given that a substantial number of other associates contend they are on a diet and thereby try to avoid the full plate.

As a further warning, there are some calorie-counting partners who, when confronted with the full-plate gambit, respond by asking to see just what's on your plate and review any alleged dietary restrictions, then proceed to make their own determination of whether an associate's plate is truly full or not. So – since credibility is everything, at least for associates – dear associate: make sure before you suggest your plate is full that it is, in fact, piled high with carbohydrates and cholesterol and saturated fats and other stick-to-the-ribs work assignments.

Swinging Dick. A partner actually used the response I am about to share with you after I suggested my plate was full; reality is often so much more delicious and informative than fiction. You think you have just successfully fended off a partner, and smile to yourself at the skill you have displayed. All of a sudden, the partner, who has been in this predicament before, and who probably tried to use the full plate gambit in his youth, stares at you with ice-cold purpose and says, "Everyone here is working hard. I myself am killing myself. As a matter of fact, every swinging dick in this office is working his or her butt off. So, I don't care about your plate or your problems. I want the project on my desk Monday morning."

It is a short response, and I present it here to you without embellishment or editorial license. He said it, I heard it, just like that. My first reaction to the partner response was *how vulgar*. But, as time passed, and with it passed my initial offense to the vulgarity of the response, I did what law school taught me to do: critical analysis. So, as we analyze the phrase together today, dear associates, you can readily see it is replete with failed attempts at sexual equality, poor grammar and mixed metaphors.

As we unpack the partner's statement word by word, let's first start with the words *"swinging dick."* The Urban Dictionary says that the phrase:

> *refers literally to a man, but specifically to someone whose skills or physical stature make him especially intimidating. A badass. It can be used metaphorically to refer to a woman, as long as she is a total badass at something.*

There is a common misconception that this term refers to any male because it references the male organ, but the more important part of the term is "swinging." That is, not just any man, but an especially potent or imposing man. Hence, a badass.

Observe that in the modern era, someone on the editorial staff at Dictionary Central tried to normalize the phrase to include females as well as males. What a long way we've come; who would have thought the suffragettes were fighting for the right to be called a swinging dick?

The origins of the law firm partner's swinging-dick response, however, can be traced to the days when law firms were the bastions of male protectionism, when every partner in the office practiced the art of intimidation and fancied himself a badass who, therefore, by definition, had one form of a swinging dick or another. Today, of course, more than half of the attorneys escaping from law school into the real world are females, so the astute partner has tried to modify the swinging dick response to take into account the advent of the female attorney population. But in any case, kudos to the partner in this story who tried to include both males and females even as the partner delivered the bad news.

"I myself am killing myself" Bad grammar, but what does it mean? At first, the associate may get the impression the partner is so mad that he is unable to form a proper sentence. This is the reaction the partner hopes for; he wants to convey a certain frothing-at-the-mouth state of affairs. Do not be fooled, however. The partner, of course, has the skillset to form a proper sentence with correct grammar to get across what is on his mind; but awkward grammar, and the threat of significant, uncontrolled froth, has a more lasting impact. The awkwardness of the grammar is likely

all preplanned.

"Every swinging dick is working his or her butt off?" How many bodily parts, and private ones at that, must be in the partner response to the "full plate" gambit? This is a mixed metaphor if I ever heard one, especially if you consider that the partner began his speech by telling you that everyone was working hard. But the sentence overreaches. There are too many bodily parts: it should be one or the other. I guess the reference to the two bodily parts is designed to emphasize just how serious the whole work assignment issue has become. A partner never drags a dick or a butt or any mid-body part into a conversation unless it is serious. Even partners know they should make judicious use of dicks and butts in their discussions with associates.

Those are the words, delivered in less than ten seconds to the unsuspecting associate: me. I have thought about this inter-action a great deal over the years. The swinging dick response is so outrageous that the unwary fully-plated associate is usu-ally stopped in his or her tracks. I was. I now know that after completion of the delivery of the words, the partner smiles inwardly, thinking he is such a badass, turns and heads for the door, confident in the knowledge that the assignment will be done by Monday. Another associate, who aspires to self-pres-ervation and merely seeks some measure of a life outside the law, shot down in his prime. After all, associates are not paid to self-preserve.

The main problem with the swinging dick response is its obvious over-testosterone approach to the problems of the work-a-day law firm world. You wouldn't shoot an ant with a gun, would you? Then why would a partner metaphorically drop the pants of everyone who worked in the office at the suggestion by a cowering associate that there can be no more work humanly consumed?

The answer is obvious: partners know they have to squelch

all uprisings immediately. There are many more associates than partners. This full-plate thing can only be permitted to work every once in a very long while. Associates must be led to believe that they have a certain amount of say, a whisper of a voice, in planning and plotting their lives. Associates have to believe that the system has some measure of equity somehow built-in and that there can be a human touch, even in a law firm, that is not a disguised human Taser gun. Word must get out that sometime in the unrecorded past, an associate stood up for his or her rights, played the full plate gambit, and won. The masses, of course, will forget that associate's name and the partners will strike the name and expunge it from the recorded law firm history, but the prospect of successfully playing the full plate gambit remains. And the prospect of success is what can make tomorrow worth living.

But too much of a say, or too loud of a voice, is beyond the scope of associate freedom. In all honesty, in my experience, the "full plate" gambit versus the "swinging dick" response is a standoff, and a tie goes to the partner. But it is worth a try. Every once in a while, to maintain the illusion that work assignments are humanely doled out, the partners have to allow the full plate gambit to succeed. Every once in a blue, blue, very blue moon.

Now, let's stop communicating like this or someone may catch us. Anyway, it is almost lunchtime.

———————————

IT IS RUMORED

Rumors — reports in general circulation with no discernible source. A law firm consummates them, procreates them, nurtures them, fosters them, and the body of humans who constitute the firm all live for them. Black market news; underground information; scuttlebutt; straight skinny; the poop; professionals' gossip; confidential chatter. Rumors are the way associates keep abreast of the important law firm news of the day. They are much more than just gossip around the coffee machine; rumors are the lifeblood of associates, who are themselves the quidnuncs of a law firm. The information that rumors provide is an associate's most valuable commodity. Without rumors, the already-low survival rate for associates would plummet. Rumors are knowledge, and knowledge is wings.

Just around three o'clock in the afternoon, the rumors begin, each one like a surfer riding a big fifty-foot information wave. One by one, the rumors catch and ride a wave down the halls. The rumor-waves pound past occupied offices, douse each associate who opens their door, and imbue each with the obligation to pass the story further down the line to at least one more associate. The players in rumor circulation are simple: there is a transmitter of the rumor and a recipient. The mechanics of rumor circulation are straightforward, too: rumors should always be communicated orally, especially in the digital age, to ensure there is no digital path, no bits and bytes, no breadcrumbs, that lead back to the source. Rumors should be passed by word-of-mouth, at lunch or during a break, or on a walk between floors, or in the library stacks, or during a friendly visit to another associate's office usually behind closed doors, known as BCD meetings in the rumor industry. But rumors are *not* always oral in the modern era, because email is so easy to use, and it has the power to expand the number of recipients both dramatically and instantaneously. Emails are dangerous, however, because they leave a trail, and rumors should never leave a trail. The rules of rumor circulation are clear: hear or read the rumor, digest it, and pass it along. Honor the sacred rule of source anonymity. Do not editorialize or embellish (just the facts, ma'am); do not summarize. Just send it along in the same state as you heard it. With these simple rules, rumors move quickly down the halls and gather a life of their own.

Some rumors will ride the wave until the end. These are the best rumors, lifeblood transfusions for iron poor associates. Other rumors will peter out, maybe because the rumor becomes public knowledge and is widely confirmed before the rumor finishes the ride. There is nothing wrong with this rumor; it is just not world-class data. And at the end of the day, the waves subside, and the tide recedes, leaving only the scattered shells and sand and treasure troves of information washed up on the shore of the law firm hallways to be explored by rumor-combers.

The law firm rumor is set apart from other rumor mills with which you may be more familiar. The typical law firm rumor is usually true; usually topical; and usually timely – The three T's of law firm rumors.

Truth

A law firm rumor must be true – it must have the highest level of reliability. Gossip may or may not be true; a rumor must be true, exact, precise. Associates work long hours, often at a laptop where they research legal questions, and sometimes they have very little human contact. They do not always know what is going on in the firm so they quickly learn to question everything they hear and see. To survive, they must observe everything but believe almost nothing. Show me: the associate's credo.

Rumors must survive this institutionalized scrutiny. A transmitter of untrue rumors soon finds that if she or he floats an inaccurate rumor, no one will believe the next one and it will never get into circulation. Such a transmitter is relegated to gossip columnist status. Absolute credibility must be maintained to survive the scrutiny and get the rumor into circulation. Rumors cannot be merely more-likely-than-not true, and they should not be beyond-a-reasonable-doubt true. The standard is higher. Attorneys are very busy people and there are not enough hours in a day to clutter rumor-time with innuendo or inference. After hearing a rumor, the associate must come away with the clear belief that it is true and correct beyond any doubt. It cannot be diluted with supposition, conjecture, inaccuracies, and mis- or dis-information; no fake news in the rumor mill.

Topical

The recipient of a good rumor should feel like Michael Douglas as Gordon Gekko in *Wall Street*. She or he receives the rumor from a rumor broker (think Charlie Sheen as Bud Fox), and it must deliver something that the recipient did not know, avoiding news that they could read about in the *National Law Journal* or some local yellow pulp legal rag. To start a rumor, the transmitter is obligated not just to send information, but to dig like an investigative reporter and develop the story to get solid information.

Make it count. *Topical* is inside information, law firm insider trading without the Securities and Exchange Commission prohibitions or penalties. In a law firm, you must be inside, because if you are not inside, you are outside, and if you are outside, you are nowhere. You have to be a player, and no one can play without trading in rumors. So to be a player, you must tell the recipient inside information, something topical, something from which any recipient can profit. It is expected; it is legal; it is part of being an associate. Successful associates manage and profit from the world of underground information. In a nutshell, the transmitter must transmit something that the recipient can use.

Tell the upcoming average associate the bonuses the firm will award this year before they are public knowledge. Tell me which real estate attorneys will be laid off. Tell the soon-to-be-but-as-yet-undisclosed profit-per-partner. Tell who will be voted into the sacred ranks of the partners, and who will not. Tell me who is leaving the firm. Deliver the scoop.

Do not convey new email policies, or vouchers for cabs, or secretarial overtime decisions or assignments, or new firm cafeteria menus, or inconsequential administrative rules and regulations rumored to be going into effect. There is no profit in such mundane trivia.

Dirt – underground black market dirt, limited only by the bounds of the imagination – is always topical. But do not weaponize the rumor. Be very careful when conveying scandalous material. Someone at our firm once floated a vicious rumor that a partner was sleeping with an associate; turned out, the rumor was untrue. It was a ruinously cruel moment in the lives of the partner and the associate, it violated the

truth tenet, and it marked the sudden end of the rumor purveyor's employment. I repeat – rumors about dirt should be
handled with extreme care.

Losses in the trenches are topical – which stellar litigating
partner has tried to hush up a recent huge jury trial loss,
complete with a judicial admonition in a published opinion, a punitive damage award, and an irate client for good
measure? Career moves are topical – who is leaving? Who
is arriving? Who is being forced out, and who is doing the
forcing? Whose star is rising, and whose star is losing its twin-
kle? Firm politics are topical – who is going to be elected to
the firm-managing committee, and who is being kicked off?
Write-offs are topical – whose client stiffed the firm for big
fees and which court disallowed whose fees? Billable hours
are topical – who is billing over the firm target; who is below?
Topical is the perception created by a law firm's daily microscopic analysis of every move the attorney makes; it is who
is crumbling under the microscopic scrutiny and who is not,
who is surviving it and who is not; it is who has power, who
has lost it, and who wants it; it is what is *not* being told. If
you want to pass on a good rumor, find out what is not being
told, and tell it.

Timely

No matter how topical, how dirty, or how good the information is, you really have to tell it while it is fresh: old news
is no news. Disseminate it before its usefulness expires. Tell
me before it happens, before it is public knowledge, before
anyone else knows. If you can tell me politics before there are
political pronouncements, if you can focus the issue before
the issue is under the public microscope of scrutiny, then
your rumor is timely. The timeliness of a rumor is fleeting;
rumors have very short shelf lives. They are only hot for a

brief period. During that brief period, and only during that brief period, they are timely.

The three T's.

Who wants to know the rumors and who needs to know? While it is beyond debate that associates thrive on rumors, scientifically, it is hard to say why. It is akin to an addiction, I suppose. Gordon Gekko and Bud Fox profited and prospered on inside information. Gekko could never have enough. He was insatiable. For associates, perhaps it is a strange combination of profit, insatiability, and survival; there is no survival without knowledge. All associates need to know, and the survivors know the need and trade in it. After years at the law firm front line, dodging incoming missiles from enemy forces, associates either get their heads blown off, get shell shock, or get to hang in by keeping their ears and eyes open. They learn how to profit, to survive, and to broker the rumor; information brokers for each other.

As well, partners, usually the younger ones, thrive on rumors. They still remember the usefulness of the rumor mill and still retain the need to know the topical truth. While there may be a partner rumor mill, it pales compared to the associate system, and the smart partners know this. Additionally, absent from the partner system is any significant, credible information about what associates are thinking. If a partner wants or needs to know how the troops are faring at the front, there must be an associate contact – someone on the inside, not so much of a snitch as a source, who can broker the rumor to the leaders in charge. So, on a "nothing is too good for the troops" pretense, a partner will cross into the front, usually on a Friday afternoon, find an associate's foxhole, and try to chat about life and love and baseball and music, and hope the banter leads to the latest rumor.

The wise associate, however, does not give up the true dirt to a partner. Satisfy the partner, yes; send the partner home with something, but preserve the integrity of the system. Know the partner's needs, but do not disclose everything the partner thinks must be known. Remember, this is a *partner*, and you can never tell what a partner will do with a rumor. It may be too big a rumor, too hot for a partner to handle. The partner may violate the rules of rumor dissemination: they may write it down or, god forbid, reveal a source. If a partner shows up at your door on a Friday, and you have to give up something, just be careful, very careful. A partner's constitution is not designed to process scuttlebutt. Can you imagine what a partner might do with dirt? The partner might share the dirt with another partner and then attribute the dirt to you. Devastating to the people that are the subject of the dirt and perhaps career ending to you if the souce of the dirt is revealed. Partners are not like Woodward and Bernstein who can be trusted to maintain the anonymity of a source. No, for the partner, part of the thrill of the rumor is the source. The prospect of a partner in possession of dirt is too frightening even to consider. The rumor mill is not a tell-all diary for partners to consume on Fridays. Respect that. Rumors are for associates. It is one of those small intangibles that separate the masses from the masters.

DAMAGE CONTROL

CAPTAIN KIRK USED TO yell after a Romulan attack, "Damage control, report!" And then Mr. Scott would reply that there was damage to the main matter/anti-matter circuits, or to the dilithium crystals and that he could only give the Captain impulse power for the next eleven hours. Yes, I'm sure of it; that's how the conversation went. Damage control.

In a law firm every once in a while, a rumor that could be particularly damaging to the law firm's reputation races up and down the corridors with the force and destruction of a deadly Romulan attack. The law firm's very power core may be disabled temporarily, and it is time for damage control. That is what partners do in the face of a rumor. They cry "damage control," get a report that assesses the damage, and then they implement repairs.

So how do rumors work in a law firm? A hot rumor might play its way out down the corridors of a large, venerable firm in waves, something like this.

Wave one of the rumor is simple: the firm has laid off five associates. The detail behind wave one: the firm asked (told) the departing associates to leave quickly, and gave them each two months of future pay to depart quietly. This can be an especially powerful rumor especially in times of trade journal reports that large, esteemed law firms had implemented associate layoffs in the face of declining revenues. This type of rumor is a hot one – one of the hottest, in fact.

Wave two: Even before anyone could ask the obvious question of who the five were, the next wave brings with it the actual names of the unlucky associates and the legal specialty areas in which they practiced. As expected in a period of economic decline, the practice areas include former boom – now economic slump – areas such as real estate and corporate takeover. Thus, the second wave of the rumor confirmed what everyone suspected – the glamour specialty fields of the past five years had become the professional graveyards of the present.

Almost before the names of the fired five could be cross-checked against the official firm picture-book and website biographies to see exactly who these people were, the third wave hits. In a quick Behind-Closed-Doors (BCD) meeting, the transmitter of the rumor might say in a hushed voice, "The latest edition of the *National Law Journal* is going to cover the layoffs."

"No? Seriously?" the recipient would reply.

"Well, I haven't seen it because it isn't out yet, but it's supposed to say that the firm is in a huge economic slump."

This third wave portion of the tripartite rumor would not be immediately confirmable, because the article would not yet have been released on *NLJ's* website. But the rumor is topical and timely, and it is beyond a reasonable doubt that it is true; although not beyond *all* doubt, as it lacks the required confirmation to make it true. Now the transmitter has a strategy decision to make. The transmitter, normally a purveyor of rock-solid, confirmed rumors, has to decide whether to go to press on this rumor and risk the fallout if the unconfirmed rumor turned out to be false. This third wave of the rumor is certainly a corollary to the originally-confirmed rumor that associates had been laid off. There never is editorial oversight for rumors, and the transmitter may feel that he owes it to the associates to send out the third wave of the rumor in its current state. The associates of the firm are always primed and ready to believe the third wave of a three-part rumor, even without confirmation.

Somehow, a partner picks up the rumor. Almost immediately the partners feel the shockwaves of the rumor's powerful consequences. The partner, sensing the problem, might be heard to yell, "Damage control, report." By any standard of assessment, there is obvious, extensive damage from the layoff rumor, and some partners later say the worst they had ever seen. It might take weeks to repair while the firm limped along on impulse power. How could the partners control the damage? Well, the firm might draw on an old army ploy when controlling a rampant, lethal rumor – plausible deniability. The firm could issue an official statement insisting, without qualification, that "No one has been laid off. Any associates whose office is now empty and dark left the firm of their own free will to pursue greener pastures – other opportunities."

Confusion among the associates would follow the firm's official statement. Every associate recipient of the original rumor would then begin the tedious process of reconfirming the original rumor. Recipients go back to their transmitter and the seminal transmitter goes back to the source. And so, the parties complete the system check, and they determine that the original rumor was not only timely and topical, but it was true. People really were laid off. Heads really rolled. Chips really fell.

The denial by the firm was not plausible. Disassociated associates had begun to find other jobs. People left quickly after they filled boxes with their belongings. The people allegedly laid off may have been told they had no future with the firm. The firm perhaps said it was in everyone's mutual interest that they find a position with another firm. Associates' pictures instantly disappeared from the firm's website. Nameplates outside offices were gone. However the firm delivered the official statement and whatever the firm's partners said in the privacy of each of the secret meetings with the discharged five, the remaining associates would believe that the firm effected an employment discharge.

The official statement did not work to quell the rumor, but still, the firm issued no additional reports or statements. From the standpoint of the brass, the firm already had effectively denied the layoff rumor: case closed. Within days, Mr. Scott finished his repairs to the dilithium crystals and the law firm ship once again operates at warp speed capacity. Or so the powers-that-be would think.

Within one week, an associate uproar will likely ensue. In the men's room, someone will etch on Stall Number One on the thirty-fifth floor, "Layoffs suck. Rise up. You have nothing to lose." An unidentified illness will spread among partners who use Stall Number One and read the etching. Mysteriously, Stall Number One will close for plumbing repairs – something about a slow draining flush and a water pressure issue.

Time for more damage control. The firm will convene a meeting of all associates, and assign a single partner to deliver a short, to-the-point message, in person – "No one was laid off." No questions will be taken and the partner view is that it is not a question of semantics. Associates departed to pursue other opportunities.

"They must think we're dummies," some associates will whisper as they exit the meeting. But the associates will return to their work – as associates always do – until one week later when another rumor begins, to the effect that the firm's economic sky is falling and the firm is on shaky financial ground. All of the associates fear – as associates always do – that there will be no raises or bonuses. All the partners will gaze at the heavens and conclude that it did not look like the sky was falling. But it did not matter whether it was falling or not. The associates made it clear that they seemed to believe it was. The partners will know that you cannot run the Enterprise without the crew, and the partners will themselves fear that the crew of the ship entered into panic mode.

So, the partners will sense that the time has come for more damage control. The engine room is certainly getting a work-out. The powers will call a high-level partner meeting in a special conference room reserved for important partner meetings. "Do you think they believed that no one was laid off?" one partner would ask. "They're not morons," another partner would crow. "Who cares what they think or believe?" another partner would say. "They're all highly paid and the remaining ones should be thankful they're still here." No one will say, "Let's tell them the truth." Or, "Let's explain the economics of law firm life." No one will utter: "Let's bring them into the fold, it will engender loyalty." No one will feel sorry. No one will feel remorse. No one will feel responsible. No one will feel like staking a smaller claim to the profits pie, to retain loyal colleagues through bad times.

The head partner, known for his ability to strategize, will listen in silence to the raging debate and finally say, "People, people. We need to rethink our damage control strategy. I think the plausible deniability of the coincidence explanation is no longer viable. We need another tack."

And they will put their collective heads together and decide that the best approach is to say nothing. Without dignifying the rumor with an explanation or a report, it would be as if nothing had ever occurred. Deniability by silent denial: sheer genius. That's why the head partner is the head partner, right? They might even decide to give the new approach a name, to distinguish it from the prior deniability strategy. Privately, of course, they would call it Operation Ostrich.

Over the next several weeks during the implementation of Operation Ostrich, several more associates, who were not part of the original five, will mysteriously disappear. Did they leave for a new opportunity that wasn't as fraught with economic concerns? No one will know for certain, but each time a new associate disappears, a hot new rumor will cascade down the hall. Associates will ask each other, "Have you seen Jill? She hasn't been in her office for three days. I think she was laid off."

"No way. She went into labor. I saw her rushed to the hospital."

"Are you sure? It could have been a new way to deliver the termination boot."

So, someone might call the hospital and learn that Jill and her new twins were alive and doing quite well. People would send her flowers of course. But before the flowers could even be delivered, another associate will be mysteriously absent.

Associates will wring their hands and cry out, "I haven't seen Bob. He hasn't reported for duty in for days. He's missing in action. He's been laid off."

"No, he hasn't. He was transferred to the New York office." A call to New York, and Bob answers the phone.

"Ok, but where's Bill?"

"He's on vacation."

A call is made to a Rocky Mountain National Park ranger to be on the lookout.

"Kate?"

"She's in a trial in Kansas City."

A call is made to the clerk of the court in the Western District of Missouri, Kansas City division. The trial is confirmed.

"Ben – where's Ben?"

No one will know. Where is Ben? Indeed, *who* is Ben? Was he laid off as well; did he leave of his own volition? No one knows. And the associates will say: "Oh Ben, we wished we'd all known him well. Best of luck, Ben, and Godspeed."

The associates might take a census and ask, "Where's Jane? She officed right next to me for years. This morning, the office was empty, and the nameplate was gone."

The partners might say, "Jane who? That office has been dark and empty for many years."

"No, no. Jane was in there."

The partners might say, "Sorry, no Jane ever occupied that office."

Some associates might think, *maybe they're right.* Jane's smiling photograph was no longer on the firm's webpage. Had it ever been?

Over the next four weeks, fueled by the rumor, the plausible denials, the meeting, the article in the still missing *National Law Journal,* and the silence, eight other associates mysteriously disappear; for the associates, the working premise would be that some were laid off, semantics be damned, and some just moved on, reason and rationale be damned. Bodies coming and going. Missing associates reports daily. It would seem that some partners had mistakenly set their phasers on vaporize, instead of just stun. Associates would simply disappear as if vaporized, their very molecules scattered. Ashes to ashes; dust to dust.

Some partners would inevitably break their code of silence, and suggest that this whole situation began when the firm appropriately "trimmed some dead wood." Dead wood? Hmmm. It would sound so naturalistic. What a wonderfully inappropriate euphemism this would be, indeed. Imagine, after years of loyal service, associates find out that they're just a dead twig, ready to fall from the tree and begin the decomposition process. One partner would give an interview to the *American Attorney* weekly rag and say no one was laid off; some people may have received "mutually agreed-upon departure deadlines." Wonderful – brilliant. When the going gets tough, the tough think of the most amazingly descriptive ways to downplay the catastrophic. If the euphemisms help the partners get through the day and look at themselves in their mirrors in the morning, then by all means, they will proceed. What's the harm?

In the aftermath, associates and pundits alike will ask the pertinent question, "Were associates laid off?" The answer will continue to be, "Who knows?"

Such is the beauty of effective damage control. Hear the rumor, digest it, and neutralize it, quickly. Let them stay informed, but... Ahead, warp factor six, Mr. Sulu.

PITS, PICS, AND PRICS

AUTHORITY. POWER. ORDERS ARE given by some that must be followed by others. Making others follow the orders: the law firm way. There is a system of authority and power in law firms because... well, just because – we are a nation of laws, and there has to be law and order. The law firm system functions based on layers of authority figures.

Generally speaking, there are three layers, comprised of Partners-In-Training, Partners-In-Charge, and Partners-Really-In-Charge: PITs, PICs, and PRICs. I was a member of each layer during my career. Meaning, at some point, I became a PRIC. I, like many PRICs may have tried to be a kinder and gentler PRIC, but it does not change the fact that I occupied the role of PRIC for many a year. A word of caution, however. I don't want you to focus on the anagrams – really – and thereby lose sight of the analysis. So I will not use them hereafter.

Each layer of authority and power has some relationship to the partner rainbow (discussed later), and the pot of gold at the end of the rainbow, the economic gain which is the reason that many people practice law and stay at a law firm, also discussed later.

Confusing? Not really. Most every partner knows the layer she or he occupies and the layers above them on the law firm totem pole. The layers of authority are arguably necessary to maintain order – a pecking order, to be more accurate. They help the mere associate to at least know who the Commanders-In-Chief are, and who are merely wannabees.

Here is the system.

Partner-In-Training

A Partner-In-Training is an associate who has begun in earnest the chase to the end of the rainbow. In every law firm, associates learn of the rainbow: the mythical bridge of bands of magical colors, ending where the pot of gold can be found. The Partner-In-Training has begun the quest for this coveted pot of gold, and hopes to gain partner status so they can begin the rainbow trek. Every day, the associate inches closer to that multicolored magic time when they supposedly will be eligible for induction into those cloistered ranks. So, one or two years before the induction vote, those associates who are not IWUPs ("Isn't Working Up to Potential") or APs ("Appropriately Placed") are permitted to start an informal training program of sorts and given various partner-like responsibilities – management and control of cases, primary contact with clients, billing, assignment of work to junior associates, strategizing, and, ultimately, full responsibility for the trial and resolution of the matter. All Partners-In-Training have some authority to exercise within the system, on a trial basis. They are eager rainbow-dreamers and devout pot-believers.

The official word is that a Partner-In-Training passes the test by acting the way a partner acts: by taking responsibility, by taking ownership of cases, and in doing so, taking on the burdens that come along with responsibility. It is someone who intercepts all the aggravations of being a Partner-In-Charge before the aggravations reach the partner. The successful

Partner-In-Training graduates once it is determined that she or he is ready for induction into the partnership ranks. The Partners-In-Training are led to believe that if they graduate from the program, they are as good as inducted as a partner.

Partners-In-Charge

When a Partner-In-Training ascends to the ranks of partner, she or he becomes a Partner-In-Charge after attending the obligatory onboarding class in which they learn some of the consequences of Partner-In-Charge status. Suffice it to say that after years of waiting and wondering, the newly-minted Partner-In-Charge oftentimes sprints across the rainbow to see what is waiting in that pot. And suffice it to observe that when they peer into the pot for the first time, they are most often disappointed. Nothing magical, and nothing in the pot for them just yet. Most find an I.O.U. of possible economic benefits to come and a warning that investment in the firm is not a guarantee of rewards, profits, and returns; a warning borrowed by the firm from one brokerage house or another. Instead of increased cash inflow, the Partner-In-Charge usually finds a cash outflow as they must immediately purchase an ownership interest in the firm.

Partners-In-Charge may lose their associate friends – the age-old noncom/officer friction, and they find themselves at the bottom of another totem pole, the lowest partners in the scramble to the top. They may feel economic harassment, social ostracism, disappointment – be it temporary or permanent – and suffer a certain amount of morale erosion, not to mention the pressure on their set of morals that results. It is always a good idea to stay out of the way of a new Partner-In-Charge. They are not very stable at the beginning of their new status; there is too much change in their lives and social and economic suffering going on.

In addition to practicing law, Partners-In-Charge immediately find themselves under economic, social and moral siege, and they also often receive assignments to various administrative duties and committees within the law firm that keep the law firm oiled, humming along, and servicing whatever client and partner needs must be serviced. These committees include finance (making other partners regularly bill clients and collect account receivables), hiring (finding new associates to hire to keep the firm staffed and competitive), and compensation (deciding how much to pay the throngs of attorneys). It is always a good idea to have Partners-In-Charge on the compensation committee because, for the first time in their lives, they realize that every dollar they pay to the masses comes out of the pie that would otherwise remain to feed the partners.

Of course, Partners-In-Charge run the lives of the associates. Someone has to. Partners-In-Charge have most of the day-to-day contact with the associates and, therefore, they have the most opportunity to issue orders from day to day.

Even with the apparent tenure that comes with partnership status, and the authority and power, Partners-In-Charge are often unfulfilled and almost always paranoid; hoarding their little piece of the partnership pie, jealously guarding the pass which admits them to the rainbow entrance and then to the road that travels over the rainbow. They keep their I.O.U. for their pot of future gold safe for redemption someday, peering through increasingly shifty eyes as they nervously clutch their newfound job security, like a fleeing bank robber who catches his breath in a dark alley as he clutches a stolen bag of money to his chest, knowing that others may soon be out to get him.

Partners-Really-In-Charge

It comes down to this – some partners in a law firm are *really* in charge. They own the rainbow and regulate passage across it. They own the pot. They fill the pot as they see fit. They guard the pot. They decide who can gaze into the pot. They approve how much gold should be removed from the pot and who should get the gold. It is the age-old adage, the golden rule: they have the gold, so they make the rules.

Everyone knows their names. Many people recognize their faces. Some people know their direct-dial telephone number; a very few call them. They speak, and colleagues listen. They are power incarnate. They run everyone's lives. They set and enforce the firm's policies. They demand and receive deference, power, and prestige, as well as a healthy chunk of the gold in the pot. From an associate's standpoint, Partners-Really-In-Charge are just names about which to whisper over lunch or drinks, far, far from the office. From a Partner-In-Training's standpoint, Partners-Really-In-Charge are names and faces about which to whisper over lunch and drinks, behind completely closed doors, but only in a very low voice and only with extreme care. From a Partner-In-Charge's standpoint, Partners-Really-In-Charge are names and faces about which to whisper over lunch and drinks, in an office, with the doors cracked open slightly, and perhaps in the washroom, but always with extreme care. A whole lot of whispering by the masses.

No one knows how the Partners-Really-In-Charge got the pot, but everyone knows they have it and everyone thinks they probably did something unmentionable to someone now unmemorable to get it. No one knows when they got the pot, but everyone thinks it was some time in the distant past.

What do they do, these Partners-Really-In-Charge? Most associates do not know; most Partners-In-Training do not know. Most Partners-In-Charge do not admit they do not know.

But whether or not anyone knows how the Partners-Really-In-Charge's days are filled, at one time or another, most everyone finds a reason to resent a Partner-Really-In-Charge for one reason or another. Of course, that resentment is not shared publicly.

Three things are clear: first, passes to the rainbow sprint are exclusively licensed and distributed by the Partners-Really-In-Charge; second, the pot belongs to the Partners-Really-In-Charge; and third, the Partners-Really-In-Charge decide who shares from the riches in the pot and how much they share. Hence, the Partners-Really-In-Charge rule everyone, are feared by the masses, and always tolerated.

So, let's review. It is all about authority and power: who can give the orders. So much authority, so little equity.

Layers of authority figures: some chasing the pot of gold in hopes of a glimpse, a taste of the contents; some finding the pot empty, missing even that glimpse; some sharing in the pot someday; some keeping the pot and glimpsing or tasting anytime they care to.

Is there something wrong with the system? Maybe, but if you judge the appropriateness of the system based on whether there is a better one, you may not be able to find anything wrong simply because no one seems to have ever come up with anything better... and we have to *have* a system. We are a nation of laws, after all.

Many acclimatize to the system as they settle into their particular layer. Others never acclimatize and instead, over time, they find themselves feeling as if they are tied to an Allman Brothers whipping post thinking: *Good Lord, I feel like I'm dying...* Maybe they are.

<hr />

SMELL THE COFFEE

One Sunday, after a particularly difficult and unrewarding week, I sat down and wrote what it was like to struggle with the perennial problem of how to balance the practice of law with a life outside of the law.

ESTABLISHING AND MAINTAINING A balance between the law and a life is not easy, especially in an otherwise unbalanced existence, but for me, the set-aside time was a critical component in the quest to survive.

It is ten o'clock on Tuesday morning. My desk is stacked with correspondence, memos, messages, charts, outlines and pleadings rising out of the weathered wood like a pyramid out of a tropical rain forest that would make the ancient Mayans of Tikal proud. My desktop dings away as emails pile up. My phone buzzes incessantly as texts arrive. I am working on at least fifteen cases at the same time. This is a new record. I may never go home. Not tonight – not ever. It has been like this for the last… well, I don't know how long. The only difference between weekdays and weekends is that I do not shave or wear a tie on the weekend. I guess God wasn't an attorney, because even God rested on the seventh day. I do not smile, because I cannot smile. I have no life because I am not allotted a life. All I have is my pyramid, a maxed-out email account, my phone, my many opposing counsel who

I cannot bring myself to love dearly, the law, an occasional daydream, and my favorite coffee cup recently filled with the law firm standard issue caffeinated liquid. As I stare into the brown liquid, I think...

I am told there is rumored to be a life outside the law. I am told that regular people have hobbies, watch and play sports, go to the gym, hike in the woods, have families, talk to their wives and friends and kids, take vacations, watch their kids grow up instead of just hearing about it, read, garden, and do whatever else they want to do in their leisure time. They may or may not drink the coffee, but they certainly smell it.

I know the rumors must be true because, for years as a kid, I watched Danny Thomas come home and have leisure time in the fifties with Marlo and the rest of his family on *Make Room for Daddy*; Ozzie Nelson come home and hang out with Ricky through the fifties into the sixties on *Ozzie and Harriet*; and Mr. Arnold come home and struggle with his kids through the seventies on *The Wonder Years*. I, of course, watched all of these shows before the law got in the way.

I do not live, however, in a thirty-minute once a week family situation comedy that takes place in any of those decades. I live in the here-and-now and barely have time to watch the television, let alone live the sitcom dream. Every morning, I awaken and brew a pot of coffee or a cup of tea. Then I feed and walk my dog. I love her – the dog. Our walk is usually eventful. At six o'clock every morning, she tries to chase the squirrels; she hates squirrels, and feels it is her purpose in life to chase all of them. If she cannot catch them, at least she can chase them up the nearest tree. She has never caught one yet, but she never gives up. She might make a great attorney with that kind of resolve.

When we return from our walk, I sit down to drink a cup of coffee or tea and brace myself for the day ahead and she lays down with a sigh to dream about whatever dogs dream about after they have been fed, walked, and chased a couple of squirrels. I can't be sure, but I bet she isn't dreaming of a life as an attorney. I bet she isn't dreaming about law partners, and court, and clients, and research, and briefs, and statutes, and judges. My best guess is that she left that to me. Her country is not one of laws, but a country of food, walks, squirrels, and a dog's life. She doesn't drink coffee but she knows how to smell it.

No, this is not some bad excuse for a coffee commercial, and this is not the point where Juan Valdez enters the room to peddle Columbia's second most popular export. The point is simply that every morning out of habit I wake up, walk the dog and smell the coffee. But when I smell the coffee, it is different from when Danny Thomas or Ozzie Nelson, or Mr. Arnold smelled it. All I smell is the brown liquid in the cup; nothing more.

You cannot find the world outside the law if, when you smell the coffee, all you smell is the brown liquid in your favorite cup.

Sometimes I have to travel to a remote place where I can hike up a deserted mountain trail to an ancient Indian mesa pueblo before I remember the world and the life outside. Sometimes I have to ride a horse for hours through the cottonwood bosques lining the Rio Grande with only the sounds of birds singing and water lazily drifting downstream before I can see things other than the law. Sometimes I have to hike so high in the mountains that there are no cell towers, and there is insufficient oxygen for both the hawk – who just glided effortlessly overhead with its motionless wings spread wide – and me, before I begin to believe that there is a life other than being an attorney. Sometimes I have to sit on the icy mountain edge of a prehistoric meteor crater, squinting into a bone-chilling, relentless wind for an hour searching for a glimpse of a big horned sheep, before it is obvious that being an attorney is not the center of the universe.

Sometimes I have to sit on a remote beach on the Otago Peninsula in New Zealand as I wait for yellow-eyed Penguins to pop out of the surf and waddle up the beach to their nests after their day of fishing at sea. Sometimes I have to be the only human being on a beach in a dense fog six feet from ten-foot storm-enhanced waves crashing before I can begin to see things as they are.

And when I have escaped far enough away from the law and there are only the hawks, and the bosques and the Rio Grande and the surf, and the penguins, and the biting wind, and the fog, I feel like I am an escaped convict outside the wall, running from the warden with every nerve alive and sensitized to the real world around me. Then, I finally begin to think that I smell the coffee, and not just the brown liquid in the cup.

Now, the process of smelling the coffee was most certainly easier before the advent of mobile phones, email, and texts. In the not-so-olden-days of less invasive communication methods, where a fax machine was the fastest way to transmit the written word, and a caller had to leave me a voice mail at work that I could return or not return, there was more peace. Then came modern technology, and – not to complain and sound like an old fogie – as glorious as tech can be, it is a stone-cold heartless killer when all you want to do is to smell the coffee. All you can do is turn off the mobile phone. That works well, but it is a scary thing. We all instinctively feel that the mobile phone is undoubtedly connected, perhaps by bluetooth, to the human brain. Turn off the phone, and the brain may well go into a coma. At the very least, turn off the phone, and withdrawal symptoms begin almost immediately.

Even if you find the inner strength necessary to turn off the tech, the experience of smelling the coffee is short-lived. Whatever I think I can see after seven days outside the wall quickly grows out of focus, fades, and then is lost the minute I return to the law. Sometimes, I cannot even remember what it was that I was so clearly seeing and smelling just a short time ago. And I brew another pot of coffee and the aroma fills the air and I walk the dog, but there are no mountains, bosques, waves, fog, or penguins; just the dog, me, the squirrels scurrying up the trees and the law reintroducing itself into my thoughts, redispersing itself through my consciousness, resaturating itself in my being, like the pentimento of an old, cracked oil painting and all the time choking out the world I so clearly saw so very recently. And when we return, the dog sighs, dozes and dreams and I smell the coffee but all I am smelling is the brown liquid once more.

I honestly believe it is this way for most attorneys. I honestly do *not* believe that most attorneys want it this way. I honestly believe that most attorneys would change the way it is if they could. I honestly believe most attorneys can't figure out why it is this way or how to change it, because this is just the way it is, and there is no way to change it. I am like most attorneys. We do not find solace in the Serenity Prayer:

> *Grant me the serenity to accept the things I cannot change; courage to change the things I can; and wisdom to know the difference.*

The law life is not serene. Attorneys are not trained to accept things; they are trained to solve problems, and in doing so, implement a change to the status quo. Attorneys are not the most courageous folks, and sadly most don't have the wisdom to know the difference between the things they can change and the things they cannot. I am just like that.

But after all of my years as an attorney, I came to know that I have had it up to the proverbial "here" (illustrated by an erect hand placed under a lifted chin) with the way it is. I have given a lot of thought to this problem and I have come to this conclusion: I can only believe that the problem must be the brown liquid. Attorneys must confuse the brown liquid with the coffee they should be smelling.

You see, attorneys drink a *lot* of brown liquid in a law firm in a year. Our firm occupies eight floors in the skyscraper we call home and we have banks of machines that brew brown liquid on each floor serviced by outside contractors who clean and tune and maintain the machines, so they always brew the perfect cup of law firm institutional brown liquid from the machine called the coffee machine. But these machines provide no chance to smell the coffee; all they provide is the caffeine rush.

My proposal for the attorneys of this nation to solve this problem is simple: eliminate the confusion. Turn off the brewing machines. Send the cleaning and tuning contractors home. Spray the hallways with Lysol. By so doing, at least there will no longer be any confusion anymore about whether the smell is the coffee aroma or just the brown liquid in the cup.

Then, Attorneys of America, after a few weeks, if you begin dreaming of Juan Valdez, and you are pretty sure you have not smelled anything worth smelling, stand up, get away from your desk, contact your travel agent, and go on a coffee-smelling leave of absence. Tell the partner-in-charge for whom you work that you are going out to smell the coffee in the ancient Mayan ruins of Guatemala. Tell the partner-really-in-charge (for whom the partner you work for works) that you are going forth to search out the perfect coffee aroma at the top of an ancient three hundred and sixty-seven-foot Acoma Indian mesa pueblo in New Mexico.

If enough of us stop drinking the coffee and start smelling it, and stop brewing the coffee and start questing for it, then, Attorneys of America, maybe we can all rejoin the human race and find a life outside the law which will undoubtedly make our lives *inside* the law richer, and more rewarding and bearable. Maybe then we can have an interest or a hobby or a pastime or an endeavor or a diversion or a sideline or whatever else regular people call it, instead of just a career. And if just fifty percent of us turn off the brewing machines and lift our heads out of our coffee cups, it might start a cause, and then a movement, and then an organization, and then maybe, friends, just maybe a revolution among attorneys. Who knows?

This is what I wrote to myself that Sunday. After that Sunday, I did not see any great revolution movement begin, but I remain hopeful. Attorneys of America, let me know when the revolution starts. I can't be part of it now because of my new status in life as a former attorney, but I remain interested especially because, like most attorneys, during my attorney life, I lost the coffee, could not seem to find it, and did not know where or how to go about looking for it. Maybe the problem was me, but I tend to think it is all of us attorneys and the law life.

MY CELL

I HAD A LITTLE cell in the law firm where I worked. It was called my office. There were no bars on the door that closed at quitting time and like a true minimum-security prison, my incarceration was based on the honor system. I came and went, mostly as I pleased, but I always had to return to the cell to do my time. I think the law firm viewed my office more as space it let me use than a cell, and of course, the firm sought no compensation from me for the space other than the sweat and labor and ulcers and sleepless nights and everyday stress my employment foisted on me.

I had different cells over the years. The longer I stayed with the firm, the bigger the cell I occupied. At one point in my career, my cell was a ten-feet by eight-feet rectangle with a large window at the far end behind my desk and it overlooked the city. I filled my eighty square feet with memorabilia and war story mementos, and I covered the walls with plaques and degrees and licenses and several paintings. When you are an attorney, the environment in which you do your time is very important. It is so important, that I thought I would offer you an open house of sorts so you will know where I served my time.

Today, friends, you will see my eighty-square-foot cell – my view, my desk, my toys, my mementos, and my wall coverings. To get to my cell, we take the same route as I did every day of my law life: I arrived in the building lobby, waved to the guard, and took an elevator up many floors to the floor where my cell resided. It didn't matter which building I was in during whichever part of my career I lived through. The daily path to the cell was the same.

We are now at my cell. So, let's start with the view of downtown that my eighty-square-foot cell afforded to me. An attorney's view is very important. It makes a statement about the attorney: it says the attorney is important enough to overlook the sprawling city. The attorney may use the view to gaze over the city like a monarch over a kingdom, ruler of all that can be seen. More accurately, as visions of grandeur fade, it is a place to look when the four walls begin to creep in. I remember reading about wall creep in some prison quarterly magazine, which reported that to combat the creep problem, many wardens had begun to allow the prisoners to have windows to see the outside world. The progressive faction in my firm prevailed on this issue, and the firm issued windows to all attorneys to see the outside world. Since my cell was on a minimum-security floor, my windows had no bars, but given that my cell was on the thirty-fifth floor and the windows did not open, there was little risk of escape through a window.

My eighty-square-foot cell was issued to me while I practiced law in Philadelphia. It overlooked the William Penn statue's rear end high atop city hall in downtown (natives call it Center City) Philadelphia, and the mighty Delaware River beyond. In the beginning, I could hardly see Mr. Penn because he was shrouded in scaffolding as he withstood the periodic cleaning that was necessary to maintain his stature to which he and the city had become accustomed. Finally, the city completed cleaning William Penn's rear end and down came the posterior scaffolding. It was liberating for me finally to be able to see Mr. Penn without the camouflage of the crisscross of so much iron erector set steel.

Beyond William Penn was Center City, Society Hill, the Old Customs House building, the Liberty Bell, Independence and Washington Squares, Olde City by the riverfront, Penn's Landing, I-95, piers, the Delaware River, the Ben Franklin Bridge spanning the river, and on the other side of the river, Camden, New Jersey, which I could see on a clear day. I thought my view was one of the best in the city and everyone who saw my office agreed.

The firm assigned my eighty-square-foot cell to me strictly by accident. I did some research on my cell only to discover that it might have been cursed, occupied by an amalgamation of associate ghosts from bygone eras. Ostensibly, every associate who did time in my eighty-square-feet before me mysteriously left the firm after only a very brief incarceration. My immediate predecessor lasted less than five weeks. Based on the oral history passed down to me, I was the only associate in the firm willing to occupy the haunted cursed space for a reasonable timespan. I knew nothing of the curse until after I moved in, but I did not believe in that sort of Stephen King stuff, knock on wood, and I had no problems in my cell other than an occasional missing book and strange noises in the walls. I liked the view and it helped to combat the wall creep.

As we traveled around the country, I had offices in Houston, Philadelphia, Kansas City, and Denver. I think the Philadelphia cell assigned to me was my favorite. I was never going to live high atop Rittenhouse Square in Philadelphia so an office high atop Center City with such a historic view was special. As I traveled from firm to firm and region to region, some larger firms changed their culture of windows and issued cells to associates that were interior. Those interior cells might have glass walls but the glass walls were no substitute for traditional windows to the outside world. All of my different cells each had an exterior window, although the view varied greatly. One of my cells had glass walls. In that cell, every passerby who looked could see my face and the harried look on it that was permanently affixed, a look that many minimum-security prisoners acquired. I didn't much like the glass walls at all. As long as I billed, why did the firm need to look in on me without coming into my office? Just saying.

The most dramatic view issued to me was in Denver where I had multiple windows, many of which faced the Front Range and snow-capped mountain tops. If I gazed out at Mount Evans from my Denver desk, I might lose forty-five minutes of work time as I gathered my thoughts while staring at the Rocky Mountains. William Penn never spoke to me in Philadelphia. I am pretty sure Mt. Evans did in Denver.

I think each of my desks was made out of some kind of nice wood, but I did not often see the wood or know what kind it was because it was so rarely exposed. In the annals of law firm history, more than one partner exclaimed that a clean desk was a sign that an associate is not busy enough. So, to mollify the warden, I cluttered my desk to show how hard I worked. I liked to think my clutter was the real McCoy and not fake news.

Like most attorneys, an in-box and an out-box sat on my desktop. There was less need for the boxes as the age of email descended on the world, but before that age, the boxes were a critical component in the law biz. My in-box was more of a holding tank for pieces of paper that I had an innate fear to discard, but at the same time, I had no idea what I should do with those papers. In the early days of my incarceration, it was common to be inundated with memos and fact sheets and papers and pleadings and things marked "FYI" or "confidential" or "forward to" or "please review" that could only be called mystery mail; for some unknown reason the mystery mail author felt compelled to send me a copy. In my first few years in the cell, I had a policy that nothing should be thrown away until I knew why I received it. This policy was not sustainable or practical, however, and eventually, I changed this policy just slightly to throw everything away unless I knew why I received it. This was my cell, so I could set and modify the policies... as long as my policies did not interfere with the warden's policies.

My out-box, on the other hand, had less drama and rules than my in-box. My out-box was just an out-box. If I put something into my out-box, it needed to find its way out of my office, quickly. Each of my secretaries over the years was wonderfully efficient at taking papers from my out-box out of my office several times a day. To each of them, a belated thank you.

In each of my cells, I had toys. I kept most of my toys on my desk apart from the clutter, not far from my boxes. One of my secrets to a long career was the ability to do time without going too crazy too often, and the secret to achieving some measure of occasional sanity was that I had immediate emergency access to enough toys to get through a bad day.

The most utilized toy on my desk was my telephone. No attorney can do time without a telephone. Mine was a standard, prison-issued, state-of-the-art wonder of modern science, silicon, and chips manufactured by a competitor of Ma Bell that the warden provided to each inmate. It did everything. It displayed the name of the person who was calling. It took messages for me when I was out of the cell, and later during the age of tech, it or some other piece of hardware somehow delivered the messages to my mobile phone. The phone did it all: parked, forwarded, conferenced, transferred, previewed callers, timed calls, speed-dialed, remembered and displayed

numbers, had a speakerphone so I could sound very important and leave callers with the feeling that I was talking to
them from the end of a tunnel, and it muted my side of the
conversation so the person on the other end of the line could
not hear me (I was never one hundred percent sure that this
function worked and in my more paranoid moments I steered
clear of the mute function). It mostly intruded, but I suppose
that was not the phone's fault. It was very sturdy. A good
attorney's phone must be able to withstand stress tests, usually when the attorney slams the receiver down with extreme
force after an extreme phone call... or every phone call. It
just depends on the attorney. The phone companies learned
to build the phones to withstand extreme forces for attorneys.
I am sure they have special attorney-stress-test departments.

With all these gizmos and gadgets built-in, it was always
by far and away the most elaborate toy I used. I would have
been perfectly happy, however, to have a good old-fashioned
telephone with a ringer, four clear buttons on it that are
depressed inward when they light up, and a red button to
put everyone else who called on hold, perhaps indefinitely, if
the mood moved me. Early on in my incarceration, I asked
the warden to requisition me such a throw-back phone, but
the warden denied my request without explanation. That
happened a lot, even in a minimum-security prison, and the
warden had no obligation to explain any such decisions.

I had silent toys on my desk to which I could turn to ease
tensions. For example, I had a kaleidoscope that I could gaze
into during an especially boring conference call. It helped me
collect my thoughts while I listened to the others on the call
argue about the language to use in one document or another.
I had a Duncan Imperial Yo-Yo. The Duncan Toy Company's
Imperial Yo-Yos are the best-balanced yo-yos in the world in
my opinion and I never grew out of the childhood habit of

playing with a Duncan. If I used the speakerphone, I could stand up and walk the dog or rock the cradle or make the yo-yo sleep in the middle of a conversation without missing a beat. It was always very therapeutic to play with a yo-yo during a phone call from an opposing counsel, especially one that screamed a great deal. The yo-yo had a calming effect, much like studies have shown pets have on inmates in maximum security prisons. I am not sure our warden ever approved the use of yo-yos by the inmates, so I tried to face my window when I placed the slip knot over my finger just in case the warden stopped by and peaked in. On more than one occasion, I wanted to send opposing counsel a yo-yo as my way of saying, "hey dude, mellow out!" But I never did. While it was beyond debate that my professionalism was not compromised when I played with the yo-yo, it would not have been professional to share a yo-yo with opposing counsel. The yo-yo, of course, was not invented for attorneys, but it was easily adapted to the law firm life.

Serving the same purpose as the yo-yo, I had a gadget that had no name but was the best toy ever invented after the attorney telephone. It was a gyroscope of sorts suspended between two parallel "U" shaped pieces of metal attached to a handle I held which formed the track along which the gyroscope moved. By moving the "U" shaped metal slowly and deliberately up and down like a wand, the gyro raced along the metal track, over and over, back and forth. On some days, the contraption was symbolic of the practice of law – slow, deliberate, repetitive waving of a magic wand while an out-of-sync-gyro attorney raced back and forth, over and over along the same track, getting nowhere and retracing steps repeatedly. But symbolism in the law biz was not always useful and sometimes the gyro was just a gyro.

I also had noisy toys. I had a slinky, possibly the third greatest toy ever invented. It was always helpful to process through a knotty problem for which there seemed to be no solution. Without fail, a solution came to me after watching the slinky do its thing for a while. I have to admit that I did not invent the use of a slinky in the practice of law. One of my former bosses used a slinky, among other things, to get him through some of the biggest oil and gas bankruptcies filed in the oil patch in the mid-eighties. I guess I just adopted his habit.

If I could diverge from the tour for a moment. I know you must be saying to yourself – attorneys should not have toys. And, I readily admit that not all attorneys have toys and it may seem somewhat unprofessional. But I like to believe I was ahead of my time. For that belief, I look no further than the tech industry's approach to office space. If you go to headquarters for tech companies such as *Google* or *Qualtrics*, or any other major tech company, you will find no offices, a sea of workstations, and toys to ease tensions and facilitate creativity and problem solving, ranging from non-motorized scooters to ping pong tables to relaxation massage chairs. The toys are simply designed to soothe tensions and increase productivity, which the tech company religiously measures with extreme precision. I suppose the idea of the toys in the workplace (or in my case, the cell) is not something I invented, but it is something I fervently defend. I needed my toys. I think more attorneys would benefit from some toys.

OK, back to the tour.

In my cell, I had a *Felix the Cat* coffee mug, but it did not do anything and all it provided was some inspiration to be able to reach into my bag of tricks. If Felix is not someone with whom you are familiar, please go watch one of the *Felix the Cat* cartoons on YouTube. You will have to admit that his bag of tricks got him out of many a problem. It was the characteristic of problem-solving that my *Felix the Cat* mug addressed, and not comedy, like the *Felix the Cat* cartoon promoted.

I had mementos. I had a belt buckle with the name and logo of a now-defunct Texas oil company cast on its face. This memento was given to me by a particularly favorite bank officer client of mine acquired in a sheriff's sale of all of the company's assets, and it helped to remind me of the oil company's owner who used to wear the buckle. After I obtained a very large judgment against the owner for the bank, I deposed the owner to find out what assets he owned, like the Rolex watch on his wrist or the ring on his wife's finger, that I could direct the sheriff to take and sell to satisfy the judgment. That sale is called a sheriff's sale. Perhaps a horrifying way to earn a living. I know. But, hey, I did not have a prison-like cell for nothing! I discovered he had moved his bank account to an offshore Caribbean island nation, beyond the reach of the sheriff. After a break, I asked the witness why he and his wife banked in the Caribbean, and not in Beaumont, Texas where they lived and had always banked, and he replied, almost apologetically, "Free checking?" I had a coffee mug from another client with two pictures on the side – one depicting what attorneys say to clients followed by legal jargon, and the other stating what clients hear followed by "blah, blah, blah, legal position, blah, blah, blah, judgments, motions, blah, blah, blah." I was given the mug after a two-year-old oil-and-gas-bankruptcy case ended, a case that beget once-a-week meetings in Dallas of eighteen banks and their attorneys, and spawned attorney speeches about the "buoyancy" of the situation, the "synergism" of the group and "closure" of the issues, along with assorted "camels in the barn" and other mixed metaphors that neither I nor my client followed at all times. Like I recently mentioned to you, attorneys do not always speak all that well.

I had pictures of my wife and son. These pictures did not

remind me so much of what they looked like – I, of course, knew what they looked like – but rather reminded me of how hard it must have been to have me as a spouse or a dad day in and day out.

I also had law licenses scattered throughout my cell. I do not know who started the custom that attorneys must frame their licenses and display them. Maybe it grew out of a concern that the client should feel at ease that their attorney was not a quack, and had indeed passed the bar exam; of course, quackery and licensing are not necessarily mutually exclusive. Maybe somewhere in the attorney regulations, it was required. The custom certainly kept the frame shops of the world quite happy. In my case, it was cumbersome to comply with the framing and hanging custom, and it was expensive. I had licenses from Kansas, Texas, Pennsylvania, Missouri, and Colorado, ten percent of the states and commonwealths that make up the United States. I was also admitted to practice in more federal courts than I could keep track of. I also had my Haverford College and Washburn Law School diplomas framed and hung. One prepared me for the work-a-day real world by giving me a liberal arts degree and no manual or instructions on how to use it, how it works, when it helps or when it doesn't. The other prepared me for a life of adversaries, adversities, clients, and confrontations with a wealth of book-knowledge and a dearth of practical suggestions of how to cope with that type of life. Ahhh, academia.

And then, one day, I removed all of the degrees and law documents – everything, from the walls and then from the frames – and I hung my sports photographs instead. Those were much more satisfying to look at. I knew I was an attorney; I didn't need reinforcement that I was an attorney by hanging the many authorization documents on my walls. It very well may be that the decision to hang sports pictures coincided with the moment I began to dream (again) in earnest of the end of my legal career, and what an afterlife might look like.

Importantly for me, when the afterlife moment finally came, I distributed my toys (and photographs) to colleagues at the firm in a "giveaway" so they would never forget me or how weird I could be at times. I am not sure they kept the toys, but the gifts were unconditional, so the toys are no longer mine to curate.

And that ends our short tour. As you can see, it was not a bad place to live when the terms of my incarceration did not permit me to live at home like a normal person. The only thing I ever considered adding to my office was a chart where I could record the number of days I had served, like in the old black and white prison break-out movies. I never did that because, like most inmates, it was more important to keep track of the remaining days of incarceration, and, like most attorneys, I was on the flex-plan – no set end date and no formula for release based on time served and good behavior, so no way to keep track of remaining days.

PAY UP

I WAS A BANKRUPTCY attorney for my entire career. I specialized in the many glories of the effect on humans of owing money. Americans did not invent debt, but we embraced it, tried to perfect it, and made it the American way. And, to protect people against the consequences of debt, we adopted bankruptcy laws so people could discharge their debts. For such a simple idea, it has always generated quite a bit of controversy. It is a stressful practice area where emotions run high, stakes are higher, and oftentimes, that can lead to extremely contentious cases comprised of creditors – many of whom want more than debtors can repay and often suspect debtors of hiding assets – and debtors who want a fresh start without creditor intervention – often with a goal of paying as little as the law will allow while discharging the remaining debt. It is a politically-charged practice area, as Congress amends the Bankruptcy Code from time to time depending on which party is in power, and which lobbying group has which senator's ear. It is made newsworthy by household names such as Texaco, United Airlines, some of the Hunt brothers, Enron, WorldCom, and others, who commence bankruptcy cases to address their debts and other issues. News of these bankruptcy cases usually find themselves on the front pages of *The New York Times* and *The Wall Street Journal*.

For the bankruptcy practitioner, the whole process is both exciting and wearing. And it has a history going back from the bible, to debtors' prisons, to modern-day theories of society's obligation to provide a safety net to debtors. With some significant literary and historical liberties, some tongue in cheek, and an attempt to find a bit of humor in debt and credit, I think that history might go something like this.

A long, long time ago, someone with very little foresight invented money as an alternative to the system of bartering that prevailed through the ages. I am not too clear on the exact evolution of money and I have never received a satisfactory explanation from any economist friends of mine; perhaps it was to address the societal problem, that not everyone has *stuff*. In the barter system, each party has stuff, and they exchange their stuff. Party A would give Party B a chicken, and in exchange Party B would give Party A some bread. Chicken for bread. But if Party A wanted bread and did not have a chicken or any other desirable stuff, there could be no exchange. Perhaps Party A then invented money, and paid for the bread. I don't know, and I don't mean to digress, but the point is simply, someone invented money and, at times, it is most certainly the root of all evil, even if it was good for a loaf of bread.

Shortly after the invention of money, some people realized they were destined to have more of it than others. To fulfill their destiny, they acquired as much of the money as they could, divvied it up among themselves, and became rich (they invented the name). The origins of the word "rich" can be traced to the Old French word *riche* which meant, "wealthy, magnificent, sumptuous," and to the Old English word *rice* which meant, "rule, reign, power, might; authority; empire."[3] I think you get the idea. "Rich" meant magnificent power, and it certainly was. After these powerful people secured

3   https://www.etymonline.com/word/rich

all the money, they floated the rumor that money wasn't everything.

But I digress. Once someone invented money, it became apparent that more than just the rich needed money, and the nouveau riche realized they could become even richer if they temporarily gave the poorer people some money and charged the poorer people a fee to use the money. The rich called it a loan, called the fee interest, and called themselves lenders. Lenders lent money – they granted temporary possession of the money to the less than rich. And God looked down, and for some unknown reason – probably because that is what God did in those days according to the Bible – decided that this was good.

Take Eve and Adam. They cultivated the Garden of Eden for years. They were not rich, and because they were farmers with little in the way of clothing, they were not likely to get rich. Each year they borrowed money from a lender to have some cash around to use while the crops matured. At harvest time, they took the crops to market, sold them and used the proceeds to pay off the loan and to live for another year.

Then Eve met the snake, ate the apple, she and Adam were thrown out of the Garden of Eden, and they left the soon-to-be-harvested crop behind. They had no money. They were broke. And so developed the first recorded cash flow crisis. They were unable to generate the necessary funds to pay back the loan they had obtained from someone; for the sake of this story, let's say Noah's great-grandfather (it has always seemed obvious to me that Noah came from a rich family. How else could he have afforded to take all that time off from work to build the Ark and pay for it out of his own pocket?). The next payment came due on the loan, but Eve and Adam did not pay: they defaulted.

The news of the first default cut through the lending industry's core like one of those William Sonoma gadgets through the heart of a pineapple and all hell broke loose in the lending business. A borrower who did not repay a loan? Unheard of!! A default? Half of the rich did not even know what "default" meant! No cash flow? Whose fault was that? Eve should never have talked to the snake or eaten the apple!

But Eve and Adam were resourceful, if they were anything, and attired in their newly-acquired fig leaf unisex jumpsuits, they met with Noah's great-grandfather and presented a plan to him of how they could repay the debt. The world's first repayment plan. No, they told him, the payment check was not in the mail, but if he would just stick with them through the hard times in the way they had been through the good times together, they were sure they could work out their problems. The next harvest, they said. Just stick with us through the next harvest. The world's first proposed repayment plan without substance or consequences to the borrowers if they defaulted.

Hmmm, thought Noah's great-grandfather. *What good times? Work out their problems? It sounds possible. It might be good for business. People who will pay back their loans on time will hear about this and come to me for a loan rather than some other rich lender.* He even thought up a name for the whole idea – a workout – from the notion of working out of a problem. And so was invented the possibility that a lender would redo a loan to work out a borrower's financial problems.

The terms of a new loan arrangement were hammered out, Eve and Adam scratched their names in a new stone tablet setting forth when and how they would repay the loan, and with a copy of the loan tablet in hand, off they went to plow, sow and harvest their new land and generate cash flow.

As the scrivener chiseled the terms of the new loan, however, Noah's great-grandfather kept hearing a little voice in his ear saying *you'll be sorry*, but he did not pay any attention to it. From time to time, many of the lenders lost their edge, their drive, their common sense, their capacity to listen to those little voices in their ear. After all, they had everything. And, remember, Noah's great-grandfather wanted a lot of loans on his books, so in exchange for a volume of loans, he was willing to ignore that little voice. Too much money to lend chasing after too few safe borrowers.

Outside the Garden, there was quite a bit of blight, pestilence, plague, rain and general natural disasters in those days that people of the time attributed to a displeased God, and all of this made for very limited harvests. The next harvest time came but the yield was very poor. Eve and Adam again had no cash flow. It cost them more to harvest their crops than they could sell them for and it took them a while to figure this out. They had always been a couple of oxen short of a fully-staffed financial plow. They defaulted again. Another payment missed.

Enough was enough, thought Noah's great-grandfather. These people are as likely to pay me back as the Red Sea is likely to part any time soon. Where is all the money I loaned them? Have they opened a hidden offshore bank account in some Philistine island? These people are crooks. God was right to banish them from the garden. Maybe we rich people should change the law, so that we execute people who fail to repay loans – not to hurt them or anything, just to make a public example; nothing personal, just business. But maybe capital punishment for default was too harsh; maybe the borrowers should be beaten? Noah took a survey among his rich friends: would it be better for Eve and Adam to be dead, or to be beaten? It became known as the famous dead/beat vote. When Eve and Adam caught wind of the deadbeat vote, they fled and never were heard from again, but all the newspaper tablets of the time reported the deadbeat vote, and eventually, "deadbeats" evolved to colloquially mean people who do not repay their loans when due.

After Adam and Eve, Moses brought the Ten Commandments back from Mount Sinai, and borrowers noted that there was no commandment decreeing that they had to pay back loans. This was a source of great disappointment for the rich lenders. They had lobbied hard when God was writing the Ten Commandments, seeking to substitute the covet commandment with one that would state that all loans must be repaid timely with all accrued interest. To default was *much* worse than to covet, or so they thought. But the angel they hired to get God's right ear failed miserably, and when chisel was put to tablet, the commandments did not talk about loans and the anti-covet provision remained. It is a little-known fact that Moses broke the Ten Commandment tablets over his knee when he read the stones and first discovered there were no loan repayment provisions. Moses, you see, had a grant from the rich lenders to conduct land-of-milk-and-honey research, and felt obligated to support their efforts to include debt repayment as one of the commandments.

Because the Ten Commandments did not expressly forbid untimely loan payments and defaults, it is widely reported that things got worse. Creditors became unfair and unreasonable in their lending and loan administration practices. Interest rates crept higher which caused wide-scale inflation (in those days, there was no Central Bank system to fight inflation and control interest rates). Borrowers became unreliable and unpredictable.

The Old Testament, in the Book of Deuteronomy, attempted a fix for these problems:

At the end of every seven years thou shalt make a release. And this is the manner of the release: every creditor shall

release that which he hath lent unto his neighbor; he shall
not exact it of his neighbor and his brother; because the
LORD's release hath been proclaimed.[4]

Releases of debt every seven years? Creditors were outraged.
How did this sneak into the Bible? Did God truly decree this,
or was it a scrivener error? Was God debtor-friendly? Who
knew, but the decree amounted to more risk. More risk meant
higher interest rates and shorter loans.

Then came Jesus, who condemned interest charges as usuri-
ous – when a lender charges an exorbitant amount of interest
on a loan. Jesus was heavily indebted to several Romans at
the time and was frustrated over the interest rate he had
to pay. He wanted to refinance but he could not get a new
loan because he was unable to purchase credit life insurance.
Something about a bad risk. In any event, God took him aside
and explained to him that the rich lenders had lost the loan
repayment lobby in Moses' time, and what was good for the
lender was good for the borrower – there was simply nothing
in the ten commandments about loans and there would be
no amendments. There would be no further discussion.

Sometime after Jesus, but before the discovery of the new
world, the whole business of loans and paybacks became
more sophisticated. The populous ignored the omission of
repayments from the Ten Commandments, and worldly
enforcement of the Lord's release in the Old Testament fell
out of favor. Rather, somewhere in the dusty books, someone
remembered that God took care of those who helped themselves. Lenders realized that if they charged a high enough
interest rate, they could make enough money off honest borrowers to cover their losses from the deadbeat borrowers.

---

4   *Book of Deuteronomy* 15:2.

Lenders also developed a system of information dissemination to deal with deadbeat borrowers. For example, in Italy, the bench outside a deadbeat merchant's establishment was used as a red flag to inform all the world that the merchant within did not repay his debts. The deadbeat's bench – the *banca*, in Italian – was broken (*rotta*): *Banca rotta*. And so was born the modern era of the bankrupt, he of the broken bench. Also, so perhaps was born the noun "broke" to signify a state of no money and insolvency.

But was it enough to inform the world, or at least the nearby community, that someone was a deadbeat? The notification did not result in the repayment of the debt. No, the descendants of Noah's great-grandfather wanted their money. If someone would not pay, what should society do with them?

Skip ahead a few years to colonial America. The English had developed a system of debt repayment and creditors' rights. But in the new world, deadbeats abounded. America was colonized by professional borrowers, and they were no fools. For example, merchants decided not to place a bench outside their establishment, so the broken bench idea was out. The lender could just repossess the bench, sell it, and keep the money. While the lenders liked the optics of a broken bench, they liked the money more.

The colonies were on the verge of credit anarchy, and lenders had to help themselves. The colonists held meetings in pubs throughout the land. Lenders decided it was a case of the golden rule – they had the gold so they should make the rules, and, following the lead of their English cousins, the rich colonists decided to throw deadbeats in jail.

What a great idea. If God could not be convinced that deadbeatery was a sin, lenders would do the next best thing – they would make it a crime, and debtors' prisons sprung up everywhere. Soon the prisons swelled with deadbeats of every kind and variety.

The problem was that someone in jail was even less likely to pay back a debt. No one considered how the prisoner would earn enough money to pay anyone anything. Someone down on their luck may have *preferred* a stint in prison, where they received three meals a day, sometimes three more than they could find on the outside. And who would foot the bill for all this incarceration and food? Why, the lenders, of course.

The lenders soon realized that debtors' prisons were a costly affair. Not only were the lenders out the money they loaned, but now they had to advance more money to incarcerate, shelter and feed the deadbeats. It was less expensive to have the nonpaying borrowers out on the street than to put them in prison, and debtors' prisons gradually faded from grace. So oftentimes it happens that people do the right thing for the wrong reason. But society, like lending, is result-oriented. Whatever the motive, no one was thrown in jail anymore for being a deadbeat. The cities and towns and boroughs and forests and swamps and coves teemed once again with deadbeats.

And the rich lenders went back to the pubs and put their collective beer steins together once more to decide how to take care of themselves. They decided if it was not a sin to default on a loan and it was not a crime, it most certainly was immoral, and the immoralizers should work off their immorality. In the Puritan scheme of things, work was moral and moralizing. It had a cleansing property – enough work purged the soul of immorality; in this case, deadbeatery.

They drank and they considered the problem of how to use some form of servitude to make people work to pay off their debts. Somewhere in colonial Virginia, a group of rich lenders decided that if jail-time was not the answer, a system of indentured servitude was.

In colonial America, many classes of people found themselves relegated to a life of involuntary servitude, such as victims of religious persecution, kidnap victims, convicts, and paupers. So it made sense to try it out on deadbeats, so thought the lenders. Deadbeats went to work for rich people without pay, sometimes working for years to repay an obligation. But problems developed with the indentured servitude system as well. Not all deadbeats were diligent workers; not all lenders were fair and just masters. Even then, it was hard for mere mortals to dole out morality to the masses.

And some rich lenders got carried away with the idea of indentured laborers. Somewhere, they got the idea these deadbeats were "free" labor and some rich lenders started lending money to poor people who, everyone knew, could not possibly repay the debt. After the inevitable default, the poor person was forced to work for the rich person for years to pay off the debt. Sure, the labor was without wages, but it was not free. Was the only way that a rich person could get any work done around the homestead to make a bad loan?

Galloping Polls conducted a survey which revealed that lenders were losing money on this indentured-servitude thing. There were too many loans being made that were not being repaid, and too many servants as a result. Lenders ignored the survey.

Then three wise men thought long and hard about the whole debt problem. They came up with a potential solution for the debtors of the world. And so, Messrs. Hamilton, Jay, and Madison gave the newly-united colonies *Bankruptcy* and documented the notion in their collective work, *The Federalist Papers*:

*The power of establishing uniform laws of bankruptcy
is so intimately connected with the regulation of commerce,
and will prevent so many frauds where the parties or their
property may lie or be removed into different States, that the
expediency of it seems not likely to be drawn into question.*[5]

The three wise men did not say much about bankruptcy in
the papers but must have written enough to plant the bug in
the ear for future generations. And the notion of bankruptcy
was penned into the Constitution.[6] Wise men, indeed.

But nothing long lasting happened with bankruptcy until
after honest Abe, a descendant of Abraham, a borrower from
Noah's great-grandfather and reportedly a direct descendant
of Eve, won the Civil War.

Thirty-three years later, in 1898, Congress followed the
lead of the three wise men, and passed a national bankruptcy
law. Borrowers had only to file papers with a bankruptcy
court and they could get out of paying, otherwise known as
discharge, their debts.

Since that fateful year, the bankruptcy laws have been
changed and changed again, like a great credit pendulum,
sometimes swinging in favor of lenders and sometimes in
favor of borrowers, depending on the trade winds blowing
in Washington D.C and the party in power. There are still
deadbeats, but through all the changes, no one goes to jail
anymore for not paying their debts; there are no more broken
benches outside defaulting merchants' establishments; no one
works for free to pay off debts. Now it has become something
of a national pastime. Huge companies file bankruptcy cases.
Middle class people run up charge accounts or become over-

---

5   *The Federalist Papers,* Essay 42 (James Madison Jan. 22, 1788).

6   U.S. Constitution, Art. I, Sec. 8, cl. 4.

whelmed with uninsured health care-related debts, and file for bankruptcy. Airlines may try to use bankruptcy to unilaterally break a collective bargaining agreement with a union – yes, the power of the Bankruptcy Code is vast. Debts are worked out, and deadbeats and their debts are processed through a system that relieves people and companies of their obligations like a great institutional novena. Bankruptcy helps balance the ledger between lenders and debtors.

It is noteworthy that it never was, and still isn't, a sin to fail to pay back debts.

What a long way America has come from the Seventeenth Century in Europe:

> *Centuries ago in Western Europe, bankruptcy was deemed "the single most scandalous phenomenon of commercial society," reviled everywhere as a "ghastly evil." In 16th-century northern Italy, for instance, a debtor seeking discharge would have to "go naked in a public and notorious place," like the piazza. There the debtor would have to "strike[ ] his backside" three times against something called "The Rock of Shame," while crying out, "I DECLARE BANKRUPTCY."[7]*

No more rocks of shame in credit-happy America. And, most of all, lucky for me: bankruptcy kept me gainfully employed for many, many years.

---

7   In re Lifschultz Fast Freight, 132 F.3d 339, 345-46 (7th Cir. 1997).

PAIN IN THE ASS

WE CALLED THEM ICEHOUSES. They were nothing more than freestanding garages, with a garage door that served as the front entry way raised on heavy-duty springs and hinges during business hours. No air conditioning, no fans. If there was no breeze, there was no air movement, and usually there was no breeze. Even if there was, it was like staring into the face of a blast furnace. The garage just contained a bar counter with bar stools, a novelty mirror or two, and sales of cold, long-necked beers dripping with condensation sweat. Nothing else. No pretzels, no nuts. But the mix of the ambiance, the brews, and the still heat somehow worked.

It was hot. When wasn't it in Houston? Like the beer bottles, the bodies dripped with sweat. Like the confluence of the mouth of a freshwater river with the Gulf of Mexico, beer-bottle condensation ran together with human-body perspiration: freshwater and saltwater in a brackish mix. It never rained, and even if it did, it would not break the humidity. The rain would just fire up the humidity even more. The sun rose; it was hot and humid. The sun set; it was hot and humid. The moon rose reluctantly in the wet evening air, and the man in the moon looked drained from the effort.

We sat at the bar under the raised garage door, clutching sweaty beer bottles, domestic, no limes. It was a toss-up whether to drink the beer or rub the bottles across our fore-heads. Of course, we did both.

Here we were: transplanted northern baby boomers who drank at a working-class icehouse anchored by our cowboy boots that we wore to fit in, while we entertained the notion that soon we would wear cowboy hats and pretend to be blue-collar Texans. We listened to Emmy Lou Harris and Patsy Cline in the background singing about love, and heart-breaks, and sweet dreams, and strangers; they sounded so damn good without having to listen too hard. Like most of the Houston residents, we had no callouses on our hands. Our bodies were not encased in dust. We had no natural twang. We owned no cattle. Neither of us could ride a horse with any skill; we were both saddle-horn grabbers. I didn't drill for oil, but he did. We had found ourselves there, and we embraced whatever it was that made Texas good and fun and exciting and different.

I was an attorney – a bankruptcy one at that. He was a geologist. At the time, everyone in Houston was either an attor-ney, a geologist, or thinking about becoming one or the other. Well, not everyone. Many of the other people at the icehouse were probably not thinking about getting into the world of geology or bankruptcy law, they were probably not from up north (maybe their pickup trucks had a bumper sticker saying "Welcome to Houston, now leave"), and they probably twanged naturally without giving it a thought. These were the authentic folks who said, perhaps to us, *Don't Mess With Texas*. And we didn't. These were the real-deal Texans who ate barbecue at Goode Company on Kirby, and agreed wholeheartedly with Jim Goode's philosophy that "You might give some serious thought to thanking your lucky stars you're in Texas."

I found that I became contemplative when I drank beer at an icehouse. I tended to contemplate during that period just after sobriety began to depart, but before the beer-buzz arrived. Sometimes it was silent contemplation. I usually contemplated my station in life, and things I felt I hadn't been able to figure out when I was sober. I sometimes confused contemplation with dreaming; they were close cousins, but not quite the same. Contemplation was just the beginning of an idea in black-and-white and it could be done in public. Dreaming was all of the tentacles of a glorious alternative possibility, a full-blown plan in technicolor, and was best done in private.

Today's contemplation topic: it occurred to me that I had never been able to soberly figure out why any of my friends put up with me. I was a big pain in the ass, and an attorney one at that, and I worried that I was growing bigger. As we drank in silence, we watched the sunset over the top of the garage door and behind us, we saw the Pasadena refineries on the distant horizon as they belched out who-knows-what. I thought back to when he and I were in college together. I didn't remember being such a big pain in the ass then. The passage of time cleanses, however, and memories tend to fade to the point where years later, everything seemed like it was the good old days. Maybe I was, in fact, a pain in the ass even in the good old days? Could very well be, but that memory had faded. I tried to reach deeper through the impending buzz of the alcohol and still could not remember being as big a pain in the ass as I found myself being these days.

This pain-in-the-ass thing had bothered me for some time. I convinced myself I was a pain in the ass because I was an attorney – I don't think I had been a pain in the ass before I went to law school. It was some kind of disease (the attorney thing, not the pain-in-the-ass thing). The disease seemed to have crawled up my arm like contagious bacteria, infected me, and now it was in the process of changing me. I fought the change, and that fight had made me a pain in the ass. Resistance was useless. Friends drifted apart and then away, fearing contamination ("Don't go near him; you can get it just by breathing!"). He didn't, though. He was immune from dealing with oil-business folks day in and day out. So we had some kind of symbiotic relationship; like a magnet, he was attracted to a pain in the ass, and an attorney one at that and I filled his need.

Other people in the 'house were talking, so I had to break our private silence. "I am one big pain in the ass."

That caught his attention, maybe just a bit, like yelling at the gorillas in the zoo to catch their attention. He slouched over the bar, rested his geological weight on his elbows, nursed a long-neck Lone Star, and began to think about the process of moving the bottle to his lips. In Texas vernacular, he was fixing to move the bottle and take a swig. And then again, based on the blank look in his eyes, maybe he was thinking about spudding wells or Spindletops or some complicated and highly technical oil production issue, and maybe he wouldn't lift it to his lips. I just couldn't tell. But I had broken the silence and he shifted his weight and turned his head slowly to stare at me. It didn't look like I had interrupted any great thought that was in the middle of being processed through the strata of his geological mind. He closed his eyes, and asked, "What the hell are you talking about?" And he turned away, very slowly (no movement is too slow when the humidity is ninety-five percent). Geologists love to swear. So do attorneys, but I think attorneys may have picked it up from the geologists, at least in Houston.

"What I'm talking about is that I'm a big pain in the ass, and I believe it's because I am an attorney."

He looked back, even more slowly. "Have another beer, and don't worry about it. You are, and I've been meaning to kick your ass because of it. Just as soon as I finish this beer, I'll take up this matter with you out back." No smile. No one else at the bar moved. No one else cared. Just as well.

There was no "out back" at this icehouse, and geologists – especially him – loved to threaten violence. We both went to a venerable Quaker college and believed that pacifism was fine, with the sole, but extremely important, exception to this Quaker absolutism: that every once in a while, violence might very well be the only answer. Not all Quaker-educated non-Quakers held this belief, but the enlightened ones did. Still, I don't think either of us had hit anyone in recent (or even in not-so-recent) memory.

"How many times have I told you I need to explore some non-attorney options I might pursue? Something that fits me well."

"Untold."

"How many times have I told you my job is not for me?"

"Uncountable. Is this a game; if I get three answers right, you buy me another beer?"

I ignored his question. "Do you believe that I have any viable non-attorneying options?"

"No idea, counselor. What you're telling me is that sometimes life sucks. I get that. I hear you. Be assured, whether you're complaining or not, I hear you. But everyone's job sucks. From time to time, life sucks, and that includes yours. I am sure there have been occasions when you've thought *I* sucked. It all sucks but luckily, not all the time. From time to time, life is fine, and that includes yours. Here's some free advice, counselor: focus on the not-all-the-time moments, and your life will be grand."

I did not listen, or if I did, I did not absorb his observation. "Chronic malcontent. Do you think I was a chronic malcontent in college?"

"Sure."

He answered much too quickly. I was? I guess I was, but he didn't have to answer so quickly. "I'm shocked. Why didn't you ever tell me?"

"You never asked. I assumed that was why you became an attorney. What better way to exorcise your malcontent-ness than by a life in which you are paid to be contentious and adversarial and unpleasant, and dismissive, and in which you get to argue everything with everyone? And, best yet, you get to call it a profession, not just a job."

"I went to law school to figure out my life. I never wanted to be contentious and adversarial and all the other things you said. I became an attorney because I couldn't think of anything else to do. You know that."

"I know that's what you've told me and I know that I even listen to you tell me that from time to time. I get it. If I didn't like you so much, I might tell you to suck it up, counselor, every time you told me that."

Silence again. I have to try to remember to break this habit of contemplation. And, by the way, I didn't like the course this conversation was taking.

He broke the silence this time. Highly unusual for him, and he said, "I need a beer if we're going to continue this."

"Then I strongly advise you to get a beer."

He ordered a beer, a long-neck Pearl this time, and said, "You see the guy over there? He's married, like you. Probably has three kids, maybe a fourth in the oven. Probably lives from week-to-week, maybe day-to-day. You think he's happy? He walks through treeless, snake-infested fields, dodging mosquitoes the size of aircraft carriers, and gets paid to mend fences all day. Then he goes home after a few beers to love his wife and yell at his kids, not necessarily in that order, like a good American. He's not content much of the time. He couldn't be, right? But I don't find him to be a fucking pain in the ass."

Ah: fuck. A geologist's favorite word. All-purpose usage. The preeminent emphasizer. I've occasionally wondered how a judge would react to its incorporation into an emotional argument: *Your Honor, my client was fucking screwed!* Probably not a good idea, but better saved for another day of long-neck-stoked contemplation. Back to the problem at hand: why wasn't the fence-mender a pain in the ass? "The fence-mender isn't a pain in the ass, but I'm such a big pain in the ass that you want to take me out back, when there isn't even an out back, and kick my ass?"

"Well, look at the size of the muscles on that guy. I'm not sure I *could* kick his ass." He grinned. Wasn't he taking this seriously?

"So, then, the point is I'm a big pain in the ass because you think you could kick my ass if you wanted to?"

Deep breath. Let it slowly hiss out through his teeth. "No. The point is, *you're* a big pain in the ass because you think you're the only one in the world who's not content or who's confused, or who always looks into the next longhorn cattle pasture for greener grounds. In my view, it's an attorney thing. All you folks have this problem with contentedness. But everyone's life sucks to some degree at times, and everyone else knows it – everyone except you. You, and every other malcontent attorney, think only yours sucks."

"If I'm such a big pain in the ass, why are you here drinking beer with me?"

"I like you. Where else should I be?"

"I think you're here because you know my life sucks and it helps you get through yours to listen to me rail on about my station in life and my failure to dream the bigger dream."

He squinted his eyes to avoid a bead of sweat and said, "There's some truth to that, I suppose. Maybe that's why people befriend attorneys. It makes them realize how much worse their own lives could be or maybe they just like to listen to an adult whine." The bead detoured around his eyebrow, through his crow's feet, and began its descent down his cheek. He slurped at the Pearl and said, "But you don't think your life is so rotten. Most of this is just a big air. It's your little way of getting attention."

"Oh, no, I think it sucks. Really, I do."

"No, goddammit." He said it softly, but slammed his Pearl down emphatically. No one noticed; no one cared. Just as well. He wiped the bead that had made its way to his chin where it was now hanging. "You're like every other god-damned attorney I've ever met. Ask them how they like what they do, and they tell you 'it could be better,' and that they'd like to do anything other than their current gig. But ask them what they're doing to rectify the situation and they start whining about how they're stuck and can't decide what else to do. They just keep on doing what they do because they can't – or don't know how to – do something else. You at least dream, I'll give you that much. Dreaming is good, but for you, to no apparent end."

I stared at the Lone Star mirror on the back wall and made no eye contact with him. He was right, of course. Partially. Well, mostly. All right, possibly completely. My dilemma: hard to stay, and harder to leave. I was a big pain in the ass. God, it was hot. I looked back at him. What a pain. Him. Me. Attorneying. Why hadn't I been born with economic freedom? That would have been the answer: trust-fund babies are all happy, right? Not.

Squiggles of heat rose from the road tar. I said, "Maybe your next oil find will go like this: you'll drill and find some oil, I'll write some leases and operating agreements, you'll give me an override for my troubles, the sun will rise over a rig instead of this garage door, and I'll live happily forever after." The Jed Clampett approach.

He smiled. "Oil? You? Happily, ever after? *You*? Not." He closed his eyes and shook his head from side to side. "Bloody hell. While I'm out looking for this oil, why don't you do something socially redeeming? Write a book or something – give yourself something to do other than getting in my hair while I'm drinking beer and losing myself in the heat."

There was an idea. A book? I'd have to file that idea under the "Prospect" folder in the storage areas in the back of my mind, and wait for my next dreaming session.

My long-neck was dry. Decision time: maybe a Tecate next round. In a can. And a lime this time. *Uno cerveza. Hecho en Mexico. Viva la* whoever invented beer – apparently someone in Iran before Christ. The sun had almost set, and the moon was just climbing into the lone star sky. Two weary ships passing in the night. Were the sun and the moon content with their lives? Did they complain to each other as they passed each day? Did they dream? I was almost past the contemplation stage, but I had enough time left to notice I was getting to be a big pain... in my own ass. I think it had been bothering me for some time. That, and the humidity. A big, humid, sometimes amusing, pain in the ass. The Tecate tasted good. The next dream would be real good. A book. About what, I wondered?

MY HOUND

EVERY ATTORNEY MUST HAVE a dog to come home to. This is my own personal, set-in-stone, no-exceptions, rule of law, my imperative. I recited my law to every associate who came to my office to lament about the pressure of the practice of law and the death of a personal life. Surviving thirty-eight years as a bankruptcy attorney without a dog is inconceivable. I reiterated my law to every partner who told me wistfully that they would leave the practice of law shortly. I told them to get a dog, and share their feelings with the dog. The dog, I said, would understand. Dogs understand everything. Dogs especially understand attorneys.

I recommend a dog to every attorney as a way to survive, plain and simple. Specifically, the wagging, barking, unwavering loyalty, and affection of a dog's greeting at the front door, no matter what time of the day or night you arrive home after fifteen hours at the entrance to Hell, is essential if you are to have any chance at all of making it through a day in the life of an attorney. I just do not see a path to getting through the day, without knowing that the canine greeting will be waiting for you when you finally get to your front door.

The dog who got me through the darkest times and who would listen to my every whine and kvetch was Scruff. Scruff was a seventeen-pound, gray, brown, white, black – and assorted other colors – cross between a schnauzer and some other kind or kinds of terrier. She did not know her heritage, and certainly didn't seem to care. I never figured out her heritage and I never cared either.

Scruff, of course, was not a colleague in the practice of law. Scruff was much more than that. Many times, she alone was the only reason I was able to rise out of bed and head for the downtown high-rise where I had my office, and resume the battle called the practice of law.

Scruff and I first met in a dog pound ten miles west of downtown Houston. At the time, I told my newly-licensed veterinarian wife that I was concerned she would struggle in her new practice unless she had a dog. I questioned how she could she dispense practical advice about dogs to her clients without her own practical experience from life with a canine practice subject in our house. I had decided I needed a dog, one to listen to my problems every day, but in selling a marital idea, sometimes it helps to come up with a reason why the idea is spouse-centric and therefore also good for the spouse. I was a younger associate at the time, and I had begun to notice that I needed an outlet to go to complain, and I was concerned that the outlet needed to be someone other than my spouse. These were, after all, attorney complaints and whines that could bubble up 24-7 at times. Dogs are the only people I know who will listen and still seem happy and loving. I needed a dog's ear and her all-knowing, soft brown eyes.

So one Saturday, Loren and I set out to visit every animal shelter in the Greater Houston area in search of the perfect companion, a practice subject for her and a canine sounding-board for me. Houston is like Los Angeles – you can drive for hours, often in bumper-to-bumper traffic, and still be within the city limits. So we had a lot of ground to cover, and we went from shelter to shelter without any luck. We saw and met and played with and visited a tremendous number

of dogs (and cats and other mammals) and had our hearts
broken and re-broken. Cage after cage of mournful, soulful
eyes and shy affection. Whoever said animals do not get sad
and depressed never visited an animal shelter. But, since we
couldn't take every dog home with us, the day was dragging
on, and we had not found our dog.

It was a long, typically steamy Houston day and as a last
resort, we entered the ramp on I-10 and drove east to what
seemed like East San Antonio to the last shelter we knew of.
I saw her, and she saw me and that was it. Scruff and me.
Her name was not really Scruff when we met; she didn't
have a name because no one at the shelter knew what it had
been. "Scruff" was exactly how she looked, wet or dry. The
rest was history.

Scruff and I had a little talk at the animal shelter outside
of Loren's view so I could screen her to see if she would fit in
with our lifestyle. I sat her on my lap, and I told her I was an
attorney. She did not seem to mind, and I was immediately
in love. You see, most people mind; most people mind quite
a bit. I tried some typical attorney grousing on her, and she
looked over her shoulder and licked me on the nose. Heaven.
I told her I would come home late at night from the dark
side and I would not have the energy to play with her. She
nuzzled her nose in the crook of my arm. Ecstasy. I told her I
was subject to brooding and dark moods and anxiety attacks
and bad dreams about bad cases and she nodded almost
imperceptibly. A match; a *perfect* match.

Then I administered the Loren-compatibility test. I told
Scruff that Loren was a veterinarian, and although most
people do not mind that Loren cares for animals, Scruff
looked a little concerned. You could see it in her eyes. People
get crows' feet around their eyes when they worry. Dogs have
their own brand of body language. The softness in dogs'

eyes fades when they worry, and their brows furrow. It is all a matter of perspective. Her concern, however, passed.

So we signed our papers, paid our suggested donation, leashed her up (or was that vice versa?), and she led us out of the shelter and jumped into the car as if she had known us for years. When we got home, she moved in with us and she ran our lives for her entire life.

Scruff's jobs at home were straightforward but very important. No matter how bad my day had been, no matter how many names I had been called by opposing counsel, no matter how many violations of my basic human rights as established by the Geneva Convention occurred, she yelped, raced across the wooden floors, skidded to a halt at my feet, jumped on my suit, wagged her tail and her butt along with it until both looked like they were ready to fall off, rolled over on her side, and, as if I had not been able to guess, she let me know how happy she was to see me. Then we went for a walk along a bayou in Houston (and later sat on the stoop in Philadelphia where I transferred the malaise of another day at the office to the east coast) while she kept a sharp watch for squirrels. Dr. Scruff was in – therapy time.

In return, she asked so little. We fed her, occasionally bathed her and brushed her coat, walked her from time to time, and gave her one or more warm places to sleep.

True to our first talk at the shelter, Scruff was one of the few Americans who did not care that I was an attorney. She was so tolerant. She was not concerned with my billing rate or my billable hours or the degree of skill or confusion I displayed or how full my plate was or the brief on which I was working. She did not care whether I made partner at any law firm, as long as food was in her bowl morning and evening and the rawhides were plentiful. She did not give me work assignments and she did not review my performance. We had a perfectly normal, human, social, non-attorney, non-aggressive, non-adversarial, non-contentious mutual admiration relationship. I had so few.

Scruff did not out-live me. The great problem with dogs, I am afraid. But I would never have gotten through my career without her, and I needed to let everyone know that. Scruff was followed by Ranger and Ranger was followed by Emily, our sweet little miss. It was as if Scruff left Ranger and Emily a manual of how to successfully live with and love an attorney and a veterinarian, and they memorized it. If you are going to make it in this work-a-day world as an attorney for any length of time, get a dog. It is a solid way for the attorneys of the world to take a first, but important, step toward learning responsibility and loyalty and respect and interdependence.

WHERE DID ALL THE SUITS AND TIES GO?

Obviously, women wear suits as well as men. But in this chapter, I speak from my own personal experience, and dispense with political correctness to focus on male attire; the salesperson and tailor I have in mind are likewise male.

I HAD TRIED TO avoid the life of ties and suits and desks. And failed. By necessity, I quickly became a consumer of the fashion requirements of the profession. Those fashions, however, were not cutting-edge, and found no unveiling each year on a fashion runway. Rather, I learned that attorneys are not the most fashion-conscious group in America. There was a time when attorneys wore suits and ties all of the time, not just in court. Clients expected their attorneys to wear suits and ties. Colleagues at the law firm expected everyone to wear suits and ties. Not so much anymore; even the stuffiest of firms have dispensed with the suit-and-tie requirement. In my view now, in contrast to my adolescent thinking, that is sad. I had two kinds of clothing in my closet: suits and ties, and raggedy jeans. I liked wearing suits and ties to work. It distinguished between work and everything else. If I had on a suit and a tie, I knew I was more than likely working. If I had on a pair of raggedy jeans, I knew I was undoubtedly *not* working. Straight forward lines of demarcation; simple rules, for a simpler time. Of course, these rules predated texts and emails, whose arrival on the scene have considerably blurred the line between working and not working. Back before tech, I only needed two kinds of clothing to maintain that line of work demarcation – formal for work, and ratty for everything else.

I came to miss those simpler clothing days as the influence of a more casual society invaded my firm. The move to casual was slow but steady. First, we had something called business casual – that could be khakis and a white shirt, or something just a notch above ratty. Then we had jeans-days. And then, at some point, we had no suit-and-tie days. And at last, every day was no suit-and-tie day, followed closely by mostly jeans-days.

Ahh, for the suits. The suits attorneys wore were mostly wool, usually lightweight tropical, dark grays or blues, sometimes pinstriped, sometimes solid, two- or three-piece numbers purchased at Boyd's in Philadelphia and Michael's in Kansas City and Norton Ditto in Houston, or Brooks Brothers anywhere, or some other equally hoity-toity purveyor of fine clothing since 1888. This was, of course, long before the days of eBay, Amazon, and online shopping.

The layout of these fine stores was almost always the same. The store had warm, but not bright, lighting, and several floors of clothing and accessories. The first floor usually displayed accessories such as ties, handkerchiefs, socks, suspenders and the like. The second through whatever floors, depending on the size of the store, usually displayed the suits in question, by size. When a customer entered the store, an older, mature, pale and mottle-complexioned, graying, maybe balding salesman targeted him immediately. The salesman almost always had dark-framed bifocal glasses hanging around his neck from whatever those string-like things that attach to glasses are called (he could also double as a mortician; maybe he was a stiff-dresser in an earlier incarnation). He would allow me to stroll around his establishment's first floor for a few moments, all the time narrowing the distance between us before coming up behind me like a dog sneaking up behind someone strolling past a front walk, and asking, "Can I be of some assistance?"

I almost always told him, "I'm interested in a suit." Big surprise.

He nodded his head and then subjected me to the age-old tradition of *can the salesman guess your size and profession?* This was the salesman's chance to show me how many years he had been in the business. Just by narrowing his eyes and scanning my bulk, he believed he could tell I was a 44 stout, or a 39 short, and just by looking at the furrows in my brow, he could tell I was an attorney. How did they do it? I never knew. It was akin to the magic show where the great Woolmeister was blindfolded and strolled through the aisles telling members of the audience their deepest, darkest secrets to wild applause. The great Woolmeister was always on the money, but everyone knew he had somehow fixed the act. My salesman never fixed the act, and as a consequence, he was occasionally correct, sometimes close, and more often wrong. No matter, it was all part of the ritual.

"Let's see," he said. Right hand on left elbow; left hand on chin. The thinker. Narrowed eyes in focused concentration. Scanning my bulk; pausing at my midsection. Move on, I thought. I knew I had a small legal paunch. But I said nothing. Not to worry, all part of the ritual. Examination over, he concluded, "I'd say you are a 42 regular. Stout? No, regular."

I could not insult him, so I raised my eyebrows, chuckled softly, and said, "Well, last time I was in I fit into a 40 short pretty nicely."

"Very well, sir." These salesmen must have been British butlers in a prior life. They were always proper. On unimportant issues they rarely disagree; the customer was usually always right.

Time was always short. I may have found myself in the store because it was located between my office and the courthouse, or I may have just finished a tough negotiating session and, without premeditation, drifted into the clothing store for solace. I always seemed to violate that life rule: never shop for groceries when hungry; never go to the clothing store after lengthy negotiations. But whatever the reason, I was there, and I had very little time. So, attired in a navy-blue suit, I got right down to the lick log and told my salesman, "I am interested in a blue suit... different from the suit I'm wearing. Do you have one of those medium charcoal-blue suits with windowpanes? I saw an ad in the Sunday *New York Times* Men's Fashion Section recently." Yes, that was the day when people read the *New York Times* on Sunday and, necessarily, the periodic fashion sections.

My salesman then looked at me. He was not *quite* hurt that I may have been looking to the *Times* for my fashion advice, but he withheld approval of my fashion choice without scowling or raising his eyebrows; nevertheless, he had an opinion. His eyes said, *oh, no sir, not windowpanes.* His manner said, *that style went out for professionals last year.* His silence said, *windowpanes are too trendy to be reliable.* Ever the diplomat, though, he inquired critically, "The most *recent* Fashion Section of the *Times*, sir?"

"I think so," I said, retreating in uncertainty.

Without saying no, without criticizing the *Times* or the fashion trends or windowpane suits, my salesman said, "Let me recommend a style that is timeless and ageless. Something that is not subject to the whims of Italian designers or *New York Times* fashion editors. Something that is trendless. It will never go out of style. Here it is," as he expertly scanned through racks of blue suits in my size, and, with a flamboyant flick of the wrist, flipped the suit in question off the rack and onto a display hook. "I sell a lot of these," he said to me.

Yeah; I could imagine. Like the one I was wearing. I stared at the proffered suit. It was pure navy, not charcoal blue. It had no windowpanes. Trendy it was not, big surprise.

"But," I said, scratching my head, "it looks just like the suit I have on," without saying, *I was hoping for something trendy and a bit more flashy with windowpanes*; or, *I don't want a suit you sell a lot of*; or, *I am aging quickly and want a suit to reverse the process*; or, *I want to be noticed*. Yes, in those long-ago days, a suit could get you noticed.

"Oh no, sir, it is very, very different from your suit. Your suit has narrow, light blue, chalk pinstripes. This suit," pointing proudly with an expertly-manicured and clear-polished pointer finger, "has slightly less narrow, slightly less chalky, slightly more white pinstripes. It will look wonderful on you. Try it on."

This was always the part of the suit salesman's pitch that was remarkably like a car salesman telling me to climb in behind the wheel of a Ford sedan, when I wanted a Mustang convertible, to "see how it feels." Nothing like the smell of fresh vinyl – or the feel of lightweight tropical wool – to change a consumer's mind. So I climbed into the suit and stood in front of one of those three-sided mirrors as the salesman doted over me from behind. Yes, in the day, before Amazon and sight-unseen clothing purchases, there were mirrors where I could eyeball how I looked before I purchased the suit.

"It's the perfect size," pulling the back vent down sharply and smoothing out the shoulders gently for me. "What do you think?"

What I thought was that notwithstanding the slightly differ-ent stripes, it was not a windowpane, not charcoal blue, not *New York Times*, not trendy, not Italian, and it would not get me noticed. But it was the right size, and I was an attorney. So, I said, "O.K. Get the tailor." The tailor was the store employee who could make any suit fit me better with a sewing machine, a needle, thread, a chalk marker, a tape measure, a small step, and a little time.

As the tailor approached, I wondered, why? Why was I buying this suit? I scanned the rack and saw a charcoal blue suit just like the one in the *Times*, so I knew the salesman had one. Was that on the non-attorney's rack? Was there some kind of discrimination going on here? I didn't see any sign proclaiming, "We reserve the right to refuse to sell charcoal blue windowpane suits to attorneys." But the salesman knew best. He was probably a consultant to the American Bar Association: Clothing Subcommittee; the pinstripe chairman. Attorneys were not trendy. No windowpanes. No charcoal blue. Not for attorneys. The ABA rule as enforced by mot-tle-complexioned, hoity-toity salesmen of hotsy-totsy navy blue pinstriped suits sold in a tony men's clothing store.

The tailor finally arrived, and I answered the standard questions about how large a break I wanted in the pants, and whether I wanted cuffs or plain bottoms. He measured the distance between my thumb and my sleeve end and marked an adjustment to be made with a white chunk of chalky soap. The tailor planned and measured for my crotch adjustment, my shoulder pinches, my waist expansion (damn the law life), the button relocations, and I paid with American Express after I fended off an attempt to sell me shirts or braces and, God forbid, a matching tie and handkerchief. I hustled out as I promised to return in a week or so to pick up my third altered navy blue pinstripe suit.

Kind of a let-down; as I exited, I sighed. I felt the same way I did every six years, when I went to the car dealer hoping to buy a sporty convertible only to leave the showroom the proud owner of yet another four-door, bench seat sedan.

And that's how, in my tailored view, attorneys have never dressed trendily. Influenced by the *New York Times*; dressed by the navy-blue-peddling salesmen. And, then came the modern era – even less trendy: jeans and a golf shirt, purchased online. No salesman, no tailor, no real panache. Maybe if we had all worn windowpane suits like we wanted to back in the day, we would have been trendier, and maybe that alone could have staved off the days of dress-down and jeans. By the end of my career, I still had my suits. I still liked my habit of wearing something at work that separated work from everything else. But that was just me; not a trendsetter, and, the truth be known, I started to buy my suits on Amazon and I was surprised, but I liked it. Progress, indeed.

IF GOD HAD MEANT
ME TO FLY

A TYPICAL DAY WHEN I practiced law:

I have been awake since 4:15 a.m. I am showered, shaved and dressed; I don't remember doing any of these rituals this morning, I just know I did them. It is now 5:15 a.m and I am in Kansas City at the airport after a rideshare through neighborhoods where sane people, unlike me, live. For them, it is too early for the showers, the newspapers, and their alarm clocks. It is still Wynken, Blynken and Nod[8] time for them.

Only fools like me are on the road. And, of course, my ride-share driver. I have to be in court this afternoon at 3 p.m. in who-knows-where. Some company somewhere filed its bankruptcy papers and owes my client $10.5 million. The company wants to use my client's money. So, off I go. My early morning, pre-caffeine, post-ride-before-the-sun-rises-as-I-wait-to-board-another-airplane reaction: no way to the money request. I will undoubtedly refine this position (I will have plenty of time, in traveling from Kansas City to wherever I have to fly and change planes), and flesh out some eloquence to my view before I reach the courthouse, and I know full

---

8   "'Wynken, Blynken & Nod'" is the childhood poem about sleep written by Eugene Field. https://poets.org/poem/wynken-blynken-and-nod

well the judge will let the company use my client's money, at least for a while. It is the way of the bankruptcy world.

The gate agent calls for the different boarding groups to board the plane. I prove to the agent that I have a seat on the plane; I walk into the jetway, take my seat, buckle up, and, finally, the plane taxis to an empty runway. The pilot announces we are third to take off although there are no other planes in sight, and after a few minutes we eventually take off. Another on-time departure. I put on my noise-canceling headphones, choose a playlist, close my eyes, and next thing I know, all of a sudden, I am at the Wherever International Airport – stop number one. I run through stop number one's airport to catch a commuter plane – same routine – and the plane takes off mostly on time. Same headphones, new playlist, and next thing I know, all of a sudden, I am where I need to be: the Destination Regional Airport. I hop into a new rideshare car, and we speed off to the courthouse for a date with the court and all the other attorneys who represent creditors who were stiffed by the debtor (we don't say "the bankrupt" anymore; too much social stigma attached).

A typical day in the life. Three hours of travel for a less than thirty-minute hearing. The judge has numerous cases on her docket this afternoon. She seems good-natured and pleasant enough; not all of them are, so I am grateful. My case is way down the list of the many cases she must hear. I refine my argument and keep it short and to the point. It is straightforward. It is just money. It is now time to daydream my typical courtroom-after-travel daydream: home, in bed, under flannel sheets, waiting for the sun to rise and smelling coffee brewing just like in the commercials. Then the alarm gently rings, my wife and I slowly stretch and rise out of bed, hug and kiss, and start our day while Art Pepper plays "You'd Be So Nice To Come Home To" softly in the background.

I spent my thirty-eight years at the law firm hoping to see my wife in the morning before I headed out the door for the airport.

I used to think I was an attorney and I practiced law for a living. Then, I came to understand that I traveled for a living and practiced law on the side. I lived while in the air. I slept while in the air. I thought while in the air. I communicated with people while in the air. I ate while in the air. I defecated and urinated and any other "ateds" you can think of while in the air. The only thing I had trouble doing was dreaming in the air. I came to believe that cabin pressure, turbulence, and getting up at 4:15 a.m. interfered with the process of a good dream.

I flew the friendly skies. I flew with people who loved to fly, and it showed. I flew with the wings of man. I flew with people who did what they did best. I flew smart and landed happy. Life was a journey and I flew it well. I got the best care in the air. You name it and I flew it. Identify an airline's tag line and I lived it. I had no idea what all tag lines meant, but I did most of them.

Newsflash: there is nothing glamorous about living in an airplane. The food is less than stellar; the seats are cramped; the noise is jarring; the cabin pressure assaults sinuses.

Some of these problems are cured by flying first class. I was told just before I became an attorney that large law firms required clients to pay for first-class arrangements, citing the age-old adage, "If you want first-class attorneys, you have to pay for first-class seats." Firms dropped the requirement as soon as I arrived and the adage remained as one of those "good old days" stories partners would tell the associates. So I usually did *not* fly first class. I flew in cramped coach.

My business travels took me to some garden spots. I had a case in Natchez, Mississippi. Itinerary: fly from Houston to Dallas to Jackson, Mississippi, rent a car, drive two hours southwest on the Natchez Trace Parkway deep into Dixie and the land of Faulkner and Sartoris as someone lay dying. I had a case in Lubbock, Texas. Itinerary: fly from Houston to Dallas to Lubbock, into the land of Buddy Holly's "Peggy Sue" and "That'll Be The Day" and Llano Vineyard Cabernets. I had a case in rural Colorado – drive forty minutes to the Kansas City airport, fly from Kansas City to Denver International Airport, and drive three hours to Nowheresville, Colorado to do battle with a farm family.

I ran from, to, and through Kansas City International, Love, DFW, Atlanta, New Orleans, Albuquerque, Santa Barbara, Midway, O'Hare, Newark, LaGuardia, JFK, DIA, MacArthur, LAX, Philadelphia, Minneapolis, Boise, Logan, San Francisco, St. Louis, several Springfields, Wichita, Oklahoma City, Nashville, Ft. Lauderdale, Ft. Meyers, Ft. Worth, Memphis, Jackson, Indianapolis, Buffalo, National, Lubbock, Pittsburgh, Austin, Houston Hobby, and George Bush International, and assorted other domestic ports of call. I ran past newsstands, and snack stands, and trinket stands that sold something somewhat indigenous to whatever city I found myself in, and past Moonies and Hari Krishna and pollsters and other privacy invaders, and probably past spies and gangsters and secret agents who surely always hang out in airports because that is what spies and secret agents do. I ran past stores that add an "e" to the end of their name, like the grille, the stande, the shoppe, the ice creame vendor, in some air travel tradition of adding class(e) to the name of an establishment to compensate for the ordinariness of the products sold within.

It is scary to think that I never even began to scratch the surface of airports through which to run, in which to get heartburn, where I could kill time and get a shoeshine, or in which to awaken with a cup of coffee. There are many, many airports I ran through but in which I have yet to sit on a toilet.

Through all this running and flying, I learned and confirmed fourteen things, and here they are. First, airport bacon is very low in cholesterol. If it was not, my arteries would have already clogged years ago. Second, news is news, and it is mostly bad no matter where it is, no matter what newspaper it is reported in, no matter what monitor at what terminal in what airport it blares from, and no matter who it affects. But, for kicks, I made it a point to try to read the local paper in whatever airport I was in. My favorite was the *New Orleans Picayune*; the attraction is all in the name and not in its reports of impending or completed news cycle events from the Crescent City.

Third, I can confirm that the most obnoxious invention in the history of all mankind is the airport golf cart that transports people from gate to gate while it beeps, honks, whistles, or spews forth a computer-generated voice, vigorously encouraging pedestrians to step aside, lest they be run over.

Fourth, many airport bars use very little alcohol in their drinks, but they make up for that by charging twice as much for the drink and giving you free stale trail mix if you ask for a bowl of it.

Fifth, airport food isn't.

Sixth, airport hot dogs might very well be, but only a fool would ask what ingredients are in a jumbo hot dog that has been greased and cooked for hours on end.

Seventh. Airport bathroom graffiti. This is not the "for a good time, call" kind of graffiti. This is the philosophical, socially conscious, sometimes iambic pentameter, sometimes Japanese haiku, usually vulgar, often thought-provoking, innovative, creative stuff. It would be crass to repeat, and could very well violate some copyright law, but I highly recommend it to the traveler killing time between flights. The best I have ever seen is in St. Louis; the wholesome, repressed midwest.

Eighth, God bless automatic toilets and sink spigots. The system is supposed to work off of some kind of sensor that somehow determines exactly when the toilet needs to flush or the sink water needs to run. But, even after all these years, the system needs tweaking. Either the toilet flushes with its occupant still residing on the seat (exhilarating) or it fails to flush for hours, constructively preventing any occupant with a functioning olfactory system from ever temporarily occupying that stall. The sink is another story. Water either turns on mysteriously when no one is trying to wash anything, or there are people soaped-up with hands under the water spout as they wait in vain for any sign of water.

Ninth, many airports are illogically designed by people who have obviously never traveled. The terminal structure might be horseshoes or spokes or straight lines or satellites, and the different buildings might be connected by subways with signs that occasionally explain where to go and how to get there in international picture language that you can't tell if it depicts a taxi or some other unknown means of transportation.

Tenth, airport parking. Can you say "hassle?" Can you say "rip-off?" You have two choices: you can park semi-near the terminal from which you will fly, and pay lots of money per day; or you can park in a reduced-rate, satellite lot that may or may not be in the same county as the airport, and ride a shuttle bus to the terminal. I am partial to the lots-of-money-a-day lot, and I choose to always park on the roof. After I have entered the lot and spiraled my way upward past one full level after another, there looms the roof level, usually empty, always cleaner-smelling than the indoor levels and almost always offering parking spots near the elevator.

Eleventh, twelfth, and thirteenth – location, location, location. Just because an airport is named after a city does not mean, and you should never assume, it is anywhere near its namesake. The goal seems to have been to build an airport as far from downtown as possible. It helps the rideshare trade, I suppose.

Lastly, I tried to avoid evangelical air pockets wherever possible. So many years ago, I took my first commuter flight on a no-longer-with-us carrier named Air Something-Or-Other from Kansas City to Hays, Kansas. We flew around a system of thunderstorms with tornadic activity within, with our brave pilot (no crew) navigating the tiny plane, as it lost and gained altitude like a yo-yo. The lady across the aisle from me clutched rosary beads and whimpered to God, or the Holy Ghost or whoever else would listen, as she sought deliverance from evil, forgiveness for her sins, and relief from the air pockets. I was good with the air pocket requests she made.

After so many years in the friendly skies, I still have a few air travel questions that remain unanswered. When you flush an airplane toilet, where do the contents of the toilet go? Back not too long ago when they had in-flight gifts catalogs, did anyone buy anything from an in-flight gift catalog? Like the "coffee survival kit" or the "dual time zone watch" or the "blood pressure monitor" or the "towel-warmer" or the "portable pant-presser valet" or the assorted wizards and electronic dictionaries, or one of my personal favorites, the "levitating world globe?" What percentage of barf bags are pressed into service annually? Does an airplane ever depart from gate number one, or is it just my luck that every flight I have ever been on departs from gate number fifty-four, one mile from the security checkpoint?

All this traveling and confirming and questioning made me old and rundown and congested and irritated and impatient and cramped and colicky and out of shape and earned me frequent flyer miles galore. The miles were supposed to make me feel better. Frequent flyer miles are the airlines' way of rewarding business passengers for flying and having their company or client pay full-fare prices. For every mile I flew and every dollar I charge on my United Airlines Visa card, I received a mile that I now can exchange for free tickets. At one point, the airlines guaranteed a minimum of 750 miles per flight, and then they tripled the mileage. What a frenzy. The good old days, indeed. I flew between Dallas and Houston roundtrip and received 4500 frequent flyer miles for a 440-mile round trip. Many a vacation was fueled by these frequent flyer miles. There was something wrong with the picture of flying for a living and then flying for vacation, but the price was right.

Traveling for a living. Law on the side.

I came out of my daydream just in time as my case was called by the court clerk. Reality set in, I spoke my mind and my client's mind, and my hearing was over. As expected, the judge let them use our money for one month. I never said, no way. I knew I would refine my reaction. So, it was back to Airport Number 2, onto Airport Number 1, some running, and finally back to my home airport. We landed at gate number fifty-two. The airport was quiet. Even the vendors went home for the evening. After what seemed like hours of pep stepping my way through the terminal past closed shoppes while the gate numbers descend to thirty-nine, then twenty-one, then finally to one, I found a rideshare, and off we go through the same neighborhoods I passed through that morning. Houses were warmly lit. Garbage was out front. Dinner dishes were in the dishwasher (Dinner. That would be nice). Families gathered around televisions to watch whatever families watched those days.

I was in my living room at 10:45 p.m. Tomorrow – Atlanta. My dog yawned and stretched. My wife hugged me. Another day at the shop.

That shop closed down this year. I still travel some for my own account, mostly to see friends. I wave at the vendors now and am working hard to forget the process of traveling for a living. I never, never run through airports, and I still have my list of unanswered questions.

BRIDGE BURNING

"WHAT DO YOU MEAN, you're leaving?" It was Monday morning. I was in the office of my only friend at the firm to tell him I had decided what to do with the rest of my life, or at least the next few years; a favorite topic, these days. Staying here at the firm was *not* part of the rest of my life, but he already knew that.

"Just what it sounds like. I'll move to the Midwest and leave this place. I have an offer and I will accept it."

He did not question the offer, nor that I thought the move was best for Loren and me. It was certainly the best option for Loren, as the move from Philadelphia to Kansas City would allow her to achieve her goal to set up a veterinary radiology practice, in a city without a radiologist and with a horse track. All he wanted to know was, "What are you going to tell *them*?" "They" were the head partners; the masters; the employers. What I was going to tell *Them* had been harder to decide than what I would do with the rest of my life.

"That I have an offer and I'm leaving," I said. I decided that was all I would say to Them. Nothing else. They would accept this explanation. They would want to accept it.

His jaw was fixed, and his mouth barely moved. "Are you going to reveal the real reason you're leaving?" he probed.

"The 'real' reason? I'm leaving because I have an offer, the move will further my wife's career, and we want to move off the east coast. That's all." I raised my eyebrows in feigned innocence when I spoke. I was trying out my explanation on him. It sounded plausible to me; he didn't buy it. I did have an offer that I would shortly accept. But the truth was that at this moment in my life, it did not take much for another offer to be better. I had been dissatisfied and disillusioned for so long. It was not all blue skies and smooth sailing in this law firm, but if I squinted, I thought I could make out some blue skies on the horizon beyond the storm in which I found myself caught. So, I had decided to turn my ship to navigate toward those blue skies. It had become much too frustrating, and finally, unbearable, in the storm. I made my decision. But none of this would shock Them. They knew how things were; They were not ignorant; but there was nothing They could do about it, and They needed to present a certain face to the associates. And so They were left with no option, except to seem indifferent. At this point in my life and from this vantage point, any other law firm seemed like it could be better. I was chasing the prospect of betterment, not betterment itself. But it was time to move on.

Most associates think there are blue skies on the horizon beyond the storm system in which they find themselves, so, the "real reason" was usually a search for those blue skies. Truth is, there *are* blue skies out there, but not necessarily at another law firm. Most of the United States firms are the same. East Coast; West Coast; No Coast: no difference. Some promote that their culture is better, and maybe some are, but most are the same. It is not the law firm; it is not the partners who run the law firm; it is the system, and it is the same system everywhere. I knew this, but I chose to ignore it as I pondered the blue skies and the hope that things would be better at a new firm. Things might be better in a new region of the country – but any possible improvement would have little to do with the new firm. I did know all of this, but it was much too long an explanation for a discussion with any of Them; no one wants a long discussion with Them during the exit interview, and neither do They.

He looked hurt. "I can't believe you're worried about burning bridges."

Burning bridges. That point of the employment relationship, when the employee decides to leave and is faced with the decision whether to make a graceful, quiet exit, or to tell the employer all the reasons why employment here was one of the worst experiences ever endured by a human being since records of employment have been kept. The bridge is the connecting structure between the firm and the rest of the world. You metaphorically walk over it to enter the firm, and you walk back over it to leave.

The associate who quits has the option to either burn the bridge, or not. Either cross the employment bridge to the next challenge, without criticism and without looking back, or, as the bridge is crossed, tell the soon-to-be-former employer the "real" reasons of how bad life was under Their control and indenture. If the associate chooses not to criticize, the theory is that the bridge remains intact even after their departure, presumably to facilitate a potential return to the firm someday. If the associate engages in a dialogue of the "real" reasons, the conversation may get heated and out of hand, the bridge will be burned after the associate crosses it *en route* to the new endeavor, and with the destruction of the bridge, any potential return to the firm in the future also goes up in flames.

They may never talk to you again; They may say bad things about you. Not too many people burn the bridge, so there may even be other retributions They would wreak. Who knows? Truth is most of Them are passive-aggressive types, who hope the departing associate just leaves without burning any bridges, so there just isn't a lot of precedent in terms of consequences of bridge-burning.

I gazed out the window. It was so nice outside. I saw serenity in the polished gray granite tops of the skyscrapers that housed people like me. It was not going to be serene inside this skyscraper today; I could feel it coming. What a rotten day to be in the office. I shrugged my shoulders and said, "I've decided I don't want to burn any bridges."

His voice was rising now. "What a chicken shit! You should tell all as you leave. Everything that has pissed you off for the last three years. Say it. Stick it to the firm. Give it to Them straight. This associate gig here is a living hell – say it! Let it be known that you're not afraid and you intend to stand up and fight back. Say everything we've talked about for the *last three years*."

He was on a path from momentary shrill to permanent hysteria. His explosion should have snapped me back into his office. But it didn't. I was still outside somewhere, serene; I asked, "For whose benefit would I say all this stuff? Not mine. I'll be gone soon."

He said, "You're right. You should fight this battle for every associate that you'll leave behind."

He had a very French Maquisard view of the world. The maquis were the rural members of the French Resistance in World War II, who valiantly fought the Nazi occupation of France and the Vichy regime that collaborated; many died for the honor of their cause. Bridge-burners tended to (metaphorically) die as well, and I wasn't interested in such a fate. Besides, his favored course of action was *not* honorable. Partners, of course, are not occupiers and the law firm is not a totalitarian regime. What he was proposing would only be a failed challenge to a system that just was what it was and could not be changed by one soon-to-be midwestern, departing associate.

I replied quickly, "Not me. I don't owe the associates anything. Associates are perfectly equipped to fend for themselves. I'm not going to try to win a fight for every associate in this firm. I fight for myself. I decide these things on my own. I'm going to leave for me, period." I could hear myself; some of what I said was true – some wasn't.

It was amazingly serene outside. It must be nice to be a skyscraper, looking down at the city and its inhabitants below. Maybe that was the feeling my dad felt when he arrived at his desk every day in the Empire State Building. Oh, the stories the skyscrapers could tell.

"But how can you leave if you know there's a laundry list of broken things here that need to be fixed?" he asked.

"Look: there *are* things broken. Maybe at the firm, and maybe in the practice of law in general. Who knows? Without question, it might temporarily satisfy some perverse fantasy to parade into the managing partner's office, confront him, maybe interrupt him, grab him by the tie, slap some sense into him, and tell him what's wrong with his firm and what They should do to fix it. But it's just a dream that, these days, occasionally infiltrates my sleep time – it's never going to happen. And I will never try to make it happen."

"I bet there are partners here who would want you to tell the M.P. off," he noted.

"I'm sure there are. But why haven't they ever done it themselves?" I asked.

"They'll want you to fight their war for them," he offered.

"Not me. If they think there's something that needs to be said, let them get their pointy-toed boots on and, pardon my crassness, kick some ass. Anyway, if you'd just calm down, you'd have to admit that it sounds more than a little preposterous for me to tell Them how to run Their institution. Even if I talked to Them, They wouldn't listen; and even if They listened, They wouldn't change anything. Mostly, They *can't* change anything. It is what it is. You know that."

He was hurt and replied, "I don't know anything of the sort, because no one ever tells Them."

"Why do you think that is?" I asked, Socratically.

"I can't believe what I'm hearing. Don't pull that Socratic B.S. on me, professor. I don't care what you *officially* tell Them. You've decided to leave because They've burned you out. You can call it whatever you want when you tell the powers-that-be, and they'll probably believe you – maybe even thank you – because they live in fear that someone will stand up and say the real reason for a departure. But if you don't tell Them the real reason – if you don't tell Them that you decided to depart because of all the things that are broke, your last act here will be to avoid the truth," he said, trying offer a guilt trip as an argument for an incendiary discussion with the partners as I exited. Such a discussion wasn't going to happen.

"What's the point? I decided to leave, so what does it matter what explanation I give? All I want to do is clean up my office, clear out my desk, take home my pictures, finish the cases I can finish, get my last few paychecks, continue to work until the last day because that's the stand-up thing to do, settle up my personal telephone call charges, and depart – quietly. I would like to call clients and thank them for the chance they gave me to serve them. I don't think, though, that They'll let me do that. No contact between clients and the dearly soon-to-be departed. Whatever. I can leave the battles to the troops who remain behind," I said.

Silence followed. I added, "If you think something's broken, why don't you go in and tell Them while you're still here?"

Low blow! Sucker punch! But it had to be said. When people before me quit, I secretly hoped they would burn a bridge for the betterment of mankind, or at least the remaining associates. But they never did. I always thought I would march right down the hall and say all the things I wished the departing associate had said. But I never did; no one ever does. So instead of marching down the hall, I always toyed with the idea of telling the partners off someday as I myself left. Who needed a bridge anyway, as long as I could use it one last time to cross it on the way out to the great beyond? Who cared whether They said bad things about me after I was gone? But now someday had finally come, and it looked like I wouldn't tell Them either. No one ever does. No point burning any bridges. It would take a lot of effort to strike a match, and I had no matches. I had no strength. I just wanted out.

He was ready to capitulate, and said dejectedly, "This place is truly rough, sometimes."

Now we both looked out at the skyscraper tops. The sun darted behind a cloud that appeared to be just a few feet above the pinnacle atop a new gothic high-rise. "No argument there," I said softly.

He said, "I'm going to leave here, too. Really, I am. It's just a question of when." I knew that. He had told me many, many times.

Silence. More silence.

I said, "Look, if I say what I think is broken, the partners will either argue with me, tell me I should have told Them sooner, or They'll pledge Their commitment to do whatever it takes to fix whatever is broken."

"Exactly!" he said instantly.

I continued, "But I don't want the argument, and They already know the problems; there may be nothing They can do. You know that."

Silence. He said nothing.

I said, "And if They pledge Their commitment to do whatever it takes to fix whatever is broken, what have They *actually* done? Not much. Not much at all."

More silence from him.

I contended, "Any comments They make will be platitudes. They won't say what They'll do to fix what is wrong, because They probably don't know what to do. They'll look surprised, hurt, sympathetic; maybe They'll even try to console me. But nothing will get done."

Yet more silence, so I filled the void by more observations: "And, I like some of them. Some of them like me. I don't want that to change when I leave." He kept listening with his eyes half shut and I continued. "Nothing will change. Whatever is wrong is institutional and systemic. It's a design defect, a glitch in the profession; a bug in all law firms' DNA for which there's no recall, no corrective line of code can be written, no new replacement part, washer, or cable can be installed. It's the practice of law, not necessarily the law firm. It's bigger than me. So why say anything?"

"I just thought it might help. I guess it wouldn't," he said slowly and very quietly.

"I have no strength left, and it isn't a question of me doing the right thing. So I'll go out quietly, and if the partners want to think I left in honor because I didn't burn my bridge, fine. They'll think I'm a great, honorable guy, who left in a class act. I don't care about class. If you and the rest of the associates want to think I avoided burning a bridge I should have burned, fine. You'll think I'm a classless act; that I'm scared. Also fine, but I'm not scared. Bridge-burning only matters if it'll change something. Nothing would change here."

"You don't know that."

"But I'm pretty certain," I replied.

"So, you'll be just like all the others. A little smile, some explanation about an offer you couldn't refuse, a new region of the
country, a stronger marriage, handshaking, back-patting, 'hell
of a guy' speeches, 'good luck in your new life' proclamations,
a departure memo wishing you all the best, a wine-and-cheese
party, and then out."

I said, "Something like that, but while I appreciate the ges-
ture, I don't need the party; let the firm donate the money to
a homeless group. I would like that. That's how it has to be.
Everyone has an agenda. Someone will use my departure to
make whatever point they want to make: let them. But not me.
I have no point to make…"

Where was the sun? It had been hidden for a while now and
the office was getting chilly. He walked over to his window. Cars
sped along the highway. People raced to work so they could park,
hustle to the elevator, squeeze in, punch their floor button, tap
their foot nervously to elevator tunes while they waited impa-
tiently for their floor to arrive; then they proceeded to their office,
closed the door behind them, put their feet up on the desk, and
gazed out at the metropolis below and the cars speeding along
the highway that took people to work who were about to do
the same thing. How many were quitting today? How many
were thinking of quitting? How many would burn a bridge?

He asked, "Why is it always like that?" Then he answered
his own question. "I think it's because the partners have
convinced everyone it's dishonorable to burn bridges." He
shook his head and went on, "There's no bridge here. You
didn't cross a bridge to get in here and you don't cross a bridge
to get out. You walked across the moat, and in through the
heavily-guarded front gate under your own steam and you
leave the same way. There's no bridge leading back; it would
take an airlift to get back here. No one ever comes back here
unless they're crazy."

I listened, and he kept going: "I bet that years ago, someone left and told the powers the exact reason why they left. The firm's management didn't much like it. So, They started the rumor that if anyone left and told Them the real reason, the departing associate would be allowed out, but their bridges would be burned. There'd be hard feelings left behind. People would say the associate left because they either didn't attend to their files, they drank too much, or they were impossible to get along with. And in doing so, the firm made it easy to leave and difficult to leave honestly. So, ever since, people just take the easy way out. They leave uneventfully."

Historical conjecture. No empirical evidence; not admissible in a court of law. But a working theory that was certainly plausible. I said, "That might all be true. But it's easier just to leave, and since the exit, and not martyrdom, is the goal, I opt just to leave. Anyone who wants out can just walk out. Ultimately, that's the most powerful thing any associate can do: vote with your feet. The ultimate op-ed piece – just leave."

Five minutes ago, my coffee had officially turned cold. Now, it had passed through the cold phase and was stale. The highway had cleared out, the skyline was still serene, I saw no smoke from any of the bridges leading to Center City, Philadelphia, and I had the feeling that thousands of people with their feet up on their desks were looking at me from the windows in the other downtown high-rises – hopefully not with binoculars. And I hoped they weren't also thinking I was going to burn a bridge for them.

Skyscrapers are so serene, especially when viewed from a nearby skyscraper. I should have been serene like the sky-scrapers. I should have found solace in my existence high atop a metropolis. I made my decision. I was content. The sun was coming out from behind the cloud again and I could see that the exit was straight ahead.

I had to admit I didn't see a bridge or even a gate, but it didn't matter. It was settled. My course was set: there would be no bridge-burning. But even though I wasn't going to burn any bridges, I couldn't help wondering what would happen if I held a propane burner in my hand when I told Them I was leaving? Would They even notice?

MIDLIFE CRISIS

ACCORDING TO THE MERRIAM-WEBSTER dictionary, a midlife crisis is "a period of emotional turmoil in middle age characterized especially by a strong desire for change." It is a fine definition as far as it goes. The dictionary editors, however, obviously did not have attorneys in mind. Here is how I would customize the definition for attorneys in general, and myself in particular:

> *A period of protracted, repeated, profound, emotional turmoil, beginning sometime in the second or third year of the practice of law, and continuing off and on, mostly on, many times for the rest of the legal career, characterized by a rather significant, continuous, and oftentimes all-consuming, desire to explore alternative possibilities; to explore a change, any change at all, and to effect the change. These periods are typically coupled with a constant search for a new dream to pursue, potentially followed by additional periods of intense regret as dreams are not fulfilled.*

I am happy with my modified definition and I will likely submit this modified definition to Merriam-Webster someday. I think I owe it to the attorneys of the world.

We all seek balance in life. In a life of the law, the balance always seemed to me to be this: if something good happens, then most assuredly, something bad is about to happen, usually brought on by something that happened in the law firm and my bankruptcy practice. In my typical midlife crisis, I sought to identify ways to change to a new, different balance. The new balance was my goal and I had many dreams over the years of how to achieve it. But try as I might, I found that I could only change the balance problem by an exit from the law firm world when it was time for me to move on. Before I moved on, however, I explored many possible paths to change within a life of the law. These all failed.

Buddhists try to follow a path to enlightenment. Different Buddhist scholars apply different meanings to the notion of enlightenment. One I like comes from the

> Chinese master Huineng (638-713), the Sixth Patriarch of Ch'an (Zen), [who] compared Buddhahood to a moon obscured by clouds. The clouds represent ignorance and defilements. When these are dropped away, the moon, already present, is revealed.[9]

I always felt that my moon was out there, but obscured by the vile, thick clouds that were the practice of law from time to time, and all I had to do was to be vigilant and hope that my dreams would make the clouds finally dissipate and reveal the hidden moon someday.

Enlightenment in order to find a dream to pursue would have been nice. But I saw no lights on the law firm roads on which I traveled. I looked for the light switch often and I tried to use fog lights, parking lights, low beams, high beams, LEDs, spotlights, a flashlight or my iPhone light to guide me, but try as I might – no lights, no enlightenment. Whenever I

---

9   https://www.learnreligions.com/what-is-enlightenment-449966

looked for the enlightened path, I found myself in a midlife crisis, and no longer content to continue to be discontented. I sometimes described my quest for enlightenment as an attempt to figure out what I would do with my life when I grew up. As time went on, however, as time is wont to do, I grew up, and I had no new plan. Disappointment followed. Disappointment stoked each and every crisis like the hot coal embers of a campfire under the Rocky Mountain stars.

When I turned thirty-eight, I was a partner in a large Kansas City-based law firm. By then, I had practiced for more than ten years. I tried to be realistic; law firms were what they were, and the practice of law was what it was. And, most assuredly, I was what I was. But realism does not equate to satisfaction, and realism is no substitute for a new dream to pursue.

I had already been through several low-level midlife crises, with no particular solution in mind, just that strong desire for change. I was disappointed in myself that I had not figured out my life path and, instead, had just sort of fallen into law school and then law firms.

Indeed, I had already attempted change several times, from region to region, job to job, and law firm to law firm. None of those changes amounted to the pursuit of a dream, and none helped to quell the desire for a more profound change. By my thirty-eighth year on planet earth, we had our son, my wife had established her veterinary practice, and there were fewer and fewer options I could see besides hanging on as best I could as a bankruptcy attorney at a large firm. Not exactly a dream and not at all a prescription for an enlightened change.

Change itself also concerned me, especially a high volume of change, as I careened in my mind from one possible solution to another and even acted out by moving regionally several times. It reminded me all too much of my parents' many moves while I was growing up, as they reacted to their many midlife crises, and I was acutely aware of the effect that so many crises could have on the people around me for whom I cared.

One morning, however, an idea came to me that I thought *might* be a dream to pursue: I would teach at a law school, and leave the business of the law firm behind. Perhaps in the separation of a law life from a law firm life, I could find the dream. The process of landing a professor position at a law school, however, is far from simple. Each year, there is a convention of sorts where law schools who have professorship openings interview candidates seeking a teaching position. Some call this convention the Meet Market, while the more observant pundits call it the Meat Market. If the interview at the Meat Market goes well, the candidate is invited to interview on the law school campus – typically by a substantial portion of the faculty who show up for a short interview, one by one, in between classes. At some law schools, the on-campus candidate then gives a lecture to the faculty during the lunch hour.

I completed and sent in my application, and a few weeks later, I learned that a school had expressed an interest to interview me. Off I went to Chicago and the Hilton Hotel; the same Hilton Hotel where the 1968 Democratic presidential candidates stayed and, on the third night of the party convention, where demonstrators clashed with law enforcement officers on national television: a historic venue. During that convention, Dan Rather was roughed up by the Chicago police and Connecticut Senator Abe Ribicoff pointed to Chicago Mayor Richard Daley and from the podium said: "How hard it is to accept the truth." So the setting was perhaps prophetic as well.

Undeterred, I brought with me my own brand of energy, a healthy dose of naivete, and of course, appropriate attire and fervent hopes for a path towards change. I arrived early so I could attend some of the preparatory lectures, in which the speakers discussed what schools looked for in candidates, and how I could better interview. All interesting and somewhat helpful and I made a checklist. But the truth I had to accept was that I could not check off many of the boxes. I was not diverse; I am a Caucasian Jewish male and there was not much I could do to satisfy the schools' interest in diverse candidates. No check. The schools wanted candidates who had published legal papers; I had authored several law journal articles, authored a short book about bankruptcy reform, and co-authored a substantial book about bankruptcy law, so I thought I had that part satisfied. Check, or so I thought. Schools wanted candidates with academic experience; other than sitting in many classes as a student, I had none. Schools wanted candidates who went to Ivy League law schools; nothing I could do there. Oh well.

Schools conducted interviews in hotel rooms. For my interview, I arrived at the appointed room a little early, and in the hallway outside the room was a lone wooden chair. Nothing in the materials I had received said what I was supposed to do, and there was no sign by the chair to give guidance. Even though I would have preferred not to sit, I went ahead and sat in the chair like a high school student hoping not to be called on in class, because that seemed like the thing to do and maybe it was some kind of test of my character... and I waited. Eventually, the door to the room opened slowly and I was invited in. My invite into the room was fifteen minutes late and as far as I could tell, there had been no interview candidate before me whose interview went a little longer than scheduled. I sat down in the only unoccupied chair in the room which looked an awful lot like the chair in the hall, surrounded by three professors... I guess they had just run late? I don't know. They never mentioned the time. Maybe it was another test of character? For the next twenty minutes, they asked me a few questions but mostly talked among themselves about me, sometimes as if I were not sitting there.

"He has no teaching experience, Bill."

"He certainly has written several articles and the two books, Helen."

"But the articles and the books are survey pieces, not analytical, Ellen."

I am reasonably sure they had not read my articles and books. I had thought I was thoughtful, and even analytical, in my writings, and I believed my publisher thought so as well. But Bill and Helen and Ellen definitely did not think so and they were in charge, so... uncheck the box.

They asked some questions, but not many, and then Bill delivered what he perceived was the dagger observation. He turned to me and said, "You know, young man, in my estimation, academia is not a place for attorneys to run to when they want to escape the practice of law." Young man?? How... well, analytical. Also, just a tad condescending and hypocritical since, from the information I had read, Bill had practiced law for years before he entered the world of academia. Nor was Bill alone; many professors ended up as professors either because they did not want to practice law from the get-go and entered academia upon graduation from law school, or because they had a midlife crisis, realized they had had enough of the law firm life, and decided they would prefer to teach rather than to practice. Also, this particular school was way up north, the winters were ten months long each year, and the temperature in the winter could approach minus thirty degrees, sometimes for days and weeks on end. Not exactly the place to which I would escape if I was on the run from the law (firm). And besides, I did not feel that I was running away from the *practice* of law; just from the law firm way of life.

In the end, I never figured out if the comments were intended to elicit responses from me; were they deliberately thought-provoking statements to see how I would react? I just don't know. I offered no reaction because I thought an interview necessarily suggested questions and answers, or, at the very least, an overt request that I comment on one topic or another. Maybe they should have read my chapter on Interviews.

The whole Meat Market process intrigued me, and the interview was certainly memorable. But needless to say, I received no call back for an on-campus interview. Just as well, I guess, and end of dream, at least at that moment. With that, back I went to the world of the law firm and its corresponding midlife crisis.

For the record, I later taught bankruptcy law at the University of Kansas for fourteen years as an adjunct bankruptcy professor. This gig served as a fix of sorts for the Meat Market iteration of my midlife crises. On my first day at KU, I stopped by the Dean's office where the professors' communal coffee pot could be found. I was both nervous and excited about beginning to teach law students. My mentor professor wished me luck, and off I went to teach bankruptcy law to sixty eager students. I walked into the large classroom, introduced myself, and then had an out-of-body experience in which I looked down at myself as I began teaching. From above, I thought: "What in God's name are you doing? Are you out of your mind?" Later that night, I answered both questions: "No idea. Yes."

The next morning, I made my way to the communal coffee urn and met my mentor again. "How did it go" he asked? I told him about the out-of-body experience, and explained that perhaps I had made a grave miscalculation. I told him I was ready to jump out of the window.

He said, "We're on the first floor. If you jump, you won't do much damage. You'll be fine. Just remember – you always know more than they do."

And, armed with no more than his sage advice, and not at all so sure that I *did* know more than the students, I gathered myself, survived my rookie year behind the podium, and taught for fourteen wonderful years at KU. I got older, of course, while the students always stayed around twenty-six years old or so, and it reminded me each year that I was aging. But I loved it, and it was my first successful identification and implementation of a dream to quell a midlife crisis. However, it was only a partial fix. I had kept my day job at the law firm, so I had two jobs for those fourteen years and therefore, while the KU gig fulfilled a dream, it did not put an end to the crises, because I was maintaining my life as a big firm bankruptcy attorney.

I applied for several judgeships, but I never got to wear a robe. It is a very competitive process, and the selection committees chose other, more worthy candidates. A judgeship would have been a significant change, but I have come to believe that I would not have made a very good judge, and certainly not a very good bankruptcy judge. A life on the bench can be lonely, as there is little contact between attorneys and the judges except in the courtroom. I like contact. In my observation, many judges struggle with their life on the bench after their life in a law firm, and a not-insignificant number of them do not seem to enjoy their life on the bench; some outright despise it. It is interesting to watch from the attorney podium, because those unhappy judges had likely thought they had found their dream and the escape route from the practice of law, only to discover that the dream was unfulfilled. Perhaps they had regrets. Perhaps the judgeship led them to more midlife crises.

So, even with a teaching gig in hand, I still plotted ways out of the law firm life. Any exit from the law firm life would have been a significant change. Those plots I devised included a scheme to leave the practice of law and move into the business sector (in this scheme, I ignored my lack of experience), a plan to go out on my own to be a solo bankruptcy law practitioner (in this strategy, I ignored the fact that I might have no clients and, therefore, would starve), a notion that I might go back to school and get a degree in anything except the law (in my notion to implement this idea, I ignored any questions as to how the family would function while I pursued whatever degree I chose). None of those ideas were truly dreams of mine, just ideas I ran up the flagpole, none of which would have ended any of the many midlife crises. When I examined each scheme, I saw no light that illuminated any potential road out.

I read a handful of "how-to-leave-the-practice-of-law" books over the years. Some are quite good, but to the extent that these books recommend an exit based on a judgeship or a full-time teaching gig, my experience is that the odds of successfully implementing these two exit plans are remarkably remote. Not a reason to refrain from trying, but I learned that it was important for me to at least give lip service to the notion of staying grounded as I dreamed up various exit plans.

I imagined, but immediately eliminated (sometimes for obvious reasons), the pursuit of the following potential escapes: baseball player; basketball player; baseball manager;

basketball coach; baseball executive; basketball executive; baseball team owner; basketball team owner; president of Haverford College; president of any college; circus performer; Broadway performer; street performer; restaurateur; politician; chief of staff for a politician; ambassador; pundit; financial advisor; mountain climber; generic musician; lead guitarist in the E Street Band; concert promoter; professional X-gamer; Broadway show promoter; world traveler; Buddhist monk. I gave some thought to each of these – often not a great deal of thought, and not high quality thought, but thought, nonetheless. I am sure there were other notions that came to me at all hours of the night and day that I did not pursue. The mind can be pretty creative when left alone to explore the universe, but it may not be very practical during those creative periods. I would characterize these potential endeavors more as daydreams (and even pipe dreams) than dreams, but when you are in a midlife crisis, consideration of any daydream is worth the time of day and you do not distinguish well between a dream, a daydream, and a pipe dream. And these dreams had an even smaller chance of success than full-time teaching or judging.

People who watched me go through midlife crisis after midlife crisis, asked me, "Why not be a professional photographer?" Those who asked me this were not attorneys. The attorneys I knew were enmeshed in their own midlife crises and not particularly focused on mine. No, the people who said to me "Why not be a professional photographer?" were non-attorneys just trying to be helpful. It was a good question, and a compliment to my images. I enjoy photography immensely, and after my problems at Northwestern University (cataloged earlier in this book), I had never wanted photography to be my profession or career, even if I was good enough for it to fulfill those roles. I came to believe that a profession or career behind the lens might destroy my love for photography, and I could not bear to lose my love for photography. Also, as the old joke goes, the difference between a pizza and professional photographer is that a pizza can feed a family of three.

Like so many attorneys, I careened from crisis to crisis, dream to dream, idea to idea, plan to plan, notion to notion, and never found the dream that led to the exit from the law firm life.

Thinking back to my childhood, I was an unwilling participant in my parents' many crises. As Nathaniel Hawthorne observed in *The House Of The Seven Gables*, "The wrongdoing of one generation lives into the successive ones." Maybe I had been conditioned to live in crisis after crisis? Perhaps. But one thing is for certain: now, after years and years of crises, I am an expert on the attorney midlife crisis syndrome, and I can observe that repeated midlife crises are not particularly good for marital and family relations. They strain the fibers of any and all relationships. People think you hate your job, and that you are perpetually unhappy. Perhaps, but that is too simplistic and therefore, perhaps to revise history a bit, I would say not at all correct, on either point. But there is no debate that a midlife crisis can strain any relationship. Eventually, I learned to manage the crises without sharing all of them with my family members. I stopped sharing my dreams, daydreams, and pipe dreams; no point making everyone else crazy. And, ultimately, I never acted on any fix for the midlife crisis *de jour* and, instead, stuck it out as a bankruptcy attorney.

My working theory is that most attorneys spend a good portion of their working lives wondering if they should be attorneys while they try to identify options. Sometimes the options are practical. Sometimes they are impractical and half-baked – the pipe dreams. Maybe in early iterations of their various midlife crises, the attorneys don't understand themselves very well – I certainly did not. At some point, they run out of midlife crises and dreams, and, while they still may not completely understand themselves or their predicament very well, they privately admit that they don't understand themselves and move forward. They are no longer slaves to dreams (to borrow from Teddy Roosevelt); perhaps because, finally, they grew out of the need to hold open the possibility of fulfilling a dream as a way out of the practice of law.

If they are good, really good, they will minimize their regrets for good dreams they failed to realize, and pipe dreams they never had a realistic chance to fulfill. I guess, then, that I am really good: I have no regrets... at least at this point. I think I grew out of the silly dreams and the regrets and moved on... finally. I think I grew into the notion that I would not retire from the law; I would retire to something *besides* the law. Indeed, I quickly hated the word "retire." While I dreamed of not being an attorney anymore, I had other ideas for the afterlife. I wanted to be busy in my next phase – just not as an attorney. That simple notion became my dream, and my new goal was to just figure out how to be busy in my next phase.

And with that, the midlife crises seemed to end. Finally, a ray of light, and the hint of a glimpse of the moon as the clouds lifted.

THE DECISION

In Texas, during the oil industry collapse of the 1980s, a real estate developer took the witness stand and tried to explain to the bankruptcy judge how he would reorganize his business during the downturn. The demise of the oil and gas industry in the early 1980s wreaked havoc on the Texas real estate market. No one was buying or leasing. No one was developing. The judge seemed dubious and asked for more details. The witness said: "Well, Judge, I'm mowin' and waitin'." The Judge asked what that meant. The witness said: "I'm just mowin' the lawn and waitin' for the real estate market to turn." That was the reality of the times and the place: mowing the weedy lawn and waiting for the economic forces to change. It was a plan – but not much of a plan. Once I decided that my dream was to retire to something else, I found myself mowin' and waitin' for the right time. This also was a plan, but again not much of one. It seemed that I was back to my early *modus operandi*, where I would just figure things out later.

Turns out, picking the right time to exit the practice of law was no easy task. In the practice of law at a big firm, there was always tomorrow – until there was not. The devil was in the detail in deciding *when* there was not. What were the factors? Were there any rules? Was there a sign I should look for? And the practice of law does not yield to this kind of plan. The law and the law firm ignore these kinds of thoughts and hopes and, instead, keep on keepin' on. Not a great environment to put meat on the bones of an exit plan.

I envy professional baseball players. The season ends on a date certain, and everyone knows the date certain. After the date certain, at least for that season, there is no tomorrow. Games end at a time certain – when a set number of innings have been played and one team has more runs than the other. Hard and fast rules. Attorneys not only like rules, they find endless comfort in sets of rules. But no published rules govern that all-important date certain in the attorney game. I sometimes wished there were published, widely-accepted rules. Because there were no rules, I developed a few departure rules that worked for me and that I share with you here for your contemplation. People at the firm got used to my rules over the years – the *NCIS* Leroy Jethro Gibbs in me, I guess. Gibbs' Rule No. 13 was *never, ever involve an attorney*. I suppose he thought that was good advice but that was a hard rule to follow in a law firm, and if that rule had had legs, I would not have had a job. Even though Gibb's Rule No. 13 was not useful for me, I still liked Gibbs' idea that he needed specific, articulated rules that governed how he lived his life.

There may very well be no universal guide on how to develop an exit plan; just on-the-job life experiences. For me, those life experiences turned into ten departure guidelines or rules that seemed to help guide me to find a departure-from-the-law-business date certain. I don't offer these as a "how-to" list, because what seemed to work for me may work *only* for me, and it represents *my* thought process, not a one-size-fits-all thought process. Indeed, I rarely shared my thought process with anyone before my departure date since it seemed so personal to me. But, over the period since I left the practice of law, the occasional former colleague has asked me about my thought process, perhaps with a bit of horror that I left the practice of law, or perhaps to assess whether I needed to be committed to an inpatient ward as a result of my decision to depart the profession. Now that I have departed, here are my guidelines or rules, setting out my thought process for what it might be worth.

Rule No. 1 – *God Will Not Help.*

The truth is, I am not a believer. The truth is, I fear that if there is a God and an afterlife when I die and ascend (I am most definitely an ascender in my opinion), I will learn that there is more of the same. These beliefs I hold cause me to ask: Isn't this worldly existence we all struggle with and through each day enough? If you are a believer, maybe you can rely on a divine sign from above or wherever your God resides. If so, I am more than a little envious, because in your system of beliefs, someone or something else will just let you know when it is time. I am afraid that divine someone or something else is not at my disposal. So for me, there is no divine help. And anyway, I would be concerned about offloading this decision on God, and I would be concerned if God then decided this issue for me. The nonbeliever in me intuits that any God would have way more important things to do in running the Universe on a day-to-day basis than decide this trivial matter of when it is time for me to leave the law life. No. For me, this was a "help-myself" problem, to be solved by me.

Rule No. 2 – *The Law Firm Will Not Help.*

Some years ago, the American Bar Association suggested that law firms should do away with mandatory age retirement requirements. Many firms had such requirements. Today, they do not. My law firm had no mandatory retirement requirement during the period all of this was roiling around in my head. Occasionally, our managing partner let the baby boomers know that he expected them to have a succession plan – a formulated way to transition clients to the younger generation and in his own way, he tried to prompt us to think about an organized wind-down to retirement. Beyond that, however, there was little my law firm could do to identify when it was time. My decision of when to stop being an attorney was a deeply personal one and, I have to believe, is different for each attorney. So the law firm did not help me and frankly, the law firm could not help, and frankly, I did not *want* the law firm to help. Help myself.

<u>Rule No. 3</u> – *Family and Friends Should Not Help.*
Family and friends sometimes think they are helpful when they make suggestions and prompt a discussion of the after-life. Certainly, my family and friends listened to me over the years and from time to time offered advice. They meant well, but they were not typically helpful. It was not their fault, but they did not have the capacity to be helpful. It was already tough enough for them to be in the same family as an attorney. Sharing a family with an attorney can make anyone a little crazy. If I had tried to involve them in my decision, I would have undoubtedly made them even crazier. I had no right or need to seek or take advice from someone I had made crazy for decades; no need to ratchet up their pain and confusion. Therefore, this rule is the same as Rules No. 1 and No. 2. Help myself.

<u>Rule No. 4</u> – *Figure Out What Else To Do.*
I particularly loved and hated this rule. I came to fear and respect it. When you are an attorney, and the world begins to learn you have decided to stop being an attorney, inevitably

you are asked: "What will you do?" While assigning no ill-will to the question or the questioner, it strikes at the core of the fear I and other attorneys have about leaving the practice of law, because the question posed is tinged with, "What else can you do since, after all, you have done nothing else as an adult except for this attorney thing?" So very true. If there is one thing that stood between the continuation of my law career, and the Afterlife, it was the fear that there was, in fact, nothing else I could do besides fight about debts, go to court, represent clients, bill, collect, attend to firm matters, get more work, etc. etc. All I could do, I feared, was all I had ever done. Sure, I had other interests. But those other interests would not fill out a week and I feared I would end up like my dad in retirement – watching Oprah re-runs and waiting for the end... of the show and of life, both of which always come. Not fun; not fulfilling; fear-inspiring.

I rated this rule as quite important, so I gave this one a great deal of (hopefully realistic) thought. For myself, I had to acknowledge that in the rear-view mirror of my life were: skiing; basketball; significant movie-going (I fall asleep in the new reclining cinema chairs); excessive eating and drinking; the continued fight against the inevitability of wrinkles and other changes that mark the march of time; and teaching (it had served its purpose and function during one of my more significant midlife crises).

I also had to concede that out the front windshield of my life were dreams that had passed me by, so I would never: hike Mount Everest; star in a slick Hollywood production of a docu-drama movie with sex and drugs and rock and roll, and a little courtroom drama in which I win the big case without expending a lot of time and without needing a lot of prepa-ration, or an international espionage thriller about British spies with numbers for names, and sex and drugs and rock and roll; live high atop Philadelphia's Rittenhouse Square; see the moon on the next mission, or any mission, to outer space; cruise around the world; live in SoHo (New York's or London's); learn six foreign languages; play Madison Square Garden with Paul Simon; meet Paul McCartney for real; have my portrait taken by Annie Liebowitz for the cover of *Rolling Stone* magazine; go out on the road like Jack Kerouac's Dean Moriarty and Sal Paradise and seek and find all of the answers to the mysteries of the universe in prolonged road trips south and west; and give an interview to Gayle King on one important topic or another. Bummer; I could count on none of these things to fill my weeks.

In other words, I needed to apply this rule with a healthy serving of honest self-evaluation, and figure out what the *realistic* future could and would hold for me.

Rule No. 5 – *Feel Free To Seek Help.*
Not from God, your friends and family, or your law firm. But I wanted real help from someone who knew their way around these issues. Strangers; kind strangers who know. For me, those strangers started off as authors of books. Many of the books I read, unfortunately, did not help much at all, but I read them. The books largely told me I was not alone in my exit feelings, but I already knew that. As well, some of the books had too much self-promotion of what a great and fulfilling life one former executive or another had after she or he left the corporate for-profit world. None of them seemed particularly restless as they explained their corporate for-profit lives. Other of the books were by former attorneys. The books were interesting but not helpful for me. Then, I stumbled on a company named *My Next Season*,[10] with a book

---

10 www.mynextseason.com.

called *Your Next Season*, which did help. The great folks at MNS helped me organize my thoughts, find purpose for my afterlife and stay calm through the process. Attorneys are not necessarily inherently calm, so thank you, MNS, very much.

Rule No. 6 – *Can I afford it?*
I was always acutely aware that we all need money, my family and I included. How much money we need depends on how much we expect to spend (you will have to figure that one out without me), and how long we will be alive to spend it (same). By way of example, based on my non-scientific calculations and our anticipated lifestyle, Loren and I need to stop living when we are about ninety-eight years old, or so. Not an exact science calculation but it is all I have, and that approximate age of demise sufficed for my purposes. I have made a note on my electronic calendar and if in 2053 I can still read and comprehend, and if we still have a planet that has not been eviscerated by man's insistence that global warming is a farce, I will be sure on November 8, 2053, to revisit whether I can continue to keep living.

Rule No. 7 – *My East and West.*
The Navajo believe that reality is divided into two sides, the east side and the west side, with good, harmony, and beauty found on the east side and evil, chaos and ugliness on the west side. Sometimes, the attorney gig felt like I woke up on the east side of reality and made the great public transportation commute each day through unending tarnished revolving turnstiles to the attorney-occupied west side where I spent my waking hours, hopefully, to return to the east side at the end of a day. I lived in both the east and the west sides of reality and it had the potential to become very confusing, which it did. But it helped form this rule for me: when the confusion

got to be too much and I felt like I woke up on the west side each day and worked on the west side each day, then returned to the west side each night – when it was all west side, then I knew that my time was drawing near.

Rule No. 8 – *I Just Knew When It Was Time.*
United States Supreme Court Justice Potter Stewart famously wrote:

> *I shall not today attempt further to define the kinds of material I understand to be embraced within that short-hand description ["hard-core pornography"], and perhaps I could never succeed in intelligibly doing so. But I know it when I see it, and the motion picture involved in this case is not that.*

Jacobellis v. Ohio, 378 U.S. 184, 194 (1964) (emphasis added). I tried not to read too much into the use of a Supreme Court quote about hardcore pornography in the context of the continuation in the practice of law. But it is a great jurist quote, and captured how I felt about the time of departure from the practice of law. When to stop being an attorney was not capable of precise definition, but I believed that I would know the end when I saw it. Really. And I did. I could trust my gut. Justice Stewart did; I did. I just knew.

Rule No. 9 – *Follow Winston Churchill's Lead.*
Paraphrasing Sir Winston, if I measure my career by what I get, I should measure my life by what I give. I had a really hard time setting aside enough time during my attorney days to give, or at least to give enough. I am not sure I made the world a better place during my years when I appeared in bankruptcy court. It became harder and harder for me to

find good in shuffling money and assets from one group of pockets to another. Don't get me wrong – money is important and the fight to distribute it where it belongs, or at least where the bankruptcy law allocates it should be, is always important, can be valiant, and even at times noble. And the clients involved in the fight are always engaged, usually responsive, and always interesting and interested. But, as my career extended into my sixties, I became much more concerned about how little good I was doing in the world outside of the bankruptcy court. I asked myself how the world was a better place every day that I returned from the courtroom. Now, however, I hope I *will* make the world a better place every day and I try to measure my new life by what I give. When I give, I feel good – every time. If I feel good, then I know I did good. The human brain is designed to provide a reward to the brain's owner after a feel-good moment, and I thank my brain for that as I hope to have many feel-good moments.

<u>Rule No. 10</u> – *Follow Steve Jobs' Lead.*

Steve Jobs said, "You have to be burning with an idea, or a problem, or a wrong that you want to right. If you're not passionate enough from the start, you'll never stick it out." I was able to know when I did not feel passionate enough anymore. Now that you know me, you will certainly be aware that I never achieved true, unadulterated passion about the law firm life, but I stuck it out, nonetheless; so, I am likely a bit duplicitous in following this rule, but passion is very important in life. Perhaps I found more passion in *what* I did as an attorney than *where* I did it. But gradually, any passion I had for what I did certainly came to an end, and as it began to end, it was time for me to follow Steve Jobs' lead and stop sticking it out. Eventually, I tried to be self-aware and recognize when it was time to stop sticking it out.

And there you have it. I developed and applied these rules after many many years of not doing so. All of a sudden, it looked like I might be on a path. Was I? Or were my rules merely a way for me to rationalize something that in the end is very personal and very irrational? I am not sure, truly. But, as for all attorneys, there is comfort in rules, and whether it was the rules or just the right time in the space-time continuum, my time was drawing near. Possibilities looked real. A dream... soon, I would be home free.

PART FOUR – THE AFTERLIFE

THE EXIT

My FIRM'S PARTNERSHIP AGREEMENT requires a full nine-months-notice before disassociation by virtue of not practicing law anymore – a fancy way of saying retirement, I suppose, written by an energetic corporate attorney some years ago. I decided to finish my career by remaining for the entire calendar year. I could have retired on January 1, but counting back nine months, the retirement notice would then have to be delivered to the managing partner on April 1. I thought that that might cause confusion, because it might be viewed as an April Fool joke. So I decided to retire on January 2, and therefore delivered the disassociation notice on April 2.

The managing partner was more than decent about the whole process, for which I was, and still am, extremely grateful. He decided that I would continue to work as usual and not let the world know of my decision until much later in the process. Since the notice period was lengthy, I privately viewed the notice as provisional and the notice period as an opportunity to continue to think about and challenge my decision. Would I get cold feet? I had nine months to figure out the answer to that question. Unlike my historical tendencies, I did not intend to use the nine months to delay my decision, but rather to critically challenge the decision often to make sure it was correct.

I regularly thought about whether my decision was right for me and came back to the same notion over and over. It was right, and therefore it was time. I believe I truly finalized my decision in November. I delivered a detailed plan under which, starting in October, I would fly around and introduce my younger colleagues to clients for whom I had responsibility. Once the transition trips began, I found them very enjoyable. Indeed, if I could just fly around and talk to clients all of the time, I might never have left the law firm... not. It was time.

The firm even had a party for me in Kansas City a few weeks before the end to celebrate my tenure; it was both extremely touching, and very much appreciated. Clients, colleagues, and friends came. For the party, I had worked hard to come up with something to say but I was surprisingly nervous, so I failed to say everything I wanted to. I am sure no one at the party felt bad that I did not prattle on and subject them to a long speech; but now I can say what I want in written form and be complete in my words, so I will:

> *After the last verse of the last song on the last album the Beatles recorded was completed, the four of them went their separate ways so, among many reasons, they could do things they were not doing as Beatles.*
>
> *I am at that moment with the practice of law. It is time for law to go its way, and for me to go mine so I can do things I am not doing as an attorney. For me to do that, I have to leave the firm. For me, it is time for my life ledger to get balanced a little better and in doing so, who knows, maybe I will get to make a little more love in the world than I have in the past.*
>
> *Watch for a book from me – I hope. Read it and either laugh or harrumph. Stop by for a photography class or two I hope to teach for returning vets.*

Let's talk about solving gangs and education and homeless-
ness by solving the housing crisis. Hopefully, I can help in my
service on Habitat-Denver's Finance and Audit Committee.
Support me as I try to help deliver the arts to inner city kids.

And if I get up the nerve, listen to me at an open mic
night somewhere on South Broadway – not real sure about
this one. We will see. My point: the world is full of things
to do, and I hope to do as many as I am able.

Thanks to Loren for putting up with me through our first
forty plus years together and for being there for me always –
none of my career would have happened without such a great
friend along for the ride. Thanks to Zachary for every day
that you are Zachary.

Thanks to each of you here tonight, and especially those
who have been in the trenches with me and for having my
back. I hope I always had yours.

Thanks to Joan Steffens [my long-term secretary/LAA]
for everything and more. I bet you never thought we would
be a team for so long. Thanks to Mark Foster and Brian
Gardner for giving me chances that I am quite sure I did not
earn. And thanks to Mark Hinderks and Allison Murdock
for everything but especially for making the ending part of
my career humane and dignified. I don't like to live in the
past but to borrow again from the Beatles – "there are places
I'll remember"… and all of you are at the top of the list
of what I will remember.

If you came to the party, please substitute this for my
shorter, more generic, remarks. *This* is what I meant to say.

After nine months of preparing to end my attorney career,
the day came without cold feet. It was time to let go and move
on. The whole day was anti-climactic. To the extent I could,
I gave selected attorneys and staff things that were significant

to me – my "giveaway." The items ranged from cartoons I retained over the years that seemed pertinent to bankruptcy and the law firm business, to my sports images that hung on my office walls, to mementos from cases I had tried, to my books. I shipped my files off to the attorneys who would take over the matters and clients, threw stuff away that I have no idea why I had retained for all those many years, and had my departure boxes down to just two.

The giveaway was not quite the reading of my last will and testament, but there were certain elements of such a reading in the process, except I was present. I suppose it is not possible to be present at a true reading of one's last will and testament, but if it could be done, I would find it most enjoyable.

I packed, I said all of my goodbyes, I made all of the client transition trips, and I was ready...

...Except for the tech stuff. No one leaves without a tech intervention. During my time as an attorney, the technology that supports an attorney's practice advanced at an incredible pace. I started with no computer and a desk phone with green blinking buttons, a red blinking hold button, and I had access to a communal telefax machine. As tech took over the world, it fascinated me, and, like so many attorneys, I was hooked on tech quickly. I first owned a Palm Pilot, and then a couple of Blackberries, the first device I could look at in the courtroom and read emails while I waited for my case to be called. From there, I owned several Windows-based mobile phones that were awful, and finally, blissfully, the iPhone came along. Thank you, Mr. Jobs. By the time of my departure, I was the proud owner of a new iPhone X. It synced wonderfully with all things law firm. But all good syncs must end in conjunction with a departure from the firm. The sync ended in our firm with a process called the "Wipe."

In our firm, the attorneys owned their mobile phones, so when they left the firm, they took their mobile phone devices with them. But much of the data on the phone – business contacts, calendar information – belonged to the firm. The departing attorney had to leave that information behind. The firm's fix for this problem was to remotely wipe all data off of the phone. That, of course, was handled by the firm's tech department. I called them the tech department but, in truth, someone had renamed the group the IT department some years ago – Information Technology. I always wondered why they changed the name from just Tech, or their nickname – the Tech Guys and Girls. I could think of only two reasons. The head of the department wanted a real corporate name – perhaps Chief Information Officer (CIO for short), or Chief Technology Officer (CTO for short), and the group wanted to distinguish itself from Best Buy's *Geek Squad* and other similar home tech repair groups.

Most everyone that worked in IT were good folks. The person who would implement the wipe – The Wiper, also a good guy – had this one task he had to do: wipe. It was the only time in my years at the firm that I had occasion to work with the Wiper. The wipe process was complicated. True, my phone contained the firm's business contacts and calendar appointments, but it also contained my personal contacts and calendar appointments as well as my many apps, most of which had nothing to do with the firm. The process of separating my stuff from the firm's stuff was not nearly as simple and straightforward as a mere remote wipe. The Wiper knew this; I was quickly learning it.

Left to my own devices, the only solution I could see to the problem of the potential loss of my personal data and apps was to back up everything on my phone that was mine in at least two different ways, and hope that after the wipe, the data and the apps that were mine would magically reappear.

The Wiper insisted that he had to perform the wipe on December 31 in the morning, which meant that for my last two-and-a-half days as an attorney, I would work at the firm, but I would have no connectivity. No connectivity in the modern era was a scary thing to contemplate, even as the end was in sight. I have no idea why the Wiper could not wait until January 2. Indeed, I was left with the impression that he was very busy with other wipes and made a concession to squeeze in my wipe to accommodate my departure. His reaction to the possibility of a January 2 wipe was an emphatic *NO*. I guess he was booked solid during the holidays. The wipe was December 31, and I said, "December 31. Splendid!" What else could I say?

On December 31 I waited for a phone call because I expected I would be told that the wipe would commence shortly – in other words, a warning that the wipe was about to start. No call. Instead, the Wiper emailed me to let me know that he had initiated the wipe, and then another email to let me know that he had completed the wipe. Of course, I could not receive the emails because during and after the wipe, my sync with the firm ended and I no longer received firm emails. Eventually, not aware the wipe was in the record books, I looked at my iPhone and it looked like an iPhone looks right out of the box. No data, and a bunch of set-up screens. The Wiper had not provided me a protocol to follow afterwards, so I started the iPhone set-up process, screen by screen, when to my surprise, the phone started to repopulate with everything the Wiper had erased. I was sure this was not protocol. I guess the Wiper's high-tech solution had failed. But I understood the firm's policy to make sure I did not leave with the firm's data. So, to help everyone out, I decided on a lower-tech solution and I did a hard reset and then another one for good measure – end of firm data. No more repopulation. I then held my breath for the restore process of my data and apps. Unlike the Wipe, the restore worked. Splendid!

The end of the sync with the firm was remarkably symbolic, somewhat dramatic, and more than a little traumatic. The Kansas City firm and I had been joined by a professional, technological umbilical cord that was the sync for almost twenty-eight years. The Wiper cut that cord and slapped me in the butt to start the process of breathing non-attorney air. For that, I thank him. I am breathing the new air just fine, but it was traumatic and even unsettling to not know what was going on at the firm for those last two days. I suppose this was the law's last-ditch way of sending me a message to let me know how dependent on the law I had been for all those years and how different my world was about to become. The law's last message to me: *you have this last chance to change your mind*. I ignored this last message from the law. I understood fully what I was doing and I had no interest in relitigating my thought process.

Two days later, I said my final, final goodbyes. I hugged my Denver LAA, Laura, and I walked out the door of our Downtown Denver office, summoned an elevator, waved to the lobby guard, and left the building. I left the building, not on a temporary basis as I had done for so many years, but for good. Since I could no longer sync, I don't know if there were any emails about the departure sent in my wake. My picture disappeared from the firm's website instantly, and with it, all public record that I had been at the firm for such a long time vanished. But that was OK; it was as if I had just shed forty-one years of the law. Just like that.

My long-time search for my answer, and my failed attempts to arrive at that answer, yielded and I simply walked out the door, and the mystery was solved. Just like that. I thought I would feel odd about the walk out the door. I did not. I thought I might feel a little remorse. I did not. Once I got past my many midlife crises, the law firm had mostly been a decent place to survive the day-to-day hazards of bankruptcy. If I was going to be a bankruptcy attorney, a notion to which I finally succumbed after years of fighting it, then the law firm met the necessary requirements for me to practice bankruptcy law, gave me the freedom to do so, and mostly left me alone. The firm was not perfect although it did the best it could. Neither was I perfect, not by a long shot, and I also like to hope that I did the best I could. When I walked out the door, I walked out easily. As I left, I could have sworn I heard a soft chorus in the ether of the firm's many corridors that whispered, "Best of luck." Not a rumor making its way down the hallowed halls, just a whisper of well-wishes. Nice.

As I walked along the Downtown Denver 16th Street Mall, I glided just a few inches off the pavement, and it felt darn good. The last live performance by the Beatles was on the top of the Apple Corp. building on Seville Street in London in broad daylight. They looked mostly happy that day when they played the soon to be released *Let It Be* songs with Billy Preston on the organ. That rooftop day was the beginning of the end for them, and the end came shortly thereafter. As the Beatles ended, their beginning phase in music ended, and they could all go on to their next phases as solo artists. My walk down the 16th Street Mall was the same. The beginning of the end of my law life had started thirty-eight years before and would officially end at 11:59 p.m. that evening. At 11:59 p.m., I would also mark the end of the beginning for me. My beginning, my law life, went on a long, long time, but now it was time for it to end and for me to get on to my next phases. The 16th Street Mall cold air in my face was all I needed for those first new phase moments. Nothing like a Rocky Mountain winter breeze to mark the start of whatever comes next.

NO, REALLY, I'M NOT COMING BACK

WHEN I LEFT THE firm, I tried to put a bit of distance between my former colleagues and myself for a while. I needed to get used to life after the law, they needed to get used to not having me around, and we all needed to get used to the notion that I no longer should know about each case, and each client, and no longer needed to know about the daily law firm goings on. I did not want to say it to their faces, but eventually I wanted them to know that I now had a new set of things about which I cared and the firm and the practice were no longer my primary concern.

A couple of months after my departure from the law firm and law life, I saw a former Kansas City colleague who, over lunch, asked, "Are you ready to come back?" I am sure he must have thought I looked surprised and confused by the question. In reality, I found myself amused. He said, "You know, now that you've pursued this wild-hare idea of a life as something other than an attorney for a little while, are you ready to come back?"

I smiled, tried not to answer too quickly or too emphatically, and said simply, no. I did not say it loudly or with anger or glee. I just said no. One word was sufficient to quell any notion that I would return. I thought the answer would be so patently obvious that the question was unnecessary. I guess not because he was not the only one to ask me. Maybe he was joking; maybe he was envious; maybe he was concerned for my well-being; maybe he was just making small talk. Maybe my decision to cease my life as an attorney seems temporary or transitional to someone still caught up in the practice of law. Maybe people back at the firm look at the decision through the lens of disbelief, and therefore feel it can't work or last. Maybe none of the above. Who knows?

For the record, there is no desire at all to return to the practice of law. I am on no sabbatical, and I am not out testing the waters with a plan to return shortly. I am happily in the moved-on mode into my next phase. How am I doing in this next phase? Doing well, thank you. Life is good. It was the correct decision for me at the correct time. And that new afterlife goes something like this.

THE POWER OF EUPHORIA

BILL PARCELLS, FORMER NEW York Giants head football coach, said "There are two things in New York, euphoria and disaster." During the first few months after I left the firm, I was quite vulnerable and I was more than a little concerned that I could not distinguish between euphoria and disaster. Was I awash in my escape from the practice of law, or was my escape from the practice of law an impending disaster that I was ignoring? I expected a certain amount of that kind of confusion, but it had been so long since I felt anything that could be called euphoria, and it confused me. It was a foreign emotion for me, and I had to learn to identify it and manage it and make sure it was not masking an impending disaster. Indeed, euphoria is not an emotion that regularly pervades an attorney's day-to-day existence, so I had little experience in how to manage it.

The level of euphoria was also a little higher than I expected. It seemed harmless, but I learned that you have to be careful with euphoria. It is kind of like being in a constant, giddy, nowhere state of affairs. Nowhere is alright for a little while, but not as a permanent address or state of being. I once wrote a song about running away from things and the chorus was, "Nowhere is the right-where to be. Somewhere's not the right-where for me." After the life of the law, however, I realized my song had it all wrong. Somewhere is ultimately a very important place for me to be and I needed the euphoria to wear off so I could get on with the business of being in the somewhere that I wanted to be. I needed the euphoria to wear off because it got in the way of me being able to make lists, and do things, and start my new life.

During the euphoria, I found that I felt like inmates Frank Morris and John and Clarence Anglin must have felt upon their escape from Alcatraz prison in 1962 if they, in fact, survived the raft ride to the mainland after their breakout. I was out on a raft in a harbor, in the cold, with my collar turned up and hoping to make landfall. Once on the mainland, were there private eyes or law firm enforcement teams or even U.S. Marshalls looking for me or following me, and reporting back to someone? Of course not, so I didn't need to look over my shoulder... did I? I made it to the shore of my new life; not sure if Morris and the Anglins did. I broke out of the law life, made it to the mainland, and after a short while, I concluded no one from any law firm seemed to have sent a search party out to look for me. Good. No... great.

Thankfully, as I eventually recognized there was no disaster, the euphoria began to wear off, although it took a couple of months. After the period of euphoria wore off, I settled into a satisfying routine. People have asked, are you busy? I am, thank you – very busy. It is an odd question, however, because no one ever asked me if I was busy during my law life. I hope they are not asking because they think only an attorney can be busy. No, I doubt it. I imagine they are just looking out for my well-being and for that, I am grateful.

WHAT I DON'T DO
AND WHAT I DO

IN MY AFTERLIFE, HERE is what I do *not* do all day. I do not practice law and I do not reside in a law firm. I don't have clients or judges or courts, or partners, or colleagues, or files, or cases, or contracts to read, or research projects, or billable time to write down and submit, or law firm numbers to crunch, or managing partner memos to read, or continuing legal education to attend. I don't read case law. I try very hard to return to a civilian life. It is not easy. The life of the law gets into your veins and invades your being. There is, as yet, no antibiotic to help purge the law from my system, and therefore it is hard to have an instant law-purification. But every day, I try *not* to argue, construe, pound the table, strategize, and I try to limit my advocacy to the things that are really important to me. I like to think I am still zealous in the causes I advocate, but hopefully in a non-lawyer kind of way.

I admit I have not been totally successful so far in the quest to return to civilian life, and I am a work-in-progress, but I am trying hard and I think am making some headway. People who know me well may tend to disagree. They are entitled to their opinions and I defer to their more learned and unbiased view of my progress.

I don't have any active law licenses. I don't fear not being an attorney. I don't fear not going into my office. I don't fill out reports of my attempts to generate law firm business. I don't fear working at home. I don't fear having actual "me" time. I don't preach about the virtues of not being an attorney; I don't preach advice about how not to be an attorney. I don't burn any bridges.

I don't watch Oprah re-runs on the telly, and don't fill my days with CNN. I don't watch reality shows or cooking shows or talk shows or TMZ or for that matter, In truth, I don't watch all that much television. I don't sleep late. I don't nap. I don't eat too much, or at least I try hard not to. I try not to drink too much... but I do like wine and Irish whiskey. I don't sit around the condo. Unless I want to, I don't sit on airplanes, run through airports, or wait for flights. I don't trade in rumors. I don't bore myself.

So, what do I do so far? First and foremost, I wrote this book – very important to me. The experience has been so satisfying that I may just try my hand at another book; perhaps my first attempt at fiction (a bankruptcy novel, perhaps).

Second, and almost as foremost, I began my service in the arts-related not-for-profit world. I am involved, finally. I make a small difference, at last. The bar is low for my involvement in causes and organizations: do I feel good about what I am doing, am I able to help in some small way, and do I fit in? If I can check all three boxes, I am happy each day that I am involved. I have found it is critically important that there is a comfortable fit for me in my board service. If I am an ambassador for the organization's mission and I believe in the mission, and the other board members and the executive director are good fits for me, then I fit in well.

I do not serve as an attorney to the boards or my organizations. I am just there as myself. I try to make that clear to my fellow board members. The former attorney life, however, helps me serve on the boards. Artists take used materials and transform and repurpose them; I guess I am a little bit like that: used, former attorney materials, that have been transformed and repurposed. Some of those used materials still work well – organization, ability to listen, and some ability to still read, write, speak and think, to name a few. Fundraising is a little like attorney business development, so my business development skills have also been repurposed.

But, at times, I need to manage some of my used attorney materials. I can be a little impatient – the not-for-profit world moves at a much different pace than an attorney's day-to-day life. Sometimes that impatience can lead to frustration; but if I feel good, can help, and fit in, I can largely manage any impatience and frustration just fine.

I am also involved with the Downtown Denver Partnership and sit on both the Mobility Council and the Housing Task Force. I enjoy both immensely, although I am hardly an expert on mobility. I do live downtown, however, so I am keenly interested in how people move into, out of, and around downtown Denver. And I am electric-scooter-aware, as it is hard to be *unaware* of these chaotic little devices and the mayhem they bring as they populate and crisscross downtown Denver. I will not use my remaining time with you to elaborate on my true feelings about electric scooters and the theory of the delivery of last-mile transportation, other than to say that I find them incredibly annoying, remarkably and inarguably quite dangerous, and their users are often shockingly lawless. Long live the pedestrian and the bicyclist, who I hope the scooter riders will someday learn to respect and emulate.

I also serve on Habitat for Humanity – Metro Denver's finance and audit committee. I am not Jimmy Carter, building houses into my nineties, but I am involved and even if all I manage to do is help a little to provide affordable housing to a needy family, I have done a good deed. Both my Habitat and DDP service have the same low bar: I feel good, I can help, and I fit in.

Because of my involvement with these organizations, I have created a very satisfying afterlife for myself where I am kept busy. I run from meeting to luncheon, to fundraiser, and to more meetings. I read bylaws and agenda and financials, and collaborate to try to make the world a little better place each day. I am not retired; I just don't go to court anymore. And for me, this is heaven. For some who have watched this process, they wonder why I am not more "retired." Not me, not now, not yet. I am having too much fun and achieving too much fulfillment to be more "retired" and I would not have it any other way. And, maybe I am a small example to the attorneys of the world who would like to start thinking about their next phase in life, but are afraid of the prospect of filling their days in the absence of a law life. As I said at the outset, I offer no advice because I am no expert. But, in a small way, maybe my path can be a comfort that attorneys are much more than one-trick ponies.

Third, I remember the times as an attorney when I had very little "me-time," so now, I have "me-time" as well, consisting largely of writing, music, photography, and reading. As mentioned already, I have written this little book, and I have started on a new one – a bankruptcy novel. I play guitar, I write songs, and I learn how to sing better with a wonderful teacher who is willing to suffer through my voice (it can be an acquired taste) and the fallout from my music past; and lately, I have taken a deep breath and started to record with a wonderful engineer. I make images. The music and photography are my constants, my places to go as a kid, my places to go as a reluctant attorney, and my places to go still now, and they provide a bridge for me between my former life and my afterlife.

I exercise a little more regularly, and I hike. I am not a fourteener, but there is so much to see in Colorado under fourteen thousand feet that I am quite happy finding myself and my thoughts between ten and twelve thousand feet.

I also have "me-travel" more often, which is travel on my own account because I *want* to travel, and in doing so I can catch up with family and friends who are scattered throughout America. I traveled plenty as an attorney but not for myself. Now I travel because I want to, and I go places that I want to go. I cook a lot. I bake bread and take cooking and baking classes. I bake to honor my dad and because I like it. I am a *Flour, Water, Salt, Yeast*, and a King Arthur guy. If you bake, you know what I am talking about. I took a business class to learn how better to serve on not-for-profit boards. I read what I want to, when I want to, and at a pace that I want to.

But do you want to know what I do a great deal of the time? I smile. Hopefully, it is not a smug smile. Hopefully, it is just a satisfied smile, and it is certainly painless to wear. I was not able to smile much after That Day in December 1965, and my life as an attorney most assuredly did not fix that problem. But now, much to my surprise and satisfaction, I smile inside and outside. I smile when I have a reason to smile. I smile when I have no reason to smile. I wear a smile because I like to smile and it turns out, I do like to smile. Hopefully, I have earned the right to smile a lot. I laughed plenty in my life as an attorney, but you can laugh without smiling inside, and I just don't think I smiled all that much in earnest in my law life. World Smile Day is celebrated on the first Friday of October each year, and I am sure I did not make it a point to smile on that Friday each year during my law life. This year, in my afterlife, I am sure I will.

In "The Only Living Boy in New York," Paul Simon sang, "Hey. I've got nothing to do today but smile." If all I had to do was smile, I'd be good with that. I find it easier to smile in the afterlife and I like that a great deal. My "me-time" is more than a little self-centered and perhaps even selfish. It is harmless, however, and I try not to give the self-centered thing too much attention and there is no point in overthinking the "me-time" question; I figure the smiles make up for any perceived selfishness.

And do you want to know what else I do a great deal of the time? I dream. Dreaming always was, and always will be, good, at least for me. There is nothing wrong with adding to the long list of things I will not necessarily be able to do in my life. Dreaming about them makes me feel good. Coming up with new pipe dreams is not such a bad thing at all.

What does the future hold for me? I hope more of the same I have experienced since the beginning of my Afterlife. But, if not, there will be new adventures, that I am sure I will dream up. Just not as an attorney. Just not in court. Just not in a law firm. Whatever those adventures might be, I can only hope they will present themselves after a good dreamer session… Just Like That.

LAST THOUGHT ON THE LAW

As I BEGIN MY journey away from the law life, you should know, or already have figured out, that I think the law looms and it consumes, fumes, presumes, entombs; it lurks in the classroom, the conference room, the boardroom, and the courtroom; sometimes it assumes; it is often the legendary professional jealous mistress, hiding within a law firm with a *nom de plume* that sounds austere and thoughtful and august and distinguished… and sometimes, just sometimes, despite itself, it manages to bloom. It is larger than life. It makes few concessions for dreamers, and perhaps dreamers have no right to expect concessions. It took me a very, very long time to learn this: while there may be better ways to go through life, at the same time, there are many, many worse ways to go through life. Really. At some point, however, it is time to part ways. And for me, it is time to move on. Just Like That.

Make An Author Happy — Please Review This Book

I would be grateful if you would take a moment to review this book on Amazon. Your review would really make my day!

Thank you,
Mark

AFTERWORD

THERE ARE SO MANY people to thank. Of prime importance, my wife, Loren, and son, Zac. You lived through my career and for that, some form of an award is due to both of you. You have put up with me. Another award. I hope it has been worthwhile. You are always there for me. Always.

The rest of the thank-yous (in no particular order and with no meaning assigned to the order) go something like this:

To Dick, Danelli, Nina, Kathy, Andy, Kris, Sid, Steve, Brent, Susan, Cathy Ann, Glenn, Roberta, Robert, Alfredo, Michael, and Ann for being the best friends that best friends could possibly be. You may be the only people to read this book, and if so, thanks in advance.

To Dickie, for being there for me every time. I hope I have been there for you.

To Judge and Jacquie, for being my mentors, teaching me, suffering through me, and letting me into your family.

To Sherryne, for being a good buddy and being so patient with such a greenhorn attorney.

To Anne, Ruben, John, John, Matt, Brad, Greg, Joe, Andy, Todd, Rick, Carol, Rosemary, Rex, and Lori, and Patrick for helping us keep our loved one and keeping him safe and us sane on the non-linear path that has been our collective life.

To Andrea, Graham and Renee, David and Martha, and all the kids – Rowan, Ethan, Ben, Jonathan, Katie, Lucy, and Dan – for being there for us.

To the great folks at *My Next Season*: Mark, Debbie, Frank, Amy, Dana, Leslie, Jeannie, for helping me help myself formulate a plan that is dignified, fulfilling, and may very well be that elusive dream. Thank you so much!

To Linda, Joan, Laura, Laurie, Bridget, and Bridgette, for being my buddies, keeping me on the straight and narrow as much as was possible, for always having my back, and for always sharing your smiles with me, the most important thing you could give me. I really did try to smile in return.

To the people who were the bosses of me: Jim, Danny, Bob, Mike, Neal, Bob, Howard, Mark, Brian, Mark, and Allison, for giving me space to be me and for putting up with me and being there for me and never saying (at least not to my face) that you had enough of me. I can only imagine that it must not have been easy.

To some special former colleagues who were not the bosses of me: Robert, Joel, Cindi, Nick, Andrew, Marc, Darrell, Paul, Tracey, John, Karen, Scott, Don, Brent, Alicia, Tom, Ben, Mike, Terry, Sara, Pat, Tim, Peter, Andrea, Mark, and Mark, for tolerating me, or at least pretending, convincingly, that you tolerated me.

To some special, special clients: Alice, Paul, Tammy, Chris, Greg, Peter, Ed, Tim, Roger, Doug, Tom, Brad, Taylor, Mike, Alan, Craig, David, Karen, Phyllis, Dawn, Barry, Paul, Rob, John, Doug, Lindsay, Phil, Scott, Gregg, Jacquie, and Chris, for letting me do what I used to do for you when I used to do it. You all made my life so much better and taught me so much.

To Barkley and Barbara, for listening to me over the years and to Barkley for pointing out that the KU window was on the first floor.

To my Stinson family in Denver, for letting me come and join and for letting me leave when it was time, and for your willingness to remain part of my life and for me to remain part of yours.

To my two special politicians: Joe and Greg. Thanks for making me feel good about our country and our prospects, not easy tasks in the current environment.

To John, Paul, George, and Ringo, for being a part of my life. I don't think I learned everything I needed to know in kindergarten, but I came pretty close to learning everything I needed to know with you.

To Rebecca and Andrew at *Design For Writers* in Great Britain, for all the help in getting the book finished, edited, designed, and published. You guys are amazing.

To Mitch, Andrea, Mike and Traci, for all the legal advice.

Finally, to whoever has gotten this far in this book, congratulations for grinding it out, and a heartfelt thanks. This has been a very productive therapy session for me. I am grateful for your couch and your time. I will look for your invoice in the mail. Cheers.

Mark Shaiken
Denver, Colorado
January, 2020
markshaiken@fastmail.com

Made in the USA
Las Vegas, NV
26 March 2021